Readings in Syrian Prison Literature

Contemporary Issues in the Middle East
Mehran Kamrava, *Series Editor*

For a full list of titles in this series,
visit https://press.syr.edu/supressbook-series
/contemporary-issues-in-the-middle-east/.

Readings in Syrian Prison Literature

The Poetics of Human Rights

R. Shareah Taleghani

Syracuse University Press

For a listing of books published and distributed by Syracuse University Press,
visit https://press.syr.edu.

ISBN: 978-0-8156-3706-6 (hardcover)
978-0-8156-3715-8 (paperback)
978-0-8156-5520-6 (e-book)

Library of Congress Cataloging-in-Publication Data

Names: Taleghani, R. Shareah, author.
Title: Readings in Syrian prison literature : the poetics of human rights / R. Shareah Taleghani.
Description: First Edition. | Syracuse : Syracuse University Press, 2021. | Series: Contemporary issues
in the Middle East | Includes bibliographical references and index. | Summary: ""Readings in Syrian
Prison Literature" is a comprehensive study of the contemporary genre of prison literature (adab
al-sujun) produced by political detainees in Syria over the past five decades. It examines the intertwined
relationships between prison writings, oppositional political movements in Syria, modern Arabic
literary experimentalism, and global human rights discourse"— Provided by publisher.
Identifiers: LCCN 2020035200 (print) | LCCN 2020035201 (ebook) | ISBN 9780815637066 (hardcover) |
ISBN 9780815637158 (paperback) | ISBN 9780815655206 (ebook)
Subjects: LCSH: Political prisoners—Syria. | Political prisoners' writings, Arabic. | Human rights—
Syria. | Social movements—Political aspects—Syria. | Syria—Politics and government—21st century.
Classification: LCC HV9777.5 .T35 2021 (print) | LCC HV9777.5 (ebook) | DDC 365/.95691—dc23
LC record available at https://lccn.loc.gov/2020035200
LC ebook record available at https://lccn.loc.gov/2020035201

For detainees and the disappeared
in/of Syria, Iran, and the US

Despite the fact that I left prison, it didn't leave
me. For the traces of its pain penetrate my blood.
Yet, my spirit still yearns for freedom, dignity,
and justice.

Rida Haddad

I want to put a sea
        in my prison cell
I want to steal all the prison cells
        and toss them into the sea

I want to compose a meter
        in my prison cell
I want to steal all the prison cells
        and recite them in the meter

Riyad al-Salih al-Hussayn

Contents

Illustrations

Acknowledgments

This book has been many years in the making, and I am deeply grateful for the support I have received in the process of writing it. Research for the original dissertation that forms the foundation of this study was supported by a 2005 summer research grant from the Graduate School of Arts and Sciences at New York University. I would also like to thank the City University of New York's Research Foundation for a PSC-CUNY grant to conduct follow-up research in Amman and Beirut in 2017. Support for writing this book was also provided by the CUNY Faculty Fellowship Publications Program and the CUNY-Mellon Faculty Diversity Initiative Fellowship in 2017–18.

I am also lucky to live in a city that has an amazing public library system, and I would like to thank the New York Public Library for granting me a research residency in fall 2017. Over the course of a number of years, I greatly appreciated all of the efforts of the research librarians at the main Schwarzman branch, including Melanie Locay, for their help in using the library's resources, and especially in obtaining copies of Arabic-language texts.

Thank you also to Alison Brown and Michael Tencer, who provided excellent editing on earlier versions of two chapters in this book, as well as the anonymous reviewers who provided such useful feedback and constructive criticism. I am also deeply indebted to all of the editors and designers I have worked with at Syracuse University Press, both for this book and for the coedited volume *Generations of Dissent*. Thank you especially to Suzanne Guiod; to Deborah Manion, who oversaw and fast-tracked the initial proposal stage of this book; to Peggy Solic, who patiently answered a thousand and one questions and requests and guided me through the process of submitting the finalized manuscript; to Fred Wellner for his cover design; and to Mehran Kamrava for his very helpful feedback. I am also grateful for the very constructive feedback from the anonymous reviewers of this book.

I would also like to thank the members of my dissertation committee at NYU who offered their feedback on much earlier drafts of the majority of the chapters of this book: Phil Kennedy, Elias Khoury, Ella Shohat, Michael Gilsenan, and Kristin Ross. I especially thank Phil Kennedy, whose work and seminar on recognition in classical Arabic literature inspired chapter 2. I am also deeply grateful to Elias Khoury, whose class on prison literature raised my initial interest in the topic, who encouraged my research on the topic, and whose stance against the Asad and other regimes remains unwavering. I would also like to thank all those who provided support and feedback during the early dissertation writing process and in my time at NYU, including Khaled Fahmy, Sherene Seikaly, Shane Minkin, Hanan al-Kholoussy, Munir Fakher Eldin, Carole Woodall, and others.

Over the past five years I've greatly appreciated being invited to speak and receive feedback in a variety of forums on the topics covered in or related to this book in a variety of forums. Many thanks to Abed Tayyara at Cleveland State University; Carolyn Shread at Smith College; Max Weiss at Princeton; the Hagop Kevorkian Center for Near Eastern Studies at NYU, especially Greta Scharnweber, Sinan Antoon, and Hala Halim; Robert Farrell and Christa Salamandra at Lehman College–CUNY; Eman Morsi at Dartmouth College; the late Joyce Warren of the Women and Gender Studies program at Queens College; Alexa Firat at Temple University; and Beth Baron and Jeremy Randall at the Dissections Workshop at MEMEAC at the CUNY Graduate Center. I would also like to thank Friederike Pannewick and Achim Rohde for the opportunity to participate in the engaging "Reconfiguring the (Non)Political" academy in Tunis in summer 2016. I am also deeply thankful for being able to participate in the truly amazing and engaging 2015 National Endowment for the Humanities workshop "What is Gained in Translation?" that was organized by Brian Baer and Françoise Massardier-Kenney at Kent State University, where I worked on a number of translations, some excerpts of which are included in this book.

At Queens College I would like to thank the Office of the Dean of the Arts and Humanities for travel funds over a number of years to attend several conferences and present different sections of this book. I also appreciate the opportunity to participate in the CUNY Faculty Fellowship Publications Program in spring 2016 as well as the inaugural CUNY-Mellon Faculty Diversity Initiative Fellowship from spring 2017 through spring 2018. I am grateful to have had Rich McCoy as a generous faculty mentor, and to have gotten to know and to have received constructive feedback and encouragement from my CFDI colleagues: Susan Davis, Miles Grier, William Orchard, Regine Joseph, and Laura Villa. In my home department of Classical, Middle Eastern, and Asian Languages and Cultures, I am grateful especially for the cheerfulness and caring support of Meilun Chang, the humor and friendship of Mari Fujimoto and Ji Young Kim, and the encouragement and kindness of Jinyo Kim in my first years at Queens College before she retired.

I also have greatly appreciated advice from Ammiel Alcalay and his support of this project as a whole; the research for this book was in part motivated by our collective project of translating Faraj Bayraqdar's *Dove in Free Flight*. Also, many thanks to Anny Bakalian, former associate director of MEMEAC at the CUNY Graduate Center, for her warm guidance and encouragement of new Middle East Studies faculty and the invitation to give a talk on my research when I was just starting out at Queens College. In fall 2018 I had the opportunity to teach, for the first time, a seminar on prison literature and human rights at the Graduate Center, and I would like to thank all of the students in that class, especially Elsa Saade and Queenie Sukhadia, for their critical engagements and thoughtful, challenging discussions of the subject matter. We learn as we teach, and we teach as we learn.

This book would never have been written without the support of dear friends who have kept me standing while the best and worst in life happens. My deepest gratitude to you all: to F. for advice, visits, and the excursions around the Old City. To Silvia Marsans-Sakly for being a writing buddy and creating a mutual support network over so many years. To X. for laughter and lunches. To Leena Dallasheh for friendship, translation help, and shelter during storms—literal and figurative. To Eman Morsi for mutual encouragement, support, growing trees, and writing retreats. To Alexa Firat for her thoughtfulness, kindness, and steadfast coediting and coconferencing. To Jill Hutchings for friendship and for always offering a place to stay in Cairo and Istanbul. To Sarah Sullivan for always being up for reunions in Cairo, DC, or NYC, and for encouraging words, cat laughs, and last-minute reads when needed. To Nader Uthman for shared dissertation writing, engaged readings, comic relief, and beyond. To Samer El-Karanshawy for pessimism, friendship, and help during a two-month stint in Beirut back in the day. To Maya Kesrouany for wisdom and words at just the moment when I needed to hear them the most. Thank you also to Fred, Thavry, and Matthew Taleghani for reminders that the Bay Area, even after all these years, is still a site of home. To my late parents, Nancy Joleen Poos Field (1942–2001) and Esmail Taleghani (1934–2012), whose memories and absence I will always carry, I thank you for instilling in me a love of reading and, especially from my father, a love of poetry.

Most of all, my heartfelt thanks goes to the writers whose works I have read, including Hasiba 'Abd al-Rahman, Faraj Bayraqdar, Yassin al-Haj Saleh (Yassin al-Hajj Salih), 'Ali al-Kurdi, Ghassan al-Jaba'i, Ibrahim Samu'il, Bara Sarraj (Bara' al-Sarraj), and so many others. To Ibrahim Samu'il and Rim Khury, two of the kindest and most generous people in the world, your light shines always. I am also grateful to have had the opportunity to visit Faraj Bayraqdar in Homs—my thanks to him for his patience with the trials and errors of translation over so many years as well as for his generously allowing me to use his own photograph of his personal prison papers for the cover of this book. Special thanks also to Bara Sarraj, who, after only a brief virtual acquaintance, kindly allowed me to reprint some of his own maps and images from his memoir in this book. Thank you also to Hala Mohammad (Hala Muhammad) for permission to use stills from her film, *A Journey to Memory*. My sincere gratitude to Monika Borgmann and Lokman Slim for providing me with access to their film *Tadmor*, allowing me to reproduce stills from it, and providing me with UMAM's dictionary of terms of Syrian prisons.

There are many other people in and from Syria and elsewhere whose names are not given in these acknowledgments due to security concerns and loss of contact. Their names would be here if the world were a more just place—a place that we can only try to continue to create. There are those who I met along the way and welcomed me into their homes. Those who I was privileged enough to listen to and learn from and who patiently responded to my questions. I thank you for sharing your stories, writings, and art, your endless hospitality, humor, generosity, and kindness. I thank you also for teaching me and others the meaning of resilience, courage, solidarity, creativity, and determination in the face of enormous loss and injustice.

A Note on Transliteration
and Translation

Except in direct quotations, I have generally followed the system of *The International Journal of Middle East Studies* (*IJMES*) for transliterating Arabic names and titles. In some cases, when a person's name has a widely circulated spelling in English or another European language (for example, Mansour Omari) that does not follow the *IJMES* system, I have retained that more widely circulated spelling, but I have provided the *IJMES*-style transliteration in parentheses in the first instance. In some cases spelling in colloquial Syrian Arabic has been used with the transliteration for pronunciation in modern standard Arabic in parentheses (for example al-Mezzeh Prison). Translations from Arabic are my own unless otherwise indicated.

Readings in Syrian Prison Literature

Introduction

Inscriptions of Detention and Human Rights

On February 16, 2012, journalist and human rights defender Mansour Omari (Mansur al-'Umari) was arrested at the Syrian Center for Media and Freedom of Expression (SCMFE) by agents of the intelligence branch of the Syrian Air Force.[1] Detained on the same day as lawyer and rights advocate Mazen Darwish (Mazin Darwish), blogger Razan al-Ghazzawi, and other activists, Omari was forcibly disappeared, tortured, and held incommunicado in an overcrowded communal cell like thousands of other citizens and residents of Syria since the start of the 2011 Revolution. Unlike the thousands killed under torture or arbitrarily executed by the Syrian government from 2011 until 2018, he was released almost a year later, on February 7, 2013.[2] Omari's detention and the human rights violations he and others endured are recounted in the 2018 documentary *82 Names: Syria, Please Don't Forget Us*, a film directed by the Iranian-Canadian journalist Maziar Bahari, who himself had been a political prisoner of the Islamic Republic.[3]

The film *82 Names* is also about writing and its traces, about the magnitude of detainees' acts of inscription, minute or epic, as they confront the vast mechanisms of oppression, silencing, and erasure, and the well-documented, entrenched, systematic, and often deadly "politics of cruelty" of the Asad regime.[4] The title of the film alludes to small scraps of fabric that Omari managed to smuggle out of prison. Torn from his shirt, these scraps contain the names and dates of arrest of the prisoners in his cell, etched in ink made of blood and rust with a pencil fashioned from a nail. The detainees who painstakingly created this list intended it to serve

1

as a documentary record and evidence of those arrested, tortured, and killed. Most especially the list of names was needed to notify local and international human rights organizations as well as anxious and fearful family members and loved ones waiting for news of their disappeared— for word of whom, exactly, the regime had imprisoned. Faded, stained, and tattered, those scraps of fabric would eventually make their way to the US Holocaust Memorial Museum's 2017–18 exhibit that shared the title of the film.[5]

The documentary features scenes shot in the small town on the picturesque Amalfi Coast where Omari now lives in exile. Several times Omari is shown at a small table on a terrace, a laptop in front of him as he writes a book about life in Syrian prisons. While viewers see close-ups of his fingers typing on the keyboard, and the computer screen showing glimpses of the unfolding words of his memoir, Omari describes in a voice-over narrative the sense of trauma he carries from his experience. He also comments on why he feels the need to write a prison memoir: "I have this guilt; you know I was released and my friends are still there. I feel when I finish this book, and it's published, and people have read it, I'll feel that I did something." He goes on to say, "I may feel a little less guilty because I talked about the story, and people are now reading about those people who are inside. But I believe that as long as there are detainees in Syria, as long as there is one detainee, in those conditions, suffering, I will not be feeling that comfortable." As the film continues, Omari reads aloud passages from his memoir, where descriptions of interrogators' physical and psychological assaults on himself and others are juxtaposed with illustrations of torture, human bodies in pain, faces in anguish, and lines of written Arabic descriptions of the same.

As I write this introduction, Omari's memoir has yet to be published— either digitally or in conventional hard copy book form. Though dozens of testimonies of those imprisoned by the Asad regime, and later by militant opposition groups in the wake of the 2011 Revolution and the war in Syria, have circulated in written form and in videos, it is likely that accounts of arrest, torture, detention, and summary execution in prisons in Syria from 2011 to 2019 will continue appearing for decades to come.[6] Omari poignantly reflects on his need to write about his prison experience and keep alive and visible in the public sphere the memory of those who are still inside or would not make it out alive. His reflections echo the words of opposition activists and political dissidents in Syria of earlier generations—those who survived detention in Syria in the era of Hafez al-Asad (Hafiz al-Asad, 1970–2000) and during the rule of his son Bashar (2000–present) and wrote about their experiences of detention while they were in prison or afterward. It is this body of writings—produced, published, and circulated approximately between 1970 and 2015 and designated by scholars, critics, and some authors as prison literature (*adab al-sijn* or *adab al-sujūn*)—that is the subject of this book.

In the Asad era Syrian political dissidents, writers, and intellectuals have produced a vast array of literary works in, about, and through the experience of political detention. Although authors, detainees, and literary critics continue to debate the exact definition of "authentic" prison literature, this body of texts has grown exponentially since the late 1990s, especially after the death of the senior Asad in 2000.[7] Prison literature had an even greater surge in publication and dissemination after the onset of the 2011 Revolution, as former detainees who were imprisoned in the 1980s and 1990s, such as Bara Sarraj (Bara' al-Sarraj) and the late 'Abbas 'Abbas, had their writings published in the wake of the uprising. In the Arab world and in Syria, the emergence of prison literature in the 1970s and early 1980s as a specifically named genre and widely disseminated form of cultural production also coincided with the establishment of and growth in early local human rights organizations, just as dissidents increasingly adopted the language and institutions of human rights and civil society to articulate opposition to authoritarian states throughout the region, including the Asad regime.[8] Prison literature bears witness to the long history of the regime's use of torture and detention to suppress political dissent and to many of the state's human rights abuses, which have also been documented in numerous reports by human rights organizations over the past four decades.

Largely untranslated into English and unread in the US, Syrian prison literature is an essential element of the oppositional political culture created by both secular Leftist and Islamist dissidents since the 1970s—a culture that formed one of the foundations for the 2011 Syrian Revolution, the same revolution during which Omari was detained precisely for his activism—for documenting the Asad regime's human rights violations.[9]

The significance of Syrian prison literature, however, goes beyond the ways it serves as a form of witnessing, expresses creative opposition to the Asad regime, functions as an aesthetic intervention against the regime's human rights abuses, provides evidence of political subjectivities or abjection, or illuminates the larger cultural and historical backstory, the political geography of the Syrian uprising.[10] Prison literature is intertwined with the experimental shift in Arabic literature since the 1960s. Attending to the connections between literary experimentalism and detention, this study examines how diverse works of prison literature both echo and challenge the narrative structures, conventional language, and construction of the detainee as a speaking subject in modern human rights discourse.[11]

Drawing on genre, narrative, and critical theory as well as theorizations and critiques of the international, "universal" human rights regime, the chapters that follow aim to show how the truth effects generated by works of prison literature coincide with, confirm, and challenge the truth claims produced by the documentary and generic conventions of human rights.[12] Syrian prison literature produces scenes of recognition at the level of the narrative that not only heighten the reader's awareness of the acute vulnerability of the detainee but also link such stories to human rights discourse. The poetics of recognition, in the Aristotelian sense, that are at work in such texts echo and problematize the notion of political recognition that is central to twentieth-century formulations of human rights, including the Universal Declaration of Human Rights. In using the concept of poetics in the title of the book, I am intentionally evoking both the broader sense of the term as a systematic study of texts (works of literature and the documents of human rights) and the notion of poetics as an attempt to "understand how works achieve the effects that they do."[13]

The Asad Regime, Human Rights, and Adab al-Sujūn

The time period of the works examined in this study reflects the initial date of Hafez al-Asad's Corrective Movement; the conflict between the regime and the Muslim Brotherhood from 1978 to 1982; the takeover of the regime by his son, Bashar al-Asad, in 2000; the brief political opposition movement during Damascus Spring, from 2000 to 2001; the subsequent return of a systemic policy of repression of opposition movements, both secular and Islamist, in Syria; the 2011 Syrian Revolution; and the Syrian War, from 2012 to the present).[14] The Syrian government issued the State of Emergency Law with the first Ba'th Party coup in 1963 and, by doing so, formerly inscribed a "state of exception" that would last until it was nominally rescinded by the government in April 2011.[15] Under Hafez al-Asad, in the period termed the Great Repression by human rights organizations, from the mid-to-late 1970s through early 1980s, the regime perpetrated the preventative and arbitrary detention without trial of tens of thousands of Syrians, as well as other nationals, deemed to be a threat to the state; the summary and extrajudicial execution of thousands of suspected members of the Muslim Brotherhood, including those occurring during a massacre at Tadmur Military Prison in 1980; as well as the siege of and massacre at the city of Hama in 1982.[16]

In 1976 the Syrian Lawyer's Union established the first formal human rights association in the country when it formed the Committee for Human Rights.[17] Created to investigate rights abuses taking place under the Asad regime, the Committee for Human Rights was inaugurated just one year before Amnesty International won the Nobel Peace Prize and the term *human rights* gained greater dissemination in public discourse globally.[18] In the 1990s and 2000s, as the publication of Syrian prison literature increased exponentially, a number of embattled local and internationally based Syrian human rights, democratic, and civil society movements have managed to maintain their vocal and visual critical assessments of the Syrian government by deploying the language of international human rights law.[19] Such organizations include the Committees for the Defense of Democratic Freedoms and Human Rights in Syria (founded in 1989), the Syrian Human Rights Committee (1997), the Human Rights Association in Syria (2001), the Arab Organization for Human Rights in Syria (2004), the Syrian Human Rights Organization (2004), and the Syrian Observatory for Human Rights (2006).[20] Likewise, the Syrian Center for Media and Freedom of Expression (SCMFE), for which Omari worked prior to his arrest, was founded in Damascus in 2004. Although it was never formally recognized by the Syrian government, SCMFE was affiliated with Reporters without Borders and continued to operate within Syria until regime authorities closed its office and arrested its members in 2012. Some of these same organizations also serve as venues for the publication and dissemination of works of prison literature in digital form.[21]

In its most inclusive characterization, contemporary Syrian prison literature can be defined as any text that has been produced in, about, or through the experience of imprisonment, particularly political detention. Taken in this broad sense, this definition would include both fictional and nonfictional works, as well as prose, poetic, and dramatic texts. However, this definition is highly debatable and necessarily contingent. The complex question of the generic classification of what constitutes prison literature in world literature as a whole, and conceptions of *adab al-sujūn* in Arabic literature, will be taken up in more detail later in this book. The earliest use of the term I have found in Arabic literary criticism is in Syrian writer and critic Nabil Sulayman's article "Toward Prison Literature" ("Nahwa Adab al-Sujun").[22] Sulayman's article appeared just three years before the founding of the first human rights organization in Syria.

Modern writings about imprisonment in Syria are, of course, not restricted to the time period reflecting the rule of the Asad regime. Earlier twentieth-century writings about prison in Syria can be traced to the memoirs and letters of imprisoned nationalist figures under the Ottomans (especially the reign of Jamal Pasha, governor of Syria from 1915 until 1918), the brief reign of Faysal (1918–20), and then the rule of the French Mandate authorities (1920–46). Such figures include 'Abd al-Rahman Shahbandar, Munir al-Rayyis, and Ibrahim Hanunu. Despite the existence of a few poems on the theme of incarceration, however, discussions of the prison experience are limited to memoir-style reportage, and the prison experience is not the primary focus of memoirs, biographies, and autobiographies that have recorded the Syrian struggle for independence against both Ottoman authorities and the French Mandate.[23]

It is, however, important to note the links, and at times the continuity, between the treatment and conditions of prisoners under colonial authorities and under postindependence states. Literary scholars have observed that different regimes co-opted and further developed the various techniques of political oppression used by colonial authorities.[24] A few novels written in the decades following independence also deal with or allude to imprisonment and torture by French Mandate authorities. These include Hanna Mina's *The Snow Comes from the Window* (*Al-Thalj Ya'ti min al-Nafidha*), as well as *The Blue Lanterns* (*al-Masabih al-Zurq*), both of which were published in the 1950s, Sidqi Isma'il's *The Rebels* (*al-'Usa*) published in the 1960s, and Salama 'Ubayd's *Abu Sabir*, published in the 1980s. Prior to the coup led by Hafez al-Asad in 1969, a number of well-known Syrian authors and intellectuals had published fictional or poetic accounts of their prison experiences. Sa'id Hawraniyya, who was imprisoned in 1959 during the period of the United Arab Republic (UAR) after temporarily fleeing to Beirut, also wrote "The Fourth Barracks" ("al-Mahja' al-Rabi'"), in which he describes the relationships among inmates in al-Mezzeh (al-Mazza) Prison.[25]

In July 1964, Syrian writer and literary critic Mut'a al-Safadi published a short story in the Lebanese literary journal *al-Adab*. Titled "The Sun Behind Bars" ("al-Shams Khalf al-Qudban"), the story describes the harrowing experiences of the narrator in a military prison. In addition, Sami al-Jundi, who was imprisoned for a brief period after Hafez al-Asad ascended to power, describes detention and references the act of writing about prison in his allegorical novella *My Friend Elias* (*Sadiqi Ilyas*), published in 1969. Beginning in 1972 with the publication of Nabil Sulayman's novel *The Prison* (*al-Sijn*), a limited number of memoirs, novels, short stories, and plays referencing political detention would be published; the great majority of texts would not emerge until after early 1990s. Many of these texts, such as al-Jundi's novella, would be published outside of Syria, with Beirut being one of the primary centers of publication for Syrian dissidents, despite the Syrian regime's military occupation of Lebanon from 1976 to 2005.

Regardless of the guarantee of the human right to freedom of expression in the Syrian constitution, theoretically the system of state censorship in Syria controls all formal aspects of cultural production before publication or exhibition, and the state security apparatus may confiscate, destroy, or shut down any work that it deems to be a threat to state stability or security.[26] Three state institutions monitor all formal literary publication and distribution: the Ministry of Culture, the Ministry of Information, and the Arab Writer's Union. By official policy, in order to be published, all texts must be approved by one of these three institutions; once they are printed, they are approved for distribution by the Ministry of Culture or the Ministry of Information. In addition, the process of censorship and surveillance of cultural production affects the critical reception of such works; if a particular work is banned, then reviews and studies of it are not likely to appear in the domestic press. However, this has changed with the introduction of the internet into Syria in 1997. Despite government attempts at restriction, internet access has provided authors with a broad, internationally distributed platform for publication of their works as well as of their critical reception.

In practice, the production, censorship, publication, distribution, and reception of literary works diverge from official dictates—a subject that several scholars of Syrian cultural production have examined. The system of control over cultural production permits some seemingly subversive works to be published within Syria, and authors and publishers devise various means to circumvent the system. In her seminal *Ambiguities of Domination* (1999), a study of the "cult of Asad," Lisa Wedeen has addressed the role and reach of the Syrian state in the control of cultural production. Wedeen argues that the state's use of symbolic power produces a range of everyday "as if" political practices on the part of populace; "as if" politics are politically effective for the Syrian state because they produce an acceptable range of behavior on the part of citizens, and they are frequently reinforced rather than subverted by attempts to undermine the state's power.[27]

This reinforcement of state power is demonstrated via the concept of *tanfis* (literally, deflating or letting the air out). According to Wedeen, *tanfis* is the term used to describe the "perception" of films and television serials that represent permissible criticism of political power.[28] *Tanfis* can be seen as a "safety valve" that preserves the hegemony of a repressive regime by allowing the venting of frustrations that might otherwise be translated into oppositional political action.[29] Yet Wedeen also suggests that such practices are ambiguous and cannot be characterized as either completely functioning as safety valves that preserve regime authority or as uninhibited political resistance. Thus, *tanfis* is not just "licensed critique"; rather, such practices become a locus of citizens' struggle for "control of systems of signification" and allow the regime to identify shifting levels of compliance on the part of citizens. They also can operate as a mechanism of surveillance, demonstrate various grades of opposition to the ruling apparatus, and reinforce the notion of a politics of "as if" by articulating the "recognition of that unbelief" in the symbolic power of the state within the boundaries set by the regime in the first place.[30]

While the Syrian state denies both the existence of any political prisoners in Syria and the use of torture and summary execution in civil and military prisons over the past fifty years, it simultaneously has selectively permitted the publication of literature and the production of television serials, films, and plays that directly and indirectly refer to political detention.[31] The seeming arbitrariness of Syrian state decisions to permit or ban the publication and distribution of certain works functions to consolidate state power as it saturates the cultural environment with unpredictability.[32] This arbitrariness and unpredictability can result not only in palpable gaps in the system of control over cultural production, but also in authors self-regulating or self-censorsing their own creative work.

Works of Syrian prison literature have been published outside of Syria, within Syria via the system of state control of cultural production in which *tanfis* plays a role, and also through unofficial and informal processes of production, publication, and distribution. In some cases, such as that of short story writer and playwright Ghassan al-Jaba'i, in a particular moment of relaxed political control the Ministry of Culture permitted the printing of short stories and plays about the experience of political prison and political oppression, despite the fact that those works were produced by a known political dissident. Yet it prevented the works from being widely distributed.[33] In 2004 a collection of poetry composed in prison by Faraj Bayraqdar could be found at a book exhibition by the Ministry of Culture in Damascus. In the case of another writer's works, publication permission was given because the individual censor who was assigned his texts admired his work and was sympathetic with his political position.

Writers do, of course, devise alternatives to official or conventional publication, and such alternatives function as a parallel system of cultural production, with digital publication now widely used to completely circumvent the state apparatus of censorship. Bara Sarraj, for example, first began dessiminating short excerpts from his prison memoir on Twitter in 2011 and 2012, then published an initial PDF version on 4shared, and finally self-published a lengthier version through Amazon in 2016. On one hand, a number of works have been published and distributed within Syria with regime consent, such as Ibrahim Samu'il's first two story collections, *The Stench of the Heavy Step* (*Ra'ihat al-Khatw al-Thaqil*) and *Ahem, Ahem* (*al-Nahnahat*), and thus can be considered to be approved by a state. On the other hand, a number of works, such as Mustafa Khalifa's *The Shell* (*al-Qawqa'a*), have been banned and have only circulated within Syria in an unofficial capacity, and some have received more critical attention abroad, either in the Arab world or in Europe, than they have at home. Yet authors raise funds for private printings and, as has become more widespread, distribute their works in digital form. Despite state attempts at censorship, works still circulate, and banned works find their way into the hands and eyes of Syrian and other readers.

The Conditions of Writing in and of Syria's Prisons

The Syrian government's complex system of detention includes large civilian and military facilities, such as Saydnaya Military Prison (one of the more modern prisons), Tadmur Military Prison, 'Adra Central Prison, and Duma Women's Prison. The prison system also includes a vast network of notorious underground interrogation branches or divisions, primarily controlled by the state's four main intelligence services (referred to generally as the *mukhābarāt*): the Military Intelligence Department, the Political Security Directorate, the Air Force Intelligence Directorate, and the General Intelligence Directorate.[34] Most detainees recount that upon their arrest, they were taken to one or more of these intelligences branches and had to endure lengthy interrogations and myriad forms of physical and psychological torture, often for weeks or even months, before being transferred to one of the larger prisons. Generally prisoners face horrific conditions at these interrogation branches, such as the infamous Division 235, otherwise known as Palestine Division in Damascus, which is controlled by Syrian Military Intelligence. Sometimes held in filthy, overcrowded communal cells and other times kept in tiny solitary cells intended to keep prisoners in stress positions, detainees are confronted with either freezing cold temperatures or suffocating heat; deprived of food, water, or both for days; and have limited or no access to bathroom or hygiene facilities, or to medical care for injuries caused by torture.[35] In interrogation branches prisoners are frequently deprived of access to pen and paper or any means of comfort or entertainment.

Though consistently categorized as extremely poor by human rights organizations, conditions at the major prisons in the Syrian carceral archipelago have varied over the four decades. In the 1980s and 1990s, for example, Tadmur Military Prison (the focus of chapter 5) was Syria's most notorious detention facility; prisoners were routinely tortured to death, summarily executed with or without cursory field trials, and deprived of everything but the minimum amount of food and water they needed to barely survive. In the same time period some detainees viewed Saydnaya Military Prison as having a much less harsh and deadly environment than Tadmur, and therefore they considered it a much easier prison to survive. Not only were communal cells less crowded, but prisoners had access to more food as well as hygiene products, books, pen and paper, and visitations (and with them, clothing, money, and goods brought in from outside). However, with the onset of the 2011 Revolution and the regime's detention of tens of thousands of people, Tadmur's notoriety has been eclipsed by reports of abject conditions, mass summary executions, systematic daily torture, and lack of food and medical care for detainees at Saydnaya and other facilities.[36]

Though deprived of the conventional tools of writing in the intelligence branches and Tadmur Military Prison, detainees are able, at times, to compose and sometimes record their writings in physical form. As depicted in Mustafa Khalifa's *The Shell* and recounted in numerous memoirs, such as Sarraj's *From Tadmur to Harvard* (*Min Tadmur ila Harvard*) and Muhammad Salim Hammad's "Tadmur: Witness and Witnessed," many prisoners developed highly attuned memorization skills. Some prisoners, especially those with religious inclinations, have used these skills to memorize holy texts such as the Quran and Hadith; they memorized lists of names of those detained and executed, and others composed and memorized poetry and prose in order to record them in written form later. Some of the poems in Faraj Bayraqdar's *Dove in Free Flight* (*Hamama Mutlaqat al-Jinahayn*), 1997, for example, were memorized by cellmates who were released before he was, and they were able to transmit the poems to those outside. Prisoners also frequently use creative means to manufacture pen and paper by using whatever materials are available to them. Just as Omari recalls how he and his cellmates used scraps of fabric, ink made from blood and rust, and a nail for a pencil to record eighty-two names, other prisoners report creating ink from tea or other items and employing everything from onion peels to cigarette papers as a platform to write on.

In other major prisons, such as Duma Women's Prison or Saydnaya prior to 2011, detainees were able to obtain and use conventional notebooks and pens or pencils, and writing, whether about prison or other topics, as well as reading are a major way prisoners can productively endure their time in detention. Though prison authorities can confiscate prisoners' writings at any time, many authors have been able to preserve their papers and smuggle their writings out of prison. For example, 'Imad Shiha, who was detained for thirty years, composed three novels while in prison and was able to preserve the notebooks they were written in. Hasiba 'Abd al-Rahman's novel *The Cocoon* (*al-Sharnaqa*) is based on journals and other writings she composed while in prison. Other authors, however, such as short story writer Ibrahim Samu'il, composed some of their works only after they had been released from detention.

Reading Prison Literature and Human Rights

Although originally inspired by the life stories of the authors and by the texts of Syrian prison literature, this study draws from and seeks to contribute to scholarly examinations of prison literature and prison writings across world literatures. Of course, prison literature and prison writings are not unique to Syria, the Arab world, or the Middle East. Narratives of prison that generate critiques of regimes of power are not restricted to those written by detainees in authoritarian states or the Middle East.[37] Clear examples of this can be seen in the massive oeuvre of texts produced by those, especially from systematically marginalized, disenfranchised, and persecuted minority communities, or communities of color, who have been imprisoned in the massive carceral industrial complex of the US. Such works include those produced by George Jackson, Angela Davis, Assata Shakur, Leonard Peltier, Jimmy Santiago Baca, and countless others. More examples can be found in the writings of Guantanamo Bay detainees, such as Moazzam Begg and Mohamedou Ould Slahi, and in the case of Behrouz Boochani, the Kurdish-Iranian migrant detained for six years by Australian authorities on Manus Island who won the 2019 Victorian Prize for Literature for his memoir *No Friend but the Mountains.*

Authors of Syrian prison literature are influenced by a variety of literary works in their own writings, and the texts examined in this study circulate in an international literary field where writings about or composed through the experience of detention around the globe have been the subject of comprehensive scholarly analysis. Studies and anthologies of prison literature or prison writings, ranging from H. Bruce Franklin's *Prison Literature in America* and Tara Green's *From the Plantation to the Prison: African-American Confinement Literature* to Harold B. Segel's *The Walls behind the Curtain: East European Prison Literature, 1945–1990* and Philip F. Williams and Yenna Wu's *The Great Wall of Confinement: The Chinese Prison Camp through Contemporary Fiction and Reportage* have focused on the forms of such texts as well as their social, political, and historical functions in both classical and more recent time periods.[38] Syrian prison literature has been analyzed in English by scholars such as miriam cooke in her book *Dissident Syria*, which focuses on the context of the production of the texts, as well as the texts' content, and discusses prison literature in the broader context of oppositional cultural production.[39]

In considering the various studies and collections of texts treating or connected to detention, the difficulty of establishing a definition of prison literature or prison writings becomes clear. On the one hand, following the logic of certain anthologies, such as Pen America's 2018 Prison Writing Awards Anthology, *The Named and the Nameless*, or Judith A. Scheffler's anthology of women's writings, *Wall Tappings*, prison writing, as used in English, refers to any text, fictional or nonfictional, poetic or prose, produced by prisoners while incarcerated. The term *prison literature*, on the other hand, tends to include texts by both prisoners and nonprisoners that represent the prison experience, both briefly and in-depth, in any number of forms—memoirs, autobiographies, novels, poetry, short stories, and plays. In the critical literature the distinction between the two terms is often difficult to discern, and such texts cannot always be easily divided between the fictional and the factual.

The ambiguities, limitations, and potential imperatives of the application of such generic labels to writings by prisoners and writings about prison will be taken up in greater depth in chapter 1. At times in critical studies a near bifurcation exists in the treatment and analysis of such texts in terms of form versus content, despite the fact that many critics attempt to avoid it. A number of studies focus on the direct link between all forms of prison literature and prison writings and the articulation of universal and individual conceptions of human rights. Some critical studies, such as that offered by Kay Schaffer and Sidonie Smith in *Human Rights and Narrative Lives*, provide a sociological, historical, and political interpretation of a life-story texts related to human rights. Schaffer and Smith examine how personal life narratives (including prison memoirs) have become the predominant, documentary means through which human rights claims must be made and recognized in an ethical sense, and how such narratives are problematically transformed in a globalized context of reception. Other studies center on the treatment of prison writings in terms of form or poetics.[40]

To a certain extent early studies of Arabic prison literature reflect a tension between prison literature as politicized documentation and witness literature (resistance narratives, testimony, counternarratives, and alternatives to conventional human rights reportage) versus prison literature as a literary work of art where attention to form and creativity is the focus. Most early studies of Arabic prison literature, such as Nazih Abu Nidal's foundational *Prison Literature* (*Adab al-Sujun*, 1981), emphasize content over form and view texts about political detention as testimonies to political oppression in the Arab world and evidence of human rights abuses in specific Arab countries.

Though innately connected to its counterparts in other national literatures, as well as the global context of carceral security states in which it is produced, Syrian and Arabic prison literature is unique in its connection to a historical shift toward literary experimentalism in the Arabic literary field. In the trajectory of Syrian and Arabic literary history, prison literature has been and is produced by and productive of the designated "experimental shift" that began in modern Arabic literature in the 1960s.[41] Several heavily celebrated foundational works of experimental or avant-garde Arabic fiction are connected to, reference, allude to, or directly depict the experience of detention. The theme appears in Sun'allah Ibrahim's novella *That Smell* (*Tilka Ra'iha wa Qisas 'Ukhra*, 1966) and is subsequently encountered in novels such as Jamal al-Ghittani's *al-Zayni Barakat* (1974), 'Abd al-Rahman Munif's *East of the Mediterranean* (*Sharq al-Mutawassit*, 1976), Bensalem Himmich's (Binsalim Himmish) *The Theocrat* (*Majnun al-Hukm*, 1989), Elias Khoury's (Ilyas Khuri) *Yalu* (2002), and Sinan Antoon's (Sinan Antun) *I'jaam* (*I'jam*, 2004).

Termed a modernist shift by some critics and scholars and a postmodernist tendency by others, Arab writers' turn toward a conscious or self-reflexive manipulation of literary forms via the uses of historiographic metafiction, stream-of-consciousness narration, or cinematic realism has been engendered by systematic political oppression and, at least partially in certain foundational cases, I would argue, by the pervasive experience of political detention. Works of prison literature have not only become an essential part of the history of formal experimentation in modern Arabic literature, they have also been influenced by it.

In Syria the notions of political commitment and commitment literature remain relevant to discussions of literary production in the time period that is the focus of this book. In the 1950s, a "rallying-cry" emerged in the Arab literary world that advocated the idea that a writer should produce works that demonstrated the writer's political commitment (*iltizām*) to the progress of the nation (whether local or pan-Arab).[42] Writing in 2000, Stefan Meyer has observed that the dominant style in contemporary Syrian literature remains realism and is directly connected to the fact that "literary movements have been inseparable from political movements."[43] The connection between literary production and social realism as a vehicle for political engagement, especially in Syria, has resulted in the "intense politicization of literature," while at the same time "social criticism" has to a large extent remained controlled by "official" sponsorship and approval of writers.[44]

Meyer's reminder of the direct links between Syrian literature, official politicization of cultural production, and political movements is an important observation with which to contend in regard to discussions of prison literature.[45] This is particularly true given the attempted co-optation of the image of the politically engaged intellectual as well as the function of commitment literature in the Syrian Baʻth Party and state literary institutions.[46] However, his contention that social realism still dominated the Syrian literary scene in the 1990s is problematic given the large number of authors producing works both within and outside the genre of prison literature in the past three decades that have broken with a mode of so-called traditional social realism.[47] In Syria both earlier and more recent works of prison literature offer a clear indication of experiment with form. In turn, this experiment with form can present various challenges to the mode of reading such texts solely in terms of content or as a secondary form of human rights documentation.

This book is also inspired by and seeks to contribute to and intervene in critical scholarship on narrative, literature, and human rights—a now large and continually growing body of scholarly work that has emerged, especially in the case of the English-language academe, since September 11, 2001.[48] With a few notable exceptions, this scholarship has largely neglected the enormous corpus of literature written in Arabic and other Middle Eastern languages.[49] Additionally, certain aspects of this scholarship, despite some scholars' acknowledgment, still privileges specific literary forms, particularly the memoir and the novel, which are not necessarily the preeminent, most prominent, or most widely circulated genres in all world literatures, including Arabic literature. Some cases, such as that of Lynn Hunt's very compelling *Inventing Human Rights*, can, in part, work to reify the already well-established Eurocentrism of the origin story of a supposedly universal human rights, while also buttressing the novel's entrenched, privileged position in English language–based literary studies.[50] By including poetry and short stories in my analyses in this book, I seek to answer the call, put forward by Elizabeth Swanson Goldberg and

Alexandra Schultheis Moore, "to read for articulations of human rights in local and transnational contexts that uncover or produce alternative modernities, narratives, and ways of articulating political, economic, cultural, and social justice claims that fall outside the national-legal spheres of institutionalized human rights."[51]

Prison literature, Syrian or otherwise, and human rights discourse coalesce in numerous ways. Sophia A. McClennan and Alexandra Schultheis Moore remind us that the concept of human rights is not just "an idea, a set of discursive norms, a legal practice, and a political claim"; rather, "it attaches to a sense of community and to the construction of the victimized other; and it depends on storytelling and on practical political advocacy."[52] There is an inherent link between "human rights discourses, norms, and instruments" and "an international commitment to narratability."[53] Victims and survivors of human rights violations, including those detained in Syrian prisons, articulate their stories in narrative form, and these stories must be simultaneously narratable and readable in order to conform to the requirements of legal documentation. Human rights and international human rights law, according to Joseph Slaughter, "can be productively formulated in terms of narrative genres and narrative voices."[54] Syrian prison literature greatly broadens the spectrum of those genres and voices commonly incorporated into human rights law and discourse. In some works, such as Malik Daghastani's *The Vertigo of Freedom* (*Duwar al-Hurriyya*, 2002), the narrative can work against the notion of rendering the prison experience readable or visible, in opposition to the way it is depicted in traditional human rights discourse. In other cases, such as Faraj Bayraqdar's memoir *The Betrayals of Language and Silence* (*Khiyanat al-Lugha wa-l-Samt*, 2006) or his poetry collection *Dove in Free Flight*, stylistic or poetic elements in prison literature speak to some of the inadequacies, gaps, or limits in the normative narrative conventions of human rights.

Throughout this study, I analyze Syrian prison literature in conjunction with the reportage and legal documents of rights organizations, with the idea of viewing the concept of human rights literature as the outcome of reading practices that highlight "the interplay of literary representation and juridical-political rights work."[55] Drawing on the work of Goldberg and Moore, part of the aim of this book is to cultivate an interdisciplinary study of prison literature and human rights that analyzes the modes by which specific literary texts depict and make legible "the philosophies, laws, and practices of human rights from multiple, shifting cultural perspectives" while simultaneously challenging and evolving the narrative conventions of such rights work.[56] Like scholars working in other world literatures, I aim to develop a form of literary criticism that both examines how particular narratives interrogate and transgress the boundaries of language and representation of violence and human suffering, and accounts for the "'westcentric' history of human rights."[57]

In their overview of the history of the interdisciplinary study of human rights and literature, numerous scholars point to the heightened concerned with human rights by academics in the English-language academe following the rampant human rights violations committed by the US government in the wake of and in the wars following September 11, 2001. Yet as McClennan and Moore have pointed out, "the interdiscipline of human rights and literary studies has no definitive ontology," and approaches to the study of literary culture and human rights can include the examination of "struggles for justice and their expression through literary forms that have taken place in a global framework, across multiple languages" and that "may have different operative terms at play."[58] Decades prior to the US government's systematic perpetration of human rights violations in its pursuit of its so-called war on terror, since the mid-to-late 1970s, the growing publication and critical recognition of the genre of prison literature in Syria and across the Arab world points to such an alternative trajectory. And as noted above, production of and interest in prison literature coincided and grew with the establishment of local human rights organizations in the same time period.

There are many things this book is not and is not intended to be. This book is not a history of Syrian prisons, human rights organizations, civil society, democracy, and rights or oppositional political movements or parties in Syria. It is also not a biographical or oral history study of individuals in the Syrian opposition. It does not trace the life stories, activities, and intellectual ideologies of the deans of Syrian political prisoners; extremely important figures such as Riyad Turk, who spent almost two decades in prison and whom one biographer calls the Mandela of Syria; or major human rights activists and defenders, such as Anwar al-Bunni, Mazen Darwish, Yara Badr, and many others. All of these subjects strongly warrant further scholarly inquiry, especially in English, particularly given the limited scope of Syria studies in the US up until very recently. However, these valuable subjects are not the focus of this book. This book is intended to be an interdisciplinary, literary study of a select number of texts in a vast body of literature that represents the experience of detention in Syria. It is my hope that it will encourage further studies of Syrian cultural production, including many of the works of prison literature listed in the bibliography that, because of lack of space and time, could not be adequately discussed here. I also hope this book will encourage further study of the variegated history of the Syrian opposition and of the democracy and human rights movements in Syria, as well as the translation into English of more Syrian literature, including the works listed in the bibliography.

Finally, I must note my acute awareness of the issues of privilege and the politics of location. It is all too easy for me—an Iranian-American teacher, academic, and translator who comfortably lives and works in Queens, New York—to write a scholarly study that, of course, seeks to honor the authors and the works of literature analyzed here but also engages in a critique of the international human rights regime and discourse. This is the same international human rights establishment that people around the world, those living through everyday, systematic abuses, pervasive modes of oppression, and all too frequently lethal forms of violence, urgently turn to or engage with every day as a way to confront and combat the suffering and injustices they face. The critiques of human rights presented here are in no way intended to deprecate the work of courageous and determined human rights defenders, especially those within and from Syria who have continued to put their lives on the line to challenge violations, abuses, and atrocities perpetrated by the Asad regime, Iran's proxy militias, and, since 2012, some Syrian oppositional militias. Without the important work of determined defenders and activists, including Mansour Omari, Mazen Darwish, the still-unaccounted-for Douma (Duma) 4 (Samira al-Khalil, Razan Zeituneh [Zaytuna], Wa'il

Hamada, and Nazim Hamadi), and countless others, the world would not be aware of much of what has occurred in Syria with respect to human rights violations and crimes against humanity, including since the onset of the 2011 Syrian Revolution and the subsequent war. It is because of this critical work of human rights defenders in Syria that the international community cannot claim ignorance to the atrocities perpetrated by the Asad regime.

Evoking the distinction made by Stephen Hopgood, the intended target of criticism here is not human rights in the sense of "local and transnational activists who bring publicity to abuses they and their communities face and who try to exert pressure on governments and the United Nations for action, often at tremendous personal cost."[59] Rather, the critiques raised throughout this book are centered on a more generalized notion of Human Rights discourse and the international Human Rights establishment or regime (capitalization following Hopgood) as "a global structure of laws, courts, norms, and organizations that raise money, write reports, run international campaigns, open local offices, lobby governments, and claim to speak with singular authority in the name of humanity as a whole."[60] It is this international Human Rights regime, with its foundational reliance on the nation-state as the presumed protector of rights, and on international institutions controlled by the national interests of states such as the US, Russia, and China, that can or will only selectively intervene in crises and atrocities, along with the international community as a whole, that has failed Syria.

In the case of the humanitarian and human rights catastrophe that has unfolded in Syria since 2011, it is a failure of epic and beyond-devastating proportions. Despite the recognition of this failure, despite acknowledging the flaws of the international Human Rights system, "its imperialist origins and complicities with global power and corruption," I believe that we must still seek to understand the roles that notions of rights, human and other, play in struggles for justice and freedom.[61] Scholars, advocates, and critics of human rights frequently comment that the concept is, and has always been, an aspirational one. Through this book I hope to add my voice to others that advocate for the study of forms of cultural production globally, and Syrian prison literature in particular, to shed light on the limitations of the contemporary discourse and regime of Human Rights in order to begin to conceive of and sustain alternative, more productive, more variegated visions of human rights. In the end this book is intended to provide a series of necessarily initial and incomplete answers to two basic questions: What can we learn by reading Syrian prison literature, and what can Syrian prison literature teach us about humanity and human rights?

Overview of Chapters

Chapter 1 expands on the introduction by engaging with writers' and scholars' debates about prison literature as a genre. While I recognize the dilemmas and limitations of conceptualizing a body of writing as prison literature, there is a case to be made for the use of the generic term as a political imperative. Drawing on different trajectories of genre theory, I reflect on prison literature as a category and show how Arabic literary criticism on prison literature frequently replicates the documentary tendencies in some works of prison literature as well as human rights reportage. By privileging narrative content over form, much of the earlier literary criticism on Syrian and Arabic prison literature, I show, worked as a secondary or tertiary vehicle for documenting human rights violations. But Arabic prison literature also presents, as Nazih Abu Nidal reflects, a quest for freedom of form, and this chapter suggests that attention to alternative forms such as the short story, and the experimental, narrative structures of works such as Rosa Yaseen Hasan's (Ruza Yasin Hasan) novel *Negative* (*Nighatif*) challenge the ways in which traditional human rights reportage presents the experiences of detainees.

In March 2011, when the children of Darʿa wrote antigovernment graffiti on the wall of their school, they were detained, tortured, and held incommunicado by Syrian security services. Chapter 2 opens with reports of this event, which is widely narrated as the start of the Syrian Revolution. The way that the children's stories quickly became emblematic of the Syrian uprising is related, I posit, to the themes of recognition, vulnerability, and sentimentality in the short stories of authors such as Ibrahim Samuʾil and Ghassan al-Jabaʿi, and in a play by Wadiʿ Ismandar. Drawing on examinations of recognition in both critical and human rights theory, including the works of Terence Cave, Judith Butler, and Bryan Turner, I argue that the poetics of recognition at play in the works of Syrian prison literature evoke alternative forms of vulnerability that can reflect but sometimes fall outside the purview of human rights discourse. The evocations of vulnerability in Syrian prison literature have paved the way for a type of "sentimental education" of the readers of such works. At the same time such texts also generate allegories of the failures of political recognition that plague the international human rights system, a failure so clearly seen in the humanitarian and human rights tragedy that has enfolded Syria today.

Building on the second chapter's discussion of vulnerability and recognition, chapter 3 undertakes a comparative analysis of the representation of torture in Syrian prison literature and human rights reports. Invoking as well as critiquing Elaine Scarry's foundational analysis of the relationship between torture and voice, I argue that the laudable aim of human rights organizations, such as Amnesty International, to document, broadcast, and condemn the state's use of torture requires making the experience of torture narratable and readable. Through the case of the extraordinary rendition of Maher Arar (Mahir 'Arar), I analyze how torture is represented in the formal, generic structures of human rights reportage and court documents. Such examples show how the narrative conventions of human rights frequently mute the voices of political detainees and render them into silent objects of torture. Different authors, including the poet Faraj Bayraqdar and novelist Hasiba 'Abd al-Rahman, have represented the experience of torture in ways that go beyond the script of human rights reportage, and this chapter examines how their works interrogate the possibility of representing torture, reclaim the concept of a narrative imperative, and reassert the primacy of the voice of the tortured detainee as a speaking subject.

Beginning with a discussion of Yassin al-Haj Saleh's contention that prison is a "form of life" for thousands of Syrians, chapter 4 offers an analysis of representations of time and space in Syrian prison literature and in human rights reportage. Building on recent scholarship in the field of carceral geography, including the work of Dominique Moran, Michael

Fiddler, and others, I argue that when focusing on the physical sites of violations, human rights reportage generates a form of countermapping against the Syrian state's steadfast denial of its role in perpetrating human rights abuses. In describing prisons and detention centers, such reports emphasize that which is measurable or mappable in material and mathematical terms—cell size, deplorable prison conditions, and arbitrary sentencing—in order to make prison time and space readable and visible for their audiences. Authors of Syrian prison literature also engage in such countermapping techniques, but at the same time they articulate a profoundly different lived experience of prison time and space. Through readings of works such as Heba Dabbagh's (Hiba al-Dabbagh) memoir *Just Five Minutes,* Bara Sarraj's memoir and essay collection *From Tadmur to Harvard*, and Faraj Bayraqdar's poetry collection *Dove in Free Flight*, this chapter demonstrates how works of prison literature reproduce the affective cartographies and emotional geographies of detainees through the lived experience of detention. In doing so, they show how political prisoners individually and collectively attempt to resist the mechanisms of the carceral system to assert their creativity and individual identity.

The subject of multiple special human rights reports, Tadmur Military Prison gained its reputation as the worst prison in Syria in the 1980s. Allegedly "liberated" and then "destroyed" by the Islamic State of Iraq and Syria (ISIS/Da'ish) in May 2015 when they took over the city of Palmyra, Tadmur had been the focus of special reports by human rights organizations since the 1990s. Analyzing works such as Mustafa Khalifa's landmark novel *The Shell* and memoirs, chapter 5 extends the arguments from the previous chapter by examining how the writings about detainees' experiences in Tadmur produce forms of sousveillance in contrast to the state's denial of the human rights abuses committed there for decades. Furthermore, as with representations of torture, authors self-reflexively question the capacity of language and resort to forms of surrealism to represent the worst forms of human cruelty and suffering that took place in the prison.

Finally, many works in the ever-growing body of prison literature, such as the late Jamil Hatmal's short stories and Malik Daghastani's prison novella, *The Vertigo of Freedom*, provide self-reflexive commentaries on the relationship between prison and the act of writing itself. Incorporating scholarly analyses of postmodern metafiction by Patricia Waugh, Mark Currie, and others, I argue that the prevalence of metafictional tendencies, what I call carceral metafiction, in Syrian prison literature reflects a critical questioning of the power of narrative itself and interrogates the possibility of representing the prison experience transparently, in contrast to human rights reportage. Moreover, metafiction in Syrian prison literature is also linked to the conditions of exile faced by political dissidents before and after the 2011 Revolution. Thus this chapter shows how particular works of prison literature animate the same borderline tropes of writings about exile.

In lieu of a conclusion and in light of what now appears to be the suppression of the Syrian Revolution, the continuing reign of the Asad regime with the support of Russia and Iran, and the complicity of the international community, the coda briefly surveys the connections between recent forms of visual cultural production—such as the film *Suleima* (*Sulayma*) and the short videos of the Abounaddara (Abu Naddara) film group—and the genre of prison literature. Like texts of prison literature, these films employ various strategies to contend with forms of injustice and political oppression. Though Abounaddara, as a collective, explicitly articulates its mission in the language of human rights ("the right to the image"), some of its films reveal the failures of the international human rights regime to alleviate the suffering of Syrian citizens. Other works, such as *Suleima*, express optimism for dignity and peace for all in the future. I conclude that we must attend to the messages and modes of ambivalence, as well as articulations of additional and alternative rights (Abounaddara's "right to the image") found in these forms of cultural production and works of prison literature, along with scholarly critiques of the rights regime. We must do so in order to begin to form a more inclusive and more effective concept and practice of human rights.

1

Prison Literature, Genre, and Truth Effects

In the preface to *Negative: From the Memory of Female Syrian Detainees* (*Nighatif: Min Dhakirat al-Mu'taqalat al-Surriyat*), Rosa Yaseen Hasan begins with a reflection on the precise nature or genre of her own textual creation. She writes: "I don't know if there is such a thing called the documentary novel! But I believe that imagination is the space that novels flourish in, and documentation is the complete opposite of that. Or rather, the paths under its [documentation's] influence are already etched before writing even begins."[1] Though she expresses a preference for the "imaginary world" of fiction because it is "more beautiful in narrative," in the case of this particular text, she must "sacrifice the splendor of the novelistic imaginary" in order to "preserve the truth or, to put it more precisely, to preserve the experience."[2] Nonetheless, she insists on retaining the term *novel* as part of categorizing her own work because according to her, "what happened there (in prison) only happened to be written about in novels."[3]

Hasan's ambiguous statement suggests that what happens in prison is so unimaginable that it could only exist in a work of fiction, and yet her novel is explicitly a documentary work. Her preface and introduction frame a text that is marked by clear experimentation with form and structure. Published by the Cairo Center for Studies of Human Rights, *Negative*, sometimes fragmented and varying in style and tone, is constructed of oral testimonies of women who have been detained in Syrian prisons. A cross-genre text, it also incorporates and intertwines a number of other texts and narratives, including quotes taken from writings about prison—from Egyptian activist Farida Naqqash to Moroccan detainee

25

Malika Oufkir to South African poet Breyten Breytenbach—that serve as a reminder of the connections and solidarity between detainees who write the experience of detention around the globe.[4]

While Hasan notes that composing such a text is an important task to bring to light women's voices in a time when they have been partially silenced, she also points out that she could have continued to write it for years. No single text, the author reminds us, could capture all of the experiences of Syrian female political prisoners. Nevertheless, she asks her readers to consider her documentary novel as "an attempt to record a part of female history made absent for long years—like the experience of the opposition more generally."[5] Hasan does not mention the term *prison literature* (*adab al-sijn* or *adab al-sujūn*) in disclosing her goals in writing *Negative*. Although the text is frequently included in lists or review articles of Syrian prison literature or prison writings, and she herself has written articles about the genre, the author does not use the term in her introduction.[6]

Imprisoned from 1980 to 1996 due to his membership in the Communist Party Political Bureau, dissident writer Yassin al-Haj Saleh would finally publish a collection of his essays on prison in conventional book form in the wake of the 2011 Revolution. Though his book also frequently appears in bibliographies of prison literature, al-Haj Saleh, like Hasan, eschews the term *prison literature* in his introduction to *At Last, Boys! Sixteen Years in Syrian Prisons* (*Bi-l-Khalas, Ya Shabab! Sittin 'Aman fi al-Sujun al-Suriyya*). *At Last, Boys!* includes essays written over a number of years after the author's release from prison, as well as interviews about prison and the status of former political detainees in Syria.

Al-Haj Saleh describes this collection of texts as "faces of the experience of political prisoners in Asad's Syria," writings on "prison as a remembered experience," and reflections on the "conditions of former political prisoners in Syria."[7] The book is "placed in an uneasy position" because "it isn't comfortably classified in the abode of 'prison literature,' and neither is it social research, nor is it the autobiography of a political prisoner."[8] Likewise, this collection, according to al-Haj Saleh, is not a "political or legal document, unmasking the regime and exposing its crimes to the public."[9] Instead, the author sees *At Last, Boys!* as "an intentional effort to transform prison into a cultural subject . . . something close to divesting (it) of its magic and participating in demolishing the myths connected with it, the myth of the political prisoner, especially." Simply put, al-Haj Saleh does not consider any section of the book literature because it doesn't treat the subject of prison as "a story or tale."[10]

Hasan's and al-Haj Saleh's reflections on and categorization of their own writings are indicative of the issues and debates involved in defining just what exactly constitutes prison literature in Syria, the Middle East, or around the world more broadly. What is at stake in naming, defining, and reading it as a specific genre? Like prison literature or prison writing in English, *adab al-sijn* or *adab al-sujūn* is an amorphous and ambiguous genre in the Arabic literary field.[11] It is a genre that can be defined by subject matter (texts that represent the experience of detention, including those by authors who have never been imprisoned), but it is also demarcated by the time and place of its production (texts that authors produce while incarcerated, including those texts that may not directly refer to detention). Some writers, such as Yassin al-Haj Saleh, avoid or reject the term in reflecting on their own writings while other authors and critics embrace the genre as a literary-political imperative. When critics and readers categorize a particular work as prison literature, they can impose a kind of literary confinement or generic incarceration that can reify the structure of detention itself. They may fail to consider the text as a work of art or the creative agency of the writer in producing it. As Dylan Rodríguez cogently argues in examining the writings of imprisoned radical US intellectuals, such categorization "legitimizes and reproduces the discursive-material regime of imprisonment," where the term *prison* becomes a homogenizing and domesticating modifier.[12]

Yet for some who deliberately adopt, foster, and advocate for the term (and here I'm referring to the Arabic/Arab context), *prison literature* is a classification that intentionally and consciously marks particular texts as explicitly contesting regimes of power, including an authoritarian nation-state; the use of the generic label can demarcate such texts as forms of resistance literature. While Rodríguez makes a strong and compelling case against the generic label of *prison writing* in the case of the written cultural production of US-based prisoners, the context of the emergence and production of prison literature in Syria and the Arab world differs substantially, given the link between direct dissent against the state and the historical emergence of the genre known as *adab al-sujūn*, and especially the absence of state-sponsored creative writing and education programs in Middle East prison systems.[13] Though the state may attempt to censor or co-opt works of prison literature through the mechanisms of *tanfīs*, for some Syrian authors the use and maintenance of the term *prison literature* to describe their writings is a political imperative. Viewed as creative interventions against the political oppressions and human rights violations of the state, works of prison literature, regardless of censorship, also function as counternarratives to official state history and as witness or testimonial literature to systematic rights abuses.

In some cases, prison literature can serve as confirmation of or as an alternative to human rights reportage, especially when human rights organizations have been prevented from deploying formal mechanisms for documenting violations thoroughly or at all. Reservations about and valid critiques of the term *prison literature* notwithstanding, and with an acknowledgement of the variations in and limitations of its definitions, I argue that retaining an understanding of a body of texts called prison literature is valuable in both a literary critical and political sense. If examined through the lens of genre theory and earlier critical studies of Arabic writing about detention, the concept of prison literature can grant us a deeper understanding of the connections between the truth effects of a given literary work generated through the experience of detention and the truth claims of survivors of human rights abuses.

Generic Ambivalences: Prison Literature and Truth Effects

In its broadest and most inclusive definition, *prison literature* refers to any text, fictional or nonfictional, prose, poetic, or dramatic, that is written in, about, or through the experience of detention. Yet such a definition is necessarily contingent, problematic, and always subject to debate.[14] As noted by John Frow, in classical European criticism, genre has been equated with a system of rules and classifications that tend to be thought of "as being like standards: explicit, formalized durable rules which extend over several communities of practice."[15] The impulse toward genre classification can in some ways be linked to a kind of literary "policing" in which certain texts are excluded or viewed as an abnormal exception because they fail to fit in with a given system of classification.[16] For Frow, the biological model used to develop taxonomies of genres of European literature in the seventeenth and eighteenth centuries is extremely problematic because the "morphology of genre is open-ended and indeterminate," and genre is always "interfertile"—any genre can be crossed over with any other genre.[17] In addition, the properties of a given text cannot be directly or simply derived from its genre. Finally, no exhaustive or conclusive system of generic classification can exist because new genres and breakaway genres are always in the process of formation.

In the case of the body of texts produced through the experience of detention in Syria, the governing rules of what prison literature as a genre has been, is, or should be as pronounced by any given critic or writer are frequently met with either critical reservations or rejection by others. Despite the fact that *At Last Boys!* is nearly always included in bibliographies of Syrian prison literature and that as a dissident figure the author, Yassin al-Haj Saleh, has been compared to Václav Havel, al-Haj Saleh does not consider the book a work of prison literature.[18] Rather, he relates the term to fictional prose works—works such as Mustafa Khalifa's *The Shell* (*al-Qawqa'a*) or the short stories of Jamil Hatmal. Other authors, like Faraj Bayraqdar, consider their memoirs as part of *adab al-sujūn* but are more cautious or concerned when the label of *prison literature* is applied to other works they produced in prison, such as poetry, that might not directly represent the experience of detention. Still other authors consider everything they wrote in prison to be part of the genre while some make the case that only those who have experienced detention can write true, authentic prison literature.[19]

The questions over the definition of *adab al-sujūn* and the variety of texts that appear or disappear as part of its generic confines according to how it is being defined at a particular historical moment demonstrate what Jacques Derrida calls the "law of genre." The classifying power of generic definition is indicated as a kind of "authoritarian summons to a law of a 'do' or 'do not.'"[20] Derrida asserts that the inherent problem with generic classification is that it posits a normative position and evaluation of a given literary work that attempts to erase or avoid acknowledging the presence of texts that might destabilize the prescriptive parameters of classification. However, in reality, no genre is or remains pure because the law of genre dictates that just as norms are articulated, so too does a "law of impurity or contamination" come into play that disturbs the definition of a given genre.[21] Additionally, a given text participates in but does not solely belong to a given genre—a point that is important to consider given not only Rodríguez's salient criticisms of the term *prison writing* but also the ambivalence of some Syrian authors over the label of *prison literature* as applied to their work, and the fact that many works of prison literature incorporate different forms within a single narrative.

If genre, as Tzvetan Todorov suggests, represents "the meeting place between general poetics and event-based literary history," then the advent and invention of *adab al-sujūn* as a generic term can be identified as coming into usage in Arabic literary criticism in the early to mid-1970s as a result of both the residual effects of colonial rule in various Arab states and the suppression of political dissent in many of the same states several decades after independence from direct colonial rule.[22] The term *adab al-sujūn* serves as a link between and an enframement of the widespread and recurrent event of political detention and the literature that such an experience has generated and continues to generate. It can be constructive to think of the category of prison literature as a broadly defined complex or secondary speech genre that serves as an "aggregate of the means for seeing and conceptualizing reality" that has developed out of a particular set of historical and political circumstances in which the authors have lived.[23]

The pervasive experience of detention in Syria and elsewhere around the world has resulted in the formation of a heterogeneous body of prison literature that is connected to a specific "sphere of activity" (the experience of repression, surveillance, arrest, torture, detention) and that exists in and as a realm of "highly developed and organized cultural communication."[24] The recognition of the category of *adab al-sujūn* indicates how a genre that is always in flux and acknowledged as unstable serves as a mediation "between a social situation and the text which realizes certain features of this situation, or which responds strategically to its demands."[25] Though generic classifications may guide the "potential use values of texts," they do not strictly limit how the texts are read.[26] In other words, works of prison literature are not necessarily confined by "uses that are mapped out in advance by the genre."[27] Rather, such texts are "uses of genre, performances of or allusions to the norms and conventions which form them and which they in turn transform."[28]

In considering *adab al-sujūn* as a generic label and in identifying a series of works as tied to the experience of detention, we recognize that genres "create effects of reality and truth which are central to the different ways the world is understood. . . . The semiotic frames within which genres are embedded implicate and specify layered ontological domains—implicit realities which genres form as a pre-given reference, together with the effects of authority and plausibility which are specific to genre."[29] Considering prison literature as a broadly inclusive but amorphous and contingent genre aids us in understanding that meaning making is, indeed, often more far-reaching than the explicit content of the text. If works of *adab al-sujūn*, in all of their variation of form and content, generate truth effects, then the acknowledgement of a particular text as prison literature also shapes how these truth effects are grasped and interpreted by readers and critics. Knowing a given work is recognizable, in one way or another, as prison literature provides a "set of cues" that guides but does not entirely restrict our reading of it.[30]

Of Truth Effects and Truth Claims:
Prison Literature and Human Rights Discourse

If, as a designated genre, prison literature can be viewed as always containing and evoking a structure of implication and a series of truth effects for its readers through varying mediating forms of representation of the detention experience, it must also be recognized as a body of literature that coincides with, is intertwined with, and at times critically challenges the truth effects and truth claims generated by human rights discourse in both Arab and international contexts.[31] For many authors, readers, and critics of prison literature, the "potential use value" of such designated texts is that they serve as testimonials to or documentation of the absence of or violation of human rights.[32] This is the case despite debates over whether such literature is "truth-telling, as a representation of truth-telling, or as something imaginary that bears only a distant relationship to juridical evidence."[33] Yet I would argue that reading the many different texts that can be counted as *adab al-sujūn*, whether deemed fictional or factual by authors and critics, can both reinforce and transform our perception of the necessity as well as the adequacies of the narrative representation of the detainee as a subject and of the abuses and violations detainees endure in the discourse of human rights.[34]

Human rights discourse (including human rights reportage and the texts of international human rights law) not only is inherently tied to the notion of the right to narrate but also maintains its own generic conventions.[35] Reports, announcements, legal documents, and declarations issued by human rights organizations and international human rights institutions are written in narrative terms tend to fall in line with realist genres. Such genres "tend to assume that reality is singular and external to the forms through which we apprehend it."[36] The notion of genre itself provides "a set of 'frames' or 'fixes' on the world."[37] This suggests that the world is divisible and reinforces "the *formative* power of these representational frames."[38] In turn, the audience assumes that these frames are natural and the information provided through them transparent.[39] In order to institute its truth claims against a state, group, or individual who is in violation of international human rights standards, human rights regimes work through a discourse of transparency, visibility, and readability, and frequently in order for a rights claim to be activated, "victims need to come forward and testify."[40]

As the close readings of particular works of Syrian prison literature in the chapters that follow show, prison literature can point to the gaps, inadequacies, and effacements of detained subjects, their voices, and their experiences that occur in conventional representations of human rights abuses. One example of this is the use of the omniscient narrator or third person in human rights reportage. As Frow points out, when the third person is introduced into a speech situation, an asymmetry is produced; that third person becomes "a silent participant, an object rather than a subject of speech, and is thus sometimes designated as a grammatical non-person, unless of course they too become an interlocutor."[41] This is one of the fundamental issues involved in human rights reportage—an inevitable asymmetry of power is produced by the representation of a sometimes silent participant (the victim or survivor of human rights abuses), especially when eyewitness testimony is not available or when organizations or institutions speak for the victim. As Schaffer and Smith observe: "the pressures to conform the 'messiness' of personal testimony to protocols for the codification of a human rights abuse, to contain it within a standardized, often chronological, format . . . subsumes local knowledge and conceptual frameworks for understanding different cultural experiences and traditions to the national and international frameworks of human rights law."[42]

My purpose in pointing this out is not to suggest that the work of human rights defenders is not critically important in struggles for political freedoms around the globe. The intervention of human rights activists and institutions on behalf of prisoners of conscience can be successful in ending human rights violations, especially in individual cases, such as that of Faraj Bayraqdar.[43] Likewise, cases such as that of Mansour Omari show the dangers human rights activists face in documenting violations and reflect the fact that some defenders may also become authors of prison literature. Rather, I aim to provide an indication of how prison literature can, first, shed light on some of the narrative disruptions and erasures that occur through the discourse of human rights and, second, offer aesthetic modes of intervention against political oppression through the generation of alternative truth effects that might suggest why sometimes the discourse of human rights fails to bring about effective change or is ignored by those with the power to intervene.

Secondary Witnessing and the Quest for Freedom of Form

Though it does not refer to human rights, the literary critical designation of the genre first appears, at least to my knowledge, in a 1973 article titled "Toward Prison Literature" (Nahwa Adab al-Sujun) by Syrian novelist and critic Nabil Sulayman.[44] Eight years later the first book-length study of

Arabic texts about detention would clearly connect the genre to the 1948 Universal Declaration of Human Rights (UDHR) and the international human rights regime.

In *Prison Literature* (*Adab al-Sujun*, 1981), Nazih Abu Nidal opens his analysis with a familiar and often repeated epigraph in studies of the relationship between literature and detention. He evokes the UDHR and provides a selective citation of some of its articles. He quotes Articles 1 and 2 (stressing the inherent rights for all human beings of equality, liberty, dignity, and freedom from discrimination), Articles 3, 5, 9, 10 (emphasizing the rights of the individual, such as the right to life, the prohibition on torture and arbitrary detention, and the right to a fair, speedy, and impartial trial), Articles 12 and 14 (declaring the right of privacy and the freedom to seek asylum from persecution), Articles 18 and 19 (underscoring the rights of thought, conscience, and religion as well as freedom of expression and opinion), and finally Article 30 (asserting that no individual or state can perform any act that destroys or violates the rights embodied in the declaration), which Abu Nidal particularly highlights. Abu Nidal presents the UDHR and selected articles without directly commenting on them as the starting point for his discussion of the literature of prisons. He then provides an introduction that analyzes the historical and class roots of the crisis of Arab democracy, the oppression of intellectuals who politically oppose the prevailing regimes in the Arab world, and the absence of basic human rights in the historical period both preceding and contemporaneous with the time he was writing in. For Abu Nidal, prison literature has developed as a direct and seemingly natural by-product of this "crisis of democracy"—as a "contemporary condemnation of all forms of tyranny, dispossession, and degradations" in the Arab world and elsewhere around the globe.[45]

In the next section of his study, Abu Nidal provides summaries and brief analyses of numerous texts, ranging from Jamal al-Ghittani's novel *al-Zayni Barakat* to Muhammad Kamil al-Khatib's collection of short stories *The Coastal Cities* (*al-Mudun al-Sahiliyya*) to prison memoirs such as Farida Naqqash's (The Prison . . . The Nation) (*al-Sijn . . . al-Watn*). He also provides a brief summary of a selection of literary texts and memoirs on prison from the canon of world literature. Like other early studies of the relationship between prison and Arabic literature, this section of Abu Nidal's *Adab al-Sujun* is concerned more with a description of content and historical, political, and geographical context than with an in-depth examination of the formal features of such narratives. He describes the forms of torture various protagonists face, he summarizes depictions of censorship and surveillance, and he recounts the brutal effects of political repression on social relations as portrayed in each text. Although he offers brief remarks on the style, structure, and mode of writing of the text, Abu Nidal stresses or prioritizes the fact that each work of prison literature can be viewed as documentary testimony to the absence of those rights highlighted from the UDHR in the epigraph and introduction to his study.[46] Much of Abu Nidal's study performs as a kind of secondary or tertiary form of witness literature, documenting human rights abuses as they are represented in each text. His analysis works to "translate the knowledge produced by the literary into the fact-based vernacular that dominates much of human rights discourse."[47]

However, in contrast to the dominant stress on content in much of his study, Abu Nidal inserts into the middle of his book a short, separated chapter on "artistic form in the Arabic novel of oppression."[48] The Arab novelist, he argues, seeks to overcome and transcend oppression and terror not just through content, but also on the level of form:

> Because he, on the level of practical reality, is searching for a freedom that appears to be impossible, he strives to achieve his freedom through an attempt to flee from the classical form of the novel in the direction of a new artistic form. These attempts at escaping from the captivity of classical aesthetic forms and their chains are, consciously or unconsciously, an attempt to arrive at the equivalent of the freedom of content by possessing the freedom of form.
>
>   On the psychological level, the novelist in the moment of creativity and in order to express the intensity of the experience of prison and his sufferings in it undertakes a process of breaking the chains and shackles in both a material and abstract sense. Only the realities of fear, terror, and the chains are beyond the capacity of the human novelist, so the novelist undertakes to gain his psychological balance by breaking the chains of artistic form.[49]

For Abu Nidal, many of the texts he classifies as prison literature reflect authors' attempts to leave behind conventional forms of prose as a means of liberation from tyranny. Despite the uniqueness of each text and the individuality of each writer's experience in prison, all of the texts should be taken as a whole, and together, they provide a collective form of resistance to the political oppression they critique. At the same time, he observes that the corpus of texts can be divided into testimony (or documentation) and novels. The former elaborates the true experience of the writer while the latter is marked by creative license in depicting the prison experience, but such texts often use or incorporate documentary techniques. Although Abu Nidal categorizes some of the works in his study into one of the two categories, he asserts that the two forms—testimony and fictional novels—are generically intertwined in some works and cannot be separated.

Reading this pioneering study of modern Arabic prison literature, one is struck by the author's belated recourse to reflections on the formal or stylistic features of the texts under his consideration. Yet in this one brief chapter, he highlights the extremely significant relationship between the experience of detention and writers' recourse to literary experimentation or "freedom of form" as a revolutionary mode of writing. If "genre is essentially a socio-symbolic message" and "form is immanently and intrinsically an ideology in its own right," the emergence of various experimental forms in Arabic and Syrian prison literature within a broader movement of literary experimentalism is an important element of Arabic literary history.[50] In effect, modern Arabic prison literature has both produced and been produced by the experimental shift.

Abu Nidal's study of Arabic prison literature appeared twenty-five years after the publication of Sun'allah Ibrahim's landmark novel *That Smell* (*Tilka Ra'iha wa Qisas 'Ukhra*, 1966)—a work of literature that can be considered a foundational text in two significant ways. First, it is one of the novels most frequently identified as part of the experimental shift in Arabic literature in the 1960s.[51] Second, it is widely considered a founding text of the contemporary genre of *adab al-sujūn*. In general, according to Sabry Hafez, various works of literature produced in and after the 1960s indicated this experimental shift in Arabic narrative discourse via the use of dialogue with classical discourses, a polyphony of narrative voices, self-reflexivity, dynamic experimentation, the representation of the dissolution of time, and heterogeneous linguistic variations, among many other elements.[52] Ibrahim was imprisoned from 1959 to 1964 for his affiliation with the communist movement in Egypt. His first literary work, *That Smell*, depicts a protagonist who is completely alienated from society after being released from prison. Written in a stark and bleak style of cinematic or documentary realism, the text, as Samia Mehrez notes, defied the literary traditions of its time. Both the novel and its style indicated a disillusionment with how languages, and discourse in general, were being manipulated by the power of the state.[53]

Like many works of Arabic prison literature that would follow it, *That Smell* contains a number of innovative or unique "aestheticizing strategies" that seek to "recode or rewrite the world and its own data."[54] As a genre that has both produced and been produced by various trends in Arabic literature, in its varying versions, *adab al-sujūn* offers a political aesthetics that works to "authorize and reinforce a new representational space."[55] Barbara Harlow's observation is relevant to the case of Arabic prison literature: "the writing of political detention militates on behalf of the human and political rights of the dispossessed and disenfranchised, proposing new models and genres for politically critical literature."[56] It is in this new representational space where not only are a politics of oppression and cruelty subverted and resisted, but also the normative parameters of the generic conventions of international human rights discourse are destabilized and the traditions of literary form, the other "chains" that Abu Nidal invokes, are broken. In the Syrian case specifically, when the corpus of prison literature is not just dominated by memoirs or testimonials, but also includes fictional, dramatic, poetic, and generically hybrid works, such as Hasan's *Negative*, attention to the truth effects created by such forms is essential to understanding the critical status of the genre of prison literature and its relationship to the generic conventions of human rights.

Flashes of Light in the Darkness: Rosa Yaseen Hasan's *Negative*

In the decades after the publication of Sunʿallah Ibrahim's *That Smell*, a number of Syrian authors have produced literary works about the experience of detention that evade simple definition or classification in terms of style and form. Texts such as Hasiba 'Abd al-Rahman's fictional-autobi-ographical novel *The Cocoon* (*al-Sharnaqa*, 1999) and Faraj Bayraqdar's poetic prison memoir, *The Betrayals of Language and Silence* (*Khiyanat al-Lugha wa-l-Samt*, 2006), speak of and to the violence of torture and detention, as well as the gaps, inadequacies, and effacements that occur in the representation of human rights abuses. As narratives that experiment with how detainees as speaking subjects are represented, such texts are hybrid works that challenge the generic conventions of human rights reportage in a variety of ways. As I show in chapter 3, for example, in *The Cocoon* the disjointed and surreal stream-of-consciousness accounts of the protagonist's torture work to reassert the voice of the tortured subject while effacing the presence, power, and authority of the torturer. In *The Betrayals of Language and Silence*, the fragmented structure of the narrative and Bayraqdar's direct interrogation of language's capacity to represent torture and detention suggest the impossibility of essentialist or totalizing narratives of imprisonment.

Like the works of 'Abd al-Rahman and Bayraqdar, Hasan's *Negative* presents a mode of representation that diverges significantly from a typical individual, chronological, linear prison memoir or social realist prison novel of an earlier generation of Arab writers, such as Nabil Sulayman or Fadil al-'Azzawi. One by one, sometimes in fragmented form and without a clear chronology, Hasan introduces the reader to dozens of female prisoners by their first name and last initial only, such Lina W., Nahid B., and Hind Q. Much of the early part of the narrative is composed of transcribed oral testimonies, but these testimonies appear partial and incomplete. The novel also frequently vacillates in narrative voice between third-person and first-person (the seemingly unedited and unmediated direct voices of the detainees themselves). They describe the torture they and others endured, sometimes in graphic detail, along with their secret modes of communication between cells, their coping mechanisms and modes of resistance against the regime imposed by the prison authorities, and their emotional experience of prison spaces: the joy and sadness of visitations, hunger strikes, the birth and lives of children in detention, and the quotidian routines of prison life.

In her bid to produce a documentary novel of the women's experiences in Syrian prisons, Hasan supplements these testimonial accounts with peritextual markers beyond her preface and introduction.[57] She systematically provides footnotes, which in addition to explanatory comments and citations from other works of prison literature, detail the names, dates of arrest, and years of detention for most of the prisoners whose stories are incorporated into the narrative. Some notes include the detainee's year of birth and political affiliation. For example, the first prisoner represented in the text is introduced to the reader in a footnote that reads as follows: "Lina W. Political detainee born in 1959. Detained in 1987 until 1990."[58] Another footnote provides the following information: "Nahid B. Communist political detainee born in 1958. Detained at the end of 1987 until the end of 1991."[59] These footnotes do not merely provide a "break in the enunciative regime" of the text; they function as evidence of and corroborate the "non-fictional aspect" of Hasan's documentary novel.[60] They remind the reader of the existence of female political detainees in Syria and their very real suffering and resilience, despite the framing of the text as a novel. Most of the female prisoners whose stories are enfolded into the narrative of *Negative* were detained in the 1980s and 1990s, at a time when women made up a small percentage of the population of political detainees and were rarely given special consideration or much space in human rights reportage on Syria.[61]

In addition to offering oral testimonies and footnotes, Hasan's *Negative* integrates excerpts of previously published Syrian prison memoirs, like Heba Dabbagh's *Just Five Minutes* (*Khams Daqa'iq wa Hasb*); letters and notes (between prisoners, as well as those intended for loved ones outside the prison); and the above-mentioned quotes and excerpts from world prison literature. Hasan constructs and frames the novel as a deliberately composed and exposed "mosaic of quotations" that highlights Syrian female detainees as speaking subjects but at the same time disavows any attempt to articulate a cohesive or complete narrative of the experience of detention in Syria.[62] She acknowledges that in the process of documentation, "everything that one records is transformed, desired or undesired, into a marred copy, or rather distorted from that which is lived."[63] Rather,

she views the truth effects enacted by her text as "flashes of light continuing in the darkness," exposing, through a multitude of scenes, shots, and
frames, myriad experiences of detention. The entire "scene" of prison, as
Hasan calls it, cannot be shown clearly; it will only be gradually exposed
by "continuing those flashes and intensifying them through numerous
experiences" that reveal "the multitudes of the paths of tyrants, diverse
with the variety of their styles of torture and oppression and deep as the
depth of the dungeons of prisons."[64]

2

Vulnerability, Sentimentality, and the Politics of Recognition

According to the majority of mainstream media accounts, the Syrian Revolution began with an incident involving a group of children in the city of Darʿa in March 2011. Although other protests against the Asad regime had started a few months earlier, the uprising in Darʿa began when fifteen children and adolescents, ages ten to fifteen, inspired by protesters in Egypt and Tunisia, sprayed antigovernment graffiti on the walls of their school.[1] Their simple act of rebellion elicited a swift and brutal response from the Syrian state. The children were arrested, tortured, and held incommunicado. At first their fate was unknown, and despite consistent pleas to various police and security authorities, their parents and family members were unable to obtain their immediate release. In this small city near the Jordanian-Syrian border, the children's detention and torture ignited a protest movement that soon spread to other urban centers in Syria. At the end of April 2011, once again in Darʿa, security forces arrested thirteen-year-old Hamza ʿAli al-Khatib, who, with his father, was attending a demonstration against the government siege of the city. A month later his disfigured, almost unrecognizable, lifeless body was returned to his family.

Although government authorities denied any mistreatment of Hamza al-Khatib while he was detained, relatives maintain that he was mutilated

Material from this chapter is reprinted with permission from Taleghani, R. Shareah, "Vulnerability and Recognition in Syrian Prison Literature," *International Journal of Middle East Studies*, 49, no. 1 (2017): 91–109. Copyright © Cambridge University Press 2017.

and tortured to death while in custody. A video of his battered body quickly circulated via social media outlets, and stills from this video were often juxtaposed with a recent school photo of the boy, with a background of shades of blue, orange, and yellow and rays of light seemingly emanating from behind him. The story of Hamza al-Khatib and the widely disseminated images of him before and after he was tortured to death provoked enormous public outrage and gave further impetus to those opposing the Syrian regime. The children of Darʿa and the stories and poems that spread on social media about their courage and sacrifices became the "spark" that "lit" the Syrian Revolution.[2]

Despite the regime's specious denials, the image of adolescents or children being arrested, tortured, and arbitrarily executed continued to resonate. As one blogger stated:

> Hamza, I don't know you. But I miss your bright smile. There are no words to be said. I can't escape the pictures that assail me. I see you as a child alone, at the height of terror, the apex of pain as you live the details of what they do to you, far from the warmth and security of family and humanity. The devil takes inspiration from such acts. The shame of all shames on whoever remains silent and allows all of this sick oppression to continue.[3]

The photos and tales from Darʿa provoked many to join the protests and speak out against the regime. The same narratives and images from Darʿa also further ignited the recognition of a possible alternative future—a future in which children would be free from cruel and unusual punishment, and the economic, political, and social aspirations of ordinary Syrian citizens would finally be fulfilled.

The brutality of the state's crackdown in 2011 against first children and then adults in Darʿa was not unfamiliar to Syrians, particularly earlier generations of dissidents, or to readers of Syrian prison literature. The detention, torture, and in some cases savage murder of the children of Darʿa are echoed in and connected to numerous stories told in works of contemporary Syrian prison literature that have been published and circulated in the decades prior to the uprising. Thus the stories of the detention and torture of the children of Darʿa and the murder of Hamza al-Khatib and other children were, tragically, easily recognizable and resonated powerfully with the residents of Darʿa and others across the country.

As a form of aesthetic or creative intervention against the human rights violations perpetrated by the Syrian state, prison literature is an essential part of the backstory of the Syrian Revolution. However, rather than consider how such narratives about political detention were part of the "political geography" that "anticipated" the uprising, this chapter investigates the links between literary representations of detainees and their families as deeply moving images of human psychological and physical vulnerability.[4]

Depictions of vulnerability in most works of prison literature, including those representing the effects of human rights violations on minors, evoke for readers the power of recognition, sentiment, and empathy so prevalent in the stories of the children of Darʿa. Yet these same representations also directly intersect with the more recent focus on the vulnerability of human beings as embodied agents in critiques and retheorizations of human rights. Bryan Turner, for example, has argued for a new, universal human rights regime based on the acknowledgment of our shared, human vulnerability to physical pain. Turner includes psychological and spiritual anguish as part of this vulnerability. He also delineates the existence of a global "community of sentiment" that identifies and responds to human suffering universally through a process of critical recognition. Through examples of literary texts that especially highlight this intersection of human rights violations and the themes, tropes, and figures of vulnerability and sentimentality, including those by Ibrahim Samuʾil, Ghassan al-Jabaʿi, and Wadiʿ Ismandar, I argue that like the stories of the children of Darʿa, works of prison literature produce and portray a poetics of recognition that in turn generates a form of empathy or a type of sentimental education in readers.[5]

This poetics of recognition echoes the reliance on political recognition that is foundational to conceptions of human rights. Yet texts of prison literature also frequently emphasize the negative effects of misrecognition or the failure to recognize. In doing so, their poetics of recognition reveal in allegorical form why the foundational reliance on particular modes of political recognition in rights regimes continues to limit the current efficacy of human rights.

Vulnerability, Sentimentality, and Recognition

Of the numerous authors of Syrian prison literature, short story writer Ibrahim Samu'il is perhaps the most well-known for capturing, in sentimental form, the psychological and emotional suffering of both political prisoners and their families.[6] In "The Visit" ("al-Ziyara"), the first short story of Samu'il's collection *The Stench of the Heavy Step* (*Ra 'ihat al-Khatw al-Thaqil*), the tropes of recognition and a detainee's vulnerability are deeply intertwined, even though the text avoids any direct depiction of physical violence, and it is the parent rather than a child who is imprisoned.[7] In the story, the protagonist, a prisoner named Sa'd, is waiting nervously for a visit from family members. As the narrative unfolds, the reader discovers, via the protagonist's interior monologue, that his wife was pregnant when he was arrested, and this visit will be his first chance to meet their son, Khaldun.

Sa'd's nervous, yet optimistic, anticipation builds as he prepares to see his son. As he enters the room designated for visitations, he sees Khaldun:

> I stepped toward the bars of the first door and she came out of the room behind the second door, my wife, holding the hand of a small, enchanting child. His head was drowning in a red cap with a long brim, and his two white legs protruded out from short, white pants, banded with a belt with a small gun hanging down the side. He was stepping slightly away from his mother, surprised at the clamor of crowded voices being exchanged between the prisoners and their relatives, and he was casting about brief, confused glances, without focus.[8]

Despite Sa'd's joy at seeing his son, the meeting does not go as he anticipated. When he tries to offer a cookie as a bribe, Khaldun refuses to acknowledge him and retreats behind his mother, tugging at her dress. The mother attempts to get Khaldun to acknowledge his father, but he refuses. When she tells Khaldun that Sa'd is, in fact, his father and pleads with their son to greet him, the boy refuses, saying, "I don't wanna, I don't wanna. I want someone else!"[9]

Abruptly, Saʿd's visiting time ends, and his wife is prevented from giving him a message, the content of which is never articulated in the story. The poignancy of Saʿd's anticipation of seeing his son for the first time is disrupted by Khaldun's abrupt rejection of him. The boy's unwillingness to acknowledge and recognize his father precludes a kind of cohesive or idyllic narrative closure that might have been brought about by a successful meeting of father and son. In addition, the content of the message his wife was meant to give him is never revealed, and it is on this ambiguous point that the story ends. The fate of Saʿd, who has been deprived of both his freedom and typical social relations, and of his family is left in question as he is forced to return to his cell.

Like many of Samu'il's short stories, "The Visit" evokes a thematic triad of sentimentality, recognition, and vulnerability while depicting characters contending with the state's violations of their human rights and their human dignity. First, the motif of failed recognition defines the narrative turning point of the story. When Khaldun rejects Saʿd, both the protagonist's and the reader's expectations are instantaneously interrupted. Second, the understated but sentimental depiction of the emotional or psychological vulnerabilities of a prisoner and his family members evokes the reader's empathy for the characters and their fate. Finally, the representation of the experience of political detention through a very brief scene portraying a long-awaited family reunion indicates how the short story, as a momentary portrait, provides a contrast to other narrative genres (eye-witness or third-person-narrated reports, testimonials, declarations, interviews, memoirs, journals) that are more traditionally deployed in the documentation of human rights abuses.

Drawing on the work of Margaret Cohen, sentimentality can be defined here as a "narrative situation" portraying a scene "of suffering that solicits the spectator's sympathy."[10] Sentimentality, too, in the words of Lauren Berlant, can be viewed as a means "by which mass subaltern pain is advanced, in the dominant public sphere, as the true core of national collectivity."[11] For Berlant, sentimentality operates when the pain of others "burns into the conscience" of those in power who, theoretically, will act to "eradicate the pain," leading to "structural social change," including through the law.[12] Though Berlant's analysis of US literary and cultural production cannot neatly be mapped onto the Syrian cultural sphere or the genre of prison literature, she raises a number of significant critiques of sentimental politics. She calls attention to the fact that such politics can propagate misrecognitions, presume that suffering is universal, and "promote a dubious optimism that the law and other visible sources of inequality, for example, can provide the best remedies for their own taxonomizing harms."[13] Additionally, in using "personal stories" to confront structural effects, sentimentality can risk "thwarting its very attempt to perform rhetorically a scene of pain that must be soothed politically."[14]

However, I would caution against a dismissal of the potential power and relevance of the sentimental, particularly when it is deployed by authors who—and for readers who—already recognize that there is no recourse to those in power or the law. Despite the risks of sentimental politics that Berlant compellingly outlines, in some cases personal stories involving scenes of suffering, loss, harm, and vulnerability do give rise or further impetus to collective political action. Berlant also traces what she calls "postsentimental" narratives, with which the stories of Ibrahim Samu'il and other authors discussed in this chapter partially align; such texts present a "refusal to reproduce the sublimation of subaltern struggles into conventions of narrative satisfaction and redemptive fantasy."[15] Though postsentimental narratives retain the "contract sentimentality makes between its texts and readers—that proper reading will lead to better feeling and therefore to a better self," they are "lacerated by ambivalence" and challenge "what literature and storytelling have come to stand for in the creation of sentimental and national subjects."[16]

In addition to sentimentality, recognition is, of course, a fundamental element not only of Samu'il's short stories, but of all fiction.[17] In classical poetics, specifically in the Aristotelian tradition, recognition signifies an essential transformation in any dramatic narrative. Marking "a shift from ignorance to knowledge," recognition is the moment when "characters understand their predicament fully for the first time" and when "a sequence of unexplained and often implausible occurrences" is resolved.[18] Recognition can occur through the protagonist's discovery of a truth, often about his or her own identity or about the original source of a misunderstanding. While it can imply a "recovery of something once known," a *recognition*, it can also link a restoration of knowledge with a "disquieting sense" that what was meant to be hidden has now been revealed and that what was previously taken to be true is now demonstrably false.[19] When engaging with a text, the reader also participates in similar processes of recognition.

Parallel to these literary themes and modes, recognition is an inherent and essential element of human rights in international law. The Universal Declaration of Human Rights (UDHR) mentions the exact term *recognition* no less than four times—and this does not include derivatives or synonyms of the term.[20] In theory countries, such as the US and Syria, that are signatories to and have ratified the UDHR, have officially acknowledged that their citizens are subjects of an international human rights regime, including Article 5 (the ban against torture and cruel or unusual punishment) and Articles 6 through 14 (which include the right to a fair tribunal, presumption of innocence, and freedom from arbitrary arrest or detention). Official recognition of this regime, however, does not necessarily translate into the observation and implementation of international human rights protections on the ground. Additionally, in human rights discourse and in the debates about what human rights can potentially mean and do, recognition is always promulgated as both a political imperative and a point of contention, particularly in confrontations between human rights activists and the state. Just who is recognized as a human worthy of rights or how extensive the recognition of those rights can be is always subject to dispute. International human rights institutions have historically relied on the nation-state (the signatories to the UDHR and other conventions) to recognize the validity of human rights regimes. However, deeming the state as the purveyor and protector of rights is inherently problematic because the nation-state has always been and remains the greatest source of human rights violations.[21] The US and Syria are but two examples of this paradox. Official state recognition of human rights does not guarantee their implementation or practice on the ground.

In line with recent attempts to rethink human rights theory and address the issue of universalism versus cultural relativism, Bryan Turner has linked the notion of recognition in the political and legal sense to the vulnerability of the human body to pain and suffering. For Turner, vulnerability is a core, universal element of being human. Because all human beings "experience pain and humiliation," this vulnerability constitutes a "common ontological condition" upon which a universality of human rights can be based.[22] Thus he proposes a new human rights regime based on a "critical recognition theory," in which "recognition of the Other entails recognizing our mutual vulnerability."[23] Turner is well aware, however, that recognition "cannot take place between groups that are wholly unequal in terms of power," and because of this, he acknowledges the limits of the potential efficacy of critical recognition theory in both the construction and protection of human rights.[24]

Writing in the context of fear, mourning, and the human rights violations committed by the US in the wake of the attacks of September 11, 2001, Judith Butler has also traced the link between subjectivity, recognition, vulnerability, and humanization. Like Turner, she has noted that it is always possible that a vulnerability will not be recognized or that it will be deemed "unrecognizable."[25] In addition, Butler points out that if vulnerability is a necessary "precondition for humanization," which is a process that differs through "variable norms of recognition," then the definition of *vulnerability* is always "dependent on existing norms of recognition if it is to be attributed to a human subject."[26] The fundamental dependency on normative structures of recognition demonstrates that the very acknowledgment of vulnerability is always precarious and subject to limitations and shifts.[27] Along with Turner, Butler points to the troubling dilemmas when a complete lack of recognition of vulnerability occurs. A parallel absence of recognition appears in Samu'il's short stories and other works of Syrian prison literature. This absence works to remind readers of the harmful and far-reaching effects of a lack of recognition of the human rights of the detainee. When a state, entity, or individual fails to acknowledge or intentionally causes someone's suffering or when someone's vulnerability is ignored, the person's status as human and as the subject of and in the discourse of human rights falters.[28]

Regardless of generic contours, works of prison literature, Syrian or otherwise, produce a critical intersection of the poetics and politics of recognition. Samu'il's seemingly simple story offers a reevaluation of what constitutes a recognizable vulnerability. In the case of "The Visit," the narrative does not depict the dire physical vulnerabilities that both Turner and Butler emphasize in their discussions—for example, that of disabled human bodies or of the human body under torture —in order to raise the reader's empathy for the characters and awareness of human rights abuses perpetrated by the state. The story also does not detail the standard practice by Syrian state security authorities of indefinite detention and the refusal to grant Syrian political prisoners their rights to visitation. Instead, briefly and with tragic humor, the story sketches the unresolved alienation of a son from his father—an alienation elaborated more fully in another story in the collection, discussed below.

In such narratives of the daily suffering of detainees and their families and the violations they endure, recognition functions on several levels. On the narrative level, it is scripted as a trope and embedded within the content and the structure of the narrative. Recognition in this sense emerges again and again as a fraught process through which Samu'il's characters attempt to reformulate their identities, establish their connection to others, and articulate a sense of their own dignity, humanity, and vulnerability. But often this process of establishing the self as a dignified but vulnerable subject does not reach its full fruition, and the stories, both within their narratives and for the reader, produce an acute awareness of the dangers of failed recognition.[29]

On the level of hermeneutics and readers' response, recognition is also presented as an encounter through which the audience is forced to acknowledge and interpret the various vulnerabilities, physical and psychological, of the characters. Just as human rights organizations must rely on the political recognition of the abuses they bring to light and elicit the empathy or capture the attention of their targeted audiences, whether governments, nonstate organizations, or individual citizens, so too do works such as Samu'il's depend on, as well as transform, the "horizons of expectations" of their readers.[30] With "The Visit" the reader is left to make inferences about the reason for Sa'd's imprisonment, and with the buildup of narrative anticipation, the audience expects a moving first encounter between father and son. When the fulfillment of such a meeting is denied by Khaldun's blatant rejection of his father, we as the story's audience are forced to shift our levels of understanding in order to "bridge" the distance between the "alien horizon of the text" and our own interpretive horizon.[31] Like Sa'd, the reader struggles with recognition, but for the audience the struggle is to identify the broader social and psychological ramifications of the unexpected rejection of the father by the son. This process prompts readers to engage in an empathetic process that allows them to, as Lynn Hunt has noted, recognize themselves in the characters and "feel the same feelings that the characters are feeling."[32] At the same time, the unstated conclusions of Samu'il's stories (as well as of al-Jaba'i's short fiction, discussed below) deploy "satisfaction-denying narrative devices that generate sustained critical engagement."[33]

In "The Visit" and other stories, Samu'il suggests diverse and lamentable forms of alienation and vulnerability in the everyday experiences of political prisoners and their families. Reading such works of prison literature mimics a process of critical recognition similar to that proposed by both Turner and Butler. Readers engage in a "dialogicity of literary communication" that is based on a process of acknowledging forms of alienation and otherness, a process that is inherently political.[34] In order for our literary understanding to be more extensively dialogical, we seek out and then recognize the unexpected that differs from our own conventional horizon of assumptions.

As our interpretive horizons are expanded or transformed by the text we are reading, we come to recognize that human rights abuses can generate forms and subjects of vulnerability beyond those that are conventionally the concern of international human rights law. Through Khaldun's words, we are reminded that arbitrary political detention not only results in the physical suffering and emotional estrangement of the individual political prisoner, but also afflicts the family and society as a whole with an infinite number of trials and tribulations. It is through this interplay between vulnerability, recognition, and interpretation that we as readers enroll in a form of sentimental education. We become familiar with the experiences of the prisoners through the evocation of the sentimental that, in turn, generates empathy for their and their families' plights, much like the responses to the vulnerability of the children of Dar'a.

Unhuman Vulnerabilities

Recognition, vulnerability, and the sentimental also coalesce in the short stories of Ghassan al-Jabaʻi. His *Banana Fingers* (*Asabiʻ al-Mawz*), a collection of stories he wrote during his ten years in prison, offers a range of narratives that experiment with form. They fluctuate between social realism and surrealistic allegory, a narrative mode that clearly "says one thing and means another."[35] This vacillation from one stylistic mode to another within the same narrative space creates the sense that some of the stories remain unfinished, that perhaps much more remains to be said. For Shawqi Baghdadi, who wrote the introduction to the collection, the stories' lack of unified style is indicative of a kind of existential angst that permeates the writer's work and that is produced by writing in the environment of prison.[36]

In the title story of the collection, "Banana Fingers," al-Jabaʻi, like Ibrahim Samuʼil, tells a tale of alienation between parent and child due to political detention. The story begins with Ziyad, a prisoner, carefully saving some bananas he receives from a fellow detainee, who, in turn, received the fruit as a gift from visiting relatives. Ziyad tells his comrades that he is saving them for his son, who should be visiting him shortly with Ziyad's wife. Finally, the day of the planned visit arrives, but the joyous anticipation of the encounter dissipates when they do not show up. After several days pass, the bananas turn black. Devastated, Ziyad sinks into a depression that is depicted in the text by a momentary departure from the linear progression of the narrative. He imagines a series of scenarios where something horrible has happened to his wife and son. Later, he emerges from his grief-stricken stupor and relates to his comrade Muhammad the story behind his desire to give his son the bananas.

Ziyad begins this story by describing a scene at a school. A teacher asks the students to close their eyes and wish for something, claiming that whatever they wish for will be granted. A boy whose "father is a detainee" wishes for bananas rather than for his father's release from prison. In the end the whole story of saving the bananas is revealed to be a figment of Ziyad's imagination. The vacillation between reality and delusion in the story make it unclear if his son was ever actually going to visit him. He has been imprisoned for so long that he can no longer discern the difference between reality and his mental flights of fancy. In the text, Muhammad voices the truth that the bananas never existed at all. The narrative intervention of his revelation causes the reading audience to both recognize and witness Ziyad's acute emotional and psychological vulnerability; it is clear that Ziyad has become delusional. As a detainee, he is unable to provide for his family, including fulfilling his son's wish for a piece of fruit, and thus has no way of "ensuring for himself and his family an existence worthy of human dignity," as Article 23 of the UDHR calls for. The recognition of Ziyad's suffering caused by his and his family's loss of dignity and through his isolation and alienation from his son evokes in the reader a form of sentimentality that cultivates empathy for the plight of the characters.

The failure of recognition due to a prisoner's inability to distinguish between reality and illusion resulting from the conditions of detention is also presented in al-Jaba'i's story "The Ghoul and the Zaghlul" ("al-Ghul wa-l-Zaghlul"). This story, along with "The Memoirs of a Barrel" ("Mudhakkirat Barmil") marks a shift to a more blatantly surreal and, at times, almost naively allegorical style of representation. In a disjointed narrative, a narrator who appears to be descending into madness attempts to recount his relationship with a dependent, childlike ghoul imprisoned with him. Unlike his fellow inmates, who at first do not appear to see or recognize the creature's presence, he befriends the ghoul. It is unclear at the beginning of the story if the ghoul is a fellow prisoner who has been disfigured by torture or is merely a phantom of the narrator's imagination, but later in the story, the narrator notes that the other prisoners do not believe the ghoul to be human.

In oblique language, the narrator describes the effects of detention not on himself as a human being, but on the ghoul as a mysterious animal-monster-unhuman figure whose existence in reality appears to be the subject of debate by the community of prisoners in the story. Who or what the ghoul was and is remains ambiguous, especially at the beginning of the story. The reader could view the ghoul figure as a human detainee, a mirrorlike figure of the narrator, or a mere delusion. The ghoul's origins and status remain ambiguous in the story even when, later on, the narrator's fellow prisoners mock him for believing that the ghoul exists.

Leaving the question of the ghoul's human origin and humanity open to interpretation, al-Jabaʿi offers a portrait of the political prisoner reduced to the status of the unhuman. His allegorical narrative "disrupts or undermines meaning" and "serves as a way to describe the indescribable, or the monstrous," but in the context of political detention and the ongoing violations of the human rights of political prisoners, even the mythical monster-figure, the ghoul, is diminished and destroyed.[37] Alluding to the brutality of both the security agents and his fellow detainees, the narrator notes how the ghoul had once been a "giant" but was now a "shameful size" after "they squeezed him."[38] Through this brief reference to the torture of detainees, the narrative reminds the reader that imprisonment and torture are an attempt by the state to render human beings unhuman, as creatures whose rights and vulnerabilities remain unrecognized. Here, along with the ghoul, the narrator is reduced to a life that the state considers "unreal," a bare life that the regime can more easily target with violence and human rights violations that will never be acknowledged by the state or by fellow citizens, much like the way some of the narrator's comrades refuse to acknowledge the ghoul's presence or its potential humanity.[39]

When the narrator and the ghoul claim that they are taking care of a *zaghlūl*, or baby pigeon, the *zaghlūl* becomes the focus of their relationship. The narrator refuses to recognize that the *zaghlūl* is actually a bar of soap, as his fellow prisoners keep telling him. He asks:

> Is it reasonable that they are all wrong, and the ghoul and I are right? They are a group of reasonable men . . . men who are clever, educated, with experience. . . . Have they never seen a *zaghlūl* in their lives? Haven't they longed to see it after all of these years? Or does prison change concepts and reason. . . . I might be wrong. . . . I . . . am definitely wrong, maybe it was a piece of soap, but . . . but they. . . . It's a *zaghlūl* . . . by god, a real *zaghlūl*. . . . I heard its voice with my ear, and I saw his eye with my eye. . . . Have *zaghlūls* changed to that degree. . . . I haven't seen or heard its voice for years.[40]

Remaining adamant that both the ghoul and the *zaghlūl* exist, the narrator notes that the other inmates, seemingly out of exasperation with his behavior, expel him from the communal prison cell. Although he is initially happy with his exile, eventually two tragedies occur. The narrator reports that the ghoul accidentally kills the *zaghlūl*. Then the story concludes the next day when the narrator discovers that the ghoul, at age fifty, is dead, presumably having committed suicide, another allusion to the fact that the ghoul was, despite the disbelief of some of the other prisoners, human after all.

In "The Ghoul and the Zaghlul," al-Jabaʿi offers a portrait of a narrator-detainee who has lost his mental faculties and another of an ambiguously portrayed figure, a ghoul. The ghoul could be interpreted as the imagined creation of a detainee who has descended into madness, but it could also be seen as a prisoner who becomes reduced to the status of a debilitated creature, an unhuman yet childlike figure that highlights the Syrian state's stark dehumanization of detainees. The narrator is depicted as living in a world of delusions and so appears to be unable to acknowledge the truths that other prisoners recognize and allude to in the story: that the ghoul is not a ghoul at all, and that the *zaghlūl* is not a baby pigeon but a bar of soap. At the same time, the portrayal of the narrator and the ghoul reminds the audience that the harsh realities of political imprisonment render detainees subhuman or nonhuman. Al-Jabaʿi's tale makes recognizable the fact that the brutality of detention degrades and effaces one's sense of self, the sense of one's own humanness, and one's sense of reality. The lack of recognition of the ghoul as human can be linked to the problem of who is recognized as having human rights. The detained ghoul is deemed to be unhuman, and therefore no recognition or restoration of his rights exists. The ghoul takes his own life, and the narrator, though explicitly human, continues to languish in prison, having been relegated to the status of one whose rights remain unrecognized, just like the ghoul.

Al-Jabaʿi's story reflects the tradition and prevalence of the mode of allegory in the work of other prolific Syrian writers, such as the short story writer Zakariya Tamir and playwright Saʿd Allah Wannus. In works such as Tamir's *Tigers on the Tenth Day* (*al-Numur fi al-Yawm al-ʿAshir*, 1978) and Wannus's *The King Is the King* (*al-Malik Huwwa al-Malik*, 1977), the writers use animal or abstract historical figures to provide a coded critque of the regime and its forms of political oppression. This allegorized critique in the work of all three writers is coupled with irony as "a discursive strategy operating at the level of language and form" deploying a "critical edge," in Linda Hutcheon's terms.[41]

Al-Jaba'i's emphasis on ironic, allegorical narrative to depict the experience of imprisonment is most fully realized in "Memoirs of a Barrel," a story narrated from the point of view of a barrel that was being used for smuggling weapons and that is detained along with a group of militant political dissidents. In this case, the narrator is neither human nor animal nor monster, but an inanimate, dependent object that takes on the dehumanized status of a political detainee. Yet the question of whether the barrel is actually a human being is always just beneath the surface of the story. Hinting that it might have been human at one point, the barrel describes a security services report detailing his arrest and interrogation with another man. With ellipses serving as an indication of self-censorship or silencing, the narrator remarks: "I was a human being, and then I transformed into a barrel, and then 'three dots.' . . . Pardon me, I was not a human being exactly and I didn't change into a real barrel."[42] While describing the arrest, the barrel questions how it is that he became a political detainee and how, again ironically because of that status, he has become humanized by being imprisoned.

After recollecting his fellow inmates' initial suspicions about his political affiliations, he remarks: "My story is supposed to end because a barrel doesn't talk . . . or understand, nor can he hold a pen and write 'three dots,' but what happened to me after that . . . and, then who says that I am the one speaking and writing."[43] Although a barrel should not be able to speak and the ellipses in his speech indicate a form of self-censorship, he attempts to tell his story rather than be completely silenced. As he does so, he reveals his absolute physical vulnerability while in detention. At first, he is left outside of a communal cell and is occasionally kicked around by the guards—a passive object that suffers from physical abuse by those around him, abuse that clearly alludes to forms of torture detainees endure.

Eventually the barrel transforms into a small bucket due to a lack of water. As a bucket he describes being used for various tasks, such as carrying water and washing, and being turned upside down to serve as a step stool. He endures all of these humiliations with patience until the inmates place him in the bathroom and use him either as a water bucket or as a toilet, a situation of extreme degradation. Finally one day a prisoner stands on him in order to reach something, and the barrel-bucket's side cracks. He realizes he has suffered a "lethal blow to the stomach."[44] A guard, seeing that the bucket is cracked, puts him in the trash. A prisoner retrieves him from the trash and then cuts him into pieces. In the end the barrel-bucket is used for firewood, turned to ashes and dust—a devastating reminder that "human rights abuses disconnect and destroy the conditions that make embodiment, enselfment, and emplacement possible."[45]

In "The Ghoul and the Zaghlul" and "Memoirs of a Barrel," al-Jaba'i asserts nonhuman figures in order to provoke the reader's recognition of the inhumanity of rights violations, including torture, indefinite detention, and deprivation of due process that occur through the state's use of political detention. The ironic emphasis on nonhuman or unhuman figures works to highlight the humanity and human physical and psychological vulnerability of prisoners.[46] In narrative form, both the ghoul and the barrel are allegorical reminders that those who are rendered unhuman by the process of detention are deprived of their basic rights, including the right to not be subjected to torture or to cruel, inhuman, or degrading treatment or punishment, as promulgated in Article 5 of the UDHR. And this deprivation can have lethal results. In presenting the political prisoner as ghoul and barrel, the writer reinforces the notion that despite the Syrian state's disregard of the rights of political prisoners, the detainee still counts as "a life that qualifies for recognition," and thus a life that should be mourned if it is lost.[47]

The Perils of Misrecognition

In addition to the depiction of unhuman, sometimes childlike figures, several works of Syrian prison literature present stories of mistaken arrest—when citizens, including children, are detained due to mistaken identity or for simply being in the wrong place at the wrong time. Misrecognized as political opponents of the regime by security agents, they suffer the same carceral consequences and endure the same human rights violations as dissidents. In a short story by 'Abd al-Salam al-'Ujayli titled

"Rocky and His Mother" ("Raki wa Ummuhu"), a young boy is detained along with his father because three political fugitives use their home as a hideout.[48] Security authorities fail to recognize that Rocky, a young child, and his father have never participated in any oppositional political activity. Yet the father is forcibly disappeared; Rocky never sees him again, and he, himself, is imprisoned without trial for most of his adolescence and early adulthood. When he is finally released, he ironically acknowledges that the Syrian state is his one connection to the outside world and has thus become "his mother"; he has forgotten his real mother and the only thing he can remember about his father is his moustache. But before he is completely free, he must fulfill his duty to "his mother," the state, as a Syrian citizen. Just prior to leaving the prison, he is conscripted and forced to serve in the armed forces by the same state that violated his right, as held by Articles 11 and 9 of the UDHR, to be presumed innocent and to not be subjected to arbitrary detention.

In al-'Ujayli's story, the vulnerable child protagonist is unjustly imprisoned for fifteen years—a clear violation of his rights—and then is made to suffer even more by being forced to serve the very state that detained him. Rocky narrates his life story while he is a conscript to Ahmad, a server in the café where he must sleep during his holidays from military service because he has nowhere else to go. Ahmad does not fully believe or comprehend the protagonist's story, which concludes with Rocky laughing and then crying at the absurdity of his own situation. The reader is left with the same disquieting impression as Ahmad; the arbitrariness of Rocky's oppression and the absurd origins of his suffering grow out of the misrecognition that caused his and his father's detention in the first place. At the same time, the poignancy of Rocky's tragic tale evokes empathy from both Ahmad and the story's readers. The protagonist's vulnerability highlights the precariousness and failure of political institutions, whether those of the Syrian state or those of the international human rights regime intended to protect the individual child and young adult.[49]

Absurdity and misrecognition also permeate Wadi' Ismandar's play *The Naked Man* (*Al-Rajul al-'Ari*).[50] With clear allusion to Kafka's *The Trial*, *The Naked Man* provides a satire of social and political justice via its depiction of the ordeal of an unnamed man who interrupts the normal routine of a legal court and demands to have his complaint heard. As becomes clear in the progression of the play, the naked protagonist is none other than Christ in the immediate aftermath of his crucifixion. Yet at first his status as the Messiah goes unrecognized by the judge and the court officers. Later his designated role as the Messiah is deemed to be subversive and dangerous. The first act of the play opens with the entrance of the unknown man, who claims that the court should recognize him and take his case immediately, and in vain, he strips off his clothes in order to reveal the wounds of his crucifixion and make himself recognizable to those around him. Rather than hear his case, however, the court places him on trial. As the plot proceeds, a court officer reveals that the protagonist, now referred to as "the accused" has already been to court and that, like political detainees, he has a dossier in the archives of the government's security agencies; for this reason, he was crucified.

Having begun his reading of the man's dossier, the judge then accuses the protagonist, Christ, of a series of crimes, including practicing medicine without a license, being the leader of a "secret organization," and being paid by enemies of the state to cause public disruptions. Though the naked man attempts to make a "confession" to the audience, he refuses to acknowledge the court's charges, and then he declares that he has come to accuse the court itself of an initially unnamed crime. When he appeals to the audience for support, he is temporarily taken to prison by the secret police, and the audience is also removed from the court.

The second act opens with the naked man back in court and the judge confirming that the protagonist is, in fact, dead although he is standing before the audience. The judge's solution to the man's presence is to conceal his murder so the court can carry on with the status quo. When the protagonist refuses to cooperate, a new list of accusations against him is presented, and the court officers insist that his trial must be conducted in secret. As his trial moves on, the indications that the man is actually Christ become clear; he is two thousand years old, he is "crucified" as his stated profession, and he is accused of vagrancy. The judge orders that a witness as well as three other figures of authority (a young man, a religious leader, and a businessman) be called in. As a government informant, the witness had previously reported the protagonist as a danger to the public because he called for justice, equality, and revolution and because he had formed an underground organization that had attracted many followers among the disenfranchised population of the country. The three authority figures then discuss how he can be used for state propaganda, and thus take over the position and authority of the judge. They decide that the naked man must return to his hidden cross because he is disrupting their schemes. Thus the naked man is taken back to his cross fully clothed, and the court returns to the original case that the protagonist's entrance had disrupted.

Like Zakariya Tamir's short stories "Tigers on the Tenth Day," and "The Accused," in *The Naked Man*, Wadiʿ Ismandar presents an absurdist political allegory that incorporates the themes of vulnerability and misrecognition: Christ comes down from his crucifix in order to find justice for the case of his own murder, but he does so in front of a kangaroo court in a political system ruled by oppression, hypocrisy, and corruption. It is clear that he is incapable of receiving a fair trial. The text also offers a parody of the closed, emergency military field trials of political opponents of the Syrian regime; the court audience is dismissed, a dossier of seemingly bizarre accusations is produced, and false witnesses are called. In the end, the naked man returns to his previous position of being crucified, but this time fully clothed; the garments serve as a disguise—cloaking the crimes committed against him and his body. Much like other such texts in which raw historical and social symbolism is merged with satire and parody, Ismandar's play is another example of the use of figurative language in the representation and critique of political reality. Rather than speak of his own experiences in detention or on trial, the author provides an ironic portrait of the sacred and vulnerable figure of Christ confronting but being defeated by the Syrian judicial and political system that fails to recognize who he really is.

As seen in Samu'il's story "The Visit" and in these harrowing scenes a frequently reiterated tale is the failure of recognition between blood relatives after long periods of political detention.[51] The failure of a child to recognize the father is revisited in a particularly poignant story, "The Man Who Is No Longer a Father" ("al-Rajul Alladhi Lam Yaʿud Aban") in Samu'il's collection *The Stench of the Heavy Step*, which sentimentally evokes the devastating personal and political effects of misrecognition. Samu'il returns to the subject of the long-lasting and far-reaching effects of child-parent alienation that political detention causes. The first-person narrator presents a direct address to the reader as he tells the tragic-comedic story of a former fellow inmate. At the very opening of the story, he asks:

> Has it ever happened that you discovered that you were no longer a father to your son? Before you rush to answer, I would like to make clear that by "discovered" I don't mean what happens in Egyptian films when the hero calls out to his young son while on his deathbed. . . . No, I don't mean that of course. Rather, I mean has it ever happened to you what happened to Nadhir Rahim al-'Umar who discovered that he was no longer—after he had been—a father to his son?[52]

The narrator brings readers into the story by addressing them as if in a casual discussion. This conversational address strengthens the notion of the everydayness, the realness of this narrative. Samu'il frames the story to come as a consciously polyphonic narrative—one in which a simple anecdote reveals through multiple voices and registers the tragic psychological and emotional effects of political detention and the various vulnerabilities of both the political detainee and the detainee's family.[53]

The narrator not only stresses the notion that Nadhir was a "father to his son in the past," but he also makes metafictional references. In this case, it is the story itself that the author is writing and recording from a variety of viewpoints in order to provide greater validation of its reality:

> I say "after he had been" because he really was a father to his son Khalid, and Khalid was Nadhir's son and his name—up until the writing of this story—is still recorded in the family register in this way "Khalid bin Nadhir Rahim al-'Umar." And Maryam Rahim al-'Umar—the daughter of Nadhir's uncle before marriage—she is the wife of Khalid. She didn't marry anyone else before him and he didn't marry anyone but her. . . . This is testified to by the family register whose pages specifically for wives is void of the name of any other woman except Maryam.[54]

In this circuitous way, the narrator presents the fact that Khalid is Nadhir's son and that Maryam is his wife and the mother of Khalid in order to establish clearly their genealogical relationship to one another. There is a high level of irony in the statement that the son-father relationship has been duly and dutifully recorded, given what is about to unfold. The narrator also scripts the story as one of common occurrence, indicating that the tragic case of Nadhir and his son is not an isolated or exceptional phenomenon for political prisoners, who are held incommunicado and deprived of their rights to visitation.

The notions of hiding, revelation, and recognition will remain in play throughout the story. As the narrator says to his audience, "I won't hide from you that this discovery wouldn't have caused a problem in Nadhir's life if it had remained within its reasonable boundaries . . . except that it surpassed them greatly."[55] The narrator thus describes the central problem between father and son as being due to a failure of recognition; after years of imprisonment, Nadhir is unable to convince Khalid that he is, in fact, the child's father. Following the path of the narrator's circuitous reflections, the story is constructed via the normal digressions of daily conversation, rendering the effects of political detention an everyday or commonplace occurrence. Though the narrator deems Maryam, the wife, to be the cause of the problem between father and son, the reader easily senses that in the larger picture it is the Asad regime's environment of political repression and human rights violations that are to blame.

Eventually, the source of the problem between father and son is revealed. When Nadhir went into hiding as a political fugitive, he was forced to disguise himself with a beard, a hat, and dark glasses. When he was arrested, Maryam, who was pregnant with Khalid at the time, had only this single picture of a disguised Nadhir to show to her son after he was born. According to the narrator, that picture of Nadhir in disguise became the focus of affection and attention for Maryam and then, later, for Khalid. Maryam, "in all the years of her husband's detention," shared Nadhir's picture "in all things big and small" in Khalid's life.[56] The picture came to replace an absent Nadhir in his wife's and son's eyes. She would hold the picture nearby as she nursed Khalid, distract him with the picture if he cried, and teach him to say "Baba" before "Mama," using the picture. At Khalid's first birthday party:

> The picture was no less present than her and Nadhir's friends; rather, the picture even participated in eating the sweets as well. . . . In this way, Khalid was growing up and the picture grew with him. . . . He would say goodbye from the window before he went to nursery school, and he would greet him in the afternoon with toys and sweets. He would sit at the table with them in front of the food and sleep between them at night on the bed.[57]

Due to Nadhir's prolonged absence from the household, Khalid grew up with the idea that the man in the picture was his father; the picture, itself, as a material object, served as a substitute for his father.

According to the narrator, the picture would cause a form of indefinite and lifelong detention for Nadhir; even after he gains his freedom from the physical walls of prison, he will continue to be deprived of his dignity. The narrator details his friend's release by weaving the newly freed detainee's voice into the narrative:

> Nadhir embraced Maryam and cried, and she embraced him for a long time and cried. "But," said Nadhir despairingly, "when I turned to Khalid and hugged him to my chest, I felt a rock between him and me. I felt his frightened surprise at my hugging his mother maybe or at her crying maybe or at something else I still don't know, . . . but I felt like I was pulling a coil to my chest.[58]

Ironically this reunion between father and son, which should be filled with joy, is shaded with discomfort and rejection. The protagonist discovers that his son neither recognizes him nor feels affection for him. All of Nadhir's efforts to get his son to recognize him are "of no use."[59] At the story's conclusion, the narrator reveals to the reader that he does not know what happened to the family, but he heard from a friend that the schism between parent and child was never resolved. Khalid, to this day, continues to ignore Nadhir and act as if the picture is his father.

"The Man Who Is No Longer a Father" plays on the notion of anec-
dotal, comedic, and tragic storytelling as a kind of witnessing. Attesting to
the emotional rupture between parents and children caused by the mechanisms of the Syrian state's political oppression, detention of dissidents,
and human rights violations, the story represents the all-too-common
event of familial alienation. In this case, not only has Nadhir been forced
to endure arbitrary detention, but he has also been had been subjected to
interference in his familial relationships, relationships which are officially
recognized and protected under Article 12 of the UDHR. Though emotional states are not explicitly described in the narrative, the major characters are presented as being in pain and suffering from "a loss of dignity"
and "a loss of comfort."[60]

At the core of the story lies Nadhir's picture—a portrait of him in
disguise. The picture, though real in and of itself, becomes a masked trace
of a detained man. Maryam attempts to alleviate Nadhir's absence though
a distorted image of him. Both Nadhir and his wife are forced by political circumstances to dissimulate, and such dissimulation warps normal
familial relationships. The significance of Nadhir's photographic image is
that it exists as a real manipulatable object and as a source of distortion;
at the very least Khalid can believe he has a father even while his actual
father is imprisoned and absent. However, in the end the picture of Nadhir becomes more real to the son than the actual father himself, who no
longer has significance.

The text makes the reader aware that while Nadhir is imprisoned, his
family must make do with his photograph, which is presented as a simulacrum, in the sense of being a "semblance" that "calls into question the ability to distinguish between what is real and what is represented."[61] Rather
than his emotional loss or pain, Nadhir's frustration is briefly depicted as
he recounts how he attempted to make his son acknowledge him. Both
Nadhir and his wife have already reached a point of recognition in the
story in which they "understand their predicament fully," even if their versions of what happened differ.[62] But as a representative of the generation to
come, Khalid, at the conclusion of the story, remains in a state of denial.

The denial of the father, the older generation, that is key to the plotline,
unfolds as a recognition of the ways in which both the political prisoner

and the prisoner's family are acutely vulnerable. The reader comes to realize the painful lesson that Nadhir, having endured a series of human rights violations at the hands of the Syrian state, has been deprived of fatherhood. Similarly, Khalid remains a captive of a psychological or emotional form of detention. He has been deprived of the right to recognition as well as the right to forget. He has no memory of his real father and lives with the delusion that a photo is more real than its subject. Despite Maryam's attempts to help heal the relationship between father and son, Nadhir never fully gains his liberty; nor is he able to develop a fully integrated relationship with Khalid.

Like the works of Ghassan al-Jaba'i, 'Abd al-Salam al-'Ujayli, and Wadi' Ismandar, Ibrahim Samu'il's story "The Man Who Is No Longer a Father" provides a form of sentimental education for its readers by evoking the image of the physical, emotional, and psychological vulnerability of political prisoners and their loved ones. Samu'il's story presents the detrimental consequences of the failure of recognition between family members that is caused by prolonged absence due to political detention. This same failure in the private sphere of the family can be read as an allegory of the dilemma, if not danger, of relying on the recognition of human rights by both the state, whether Syria or other states, and the modern international human rights regime. Just as the son fails to recognize the father, so too can the state, which "holds a monopoly over legalized violence," fail to recognize the human rights of its citizens and, in turn, actively violate those rights. In the same vein, the institutions of international human rights law can fail to recognize human rights violations in particular times and places and to hold accountable those individuals, groups, or states that are responsible for such abuses.[63] The recognition of human vulnerability that occurs when the narrator of al-Jaba'i's story acknowledges and befriends the real or imaginary ghoul, much like the United Nations and its requisite institutions' recognition of human rights abuses, does not actually end the narrator's or other detainees' suffering. Sometimes, as such stories indicate, recognition fails, or when it does occur it is simply not enough.

As the narrator notes at the conclusion of "The Man Who Is No Longer a Father": "After three years passed, the prison released him *but the picture continued to detain him.*"[64] The fate of Nadhir and his family—much like the fate of many Syrian political detainees, the fate of many of the forcibly disappeared in Darʿa and elsewhere in Syria, and the fate of Syria itself—remains uncertain. The government's arrest, torture, and killing of children and adult protestors in Darʿa and elsewhere in Syria in March and April 2011 resulted in widespread and newfound recognition, both locally and internationally, of the human rights abuses of the Syrian regime, and that recognition led to or further galvanized direct political action by Syrian citizens—demonstrators, including some of the parents, relatives, and neighbors of the children who were initially arrested, peacefully protesting and calling for the end of political oppression and the recognition of their human and civil rights, including the right to dignity.

Much like the stories of the children of Darʿa, the sentimental poetics at play in the works of prison literature discussed above evoke both the vulnerability of political prisoners and the necessity and perils of recognizing such vulnerabilities. Yet many years after the start of the uprising, the international human rights regime, based as it is on a foundational reliance on the tenuous and fraught politics of recognition and the nation-state, has failed to find a resolution to the greatest human rights and humanitarian catastrophe of our time. Is it possible to conceive of alternative forms of recognition that might reformulate the notion of human rights, to fashion a human rights regime in which recognition isn't "rudimentary and defective," and "partial, contingent and transient?"[65] Could Turner's vision of a global "community of sentiment" vested in critical recognition theory come into being? Or could the concept of human rights be reenvisioned, in Kelly Oliver's terms, "beyond recognition?"[66]

3

Rescripting Torture

The Cocoons of Language

Nearly a decade prior to various forms of recognition sought by Syrians participating in the 2011 Revolution, Syrian-born Canadian citizen Maher Arar demanded official judicial acknowledgment of the torture he endured at the hands of agents and advocates of the US government's policy of extraordinary rendition. The "Complaint and Demand for Jury Trial" in the case of *Maher Arar v. US Attorney General John Ashcroft et al.* contains a nearly ten-page subsection titled "Facts Specific to the Plaintiff."[1] The facts of Arar's case are detailed in a day-by-day, sometimes hour-by-hour linear narrative offered in the third person. The account begins with Arar's detention for "suspected terrorist activity" on September 26, 2002, at John F. Kennedy International Airport by US immigration officials. It describes his initial interrogation, without legal representation, by FBI and INS agents, and goes on to offer the details of the US government decision to "render" him to Syria. We then read of Arar's "removal" first to Jordan, where he was interrogated and beaten, and then to Syria. He spent almost a year in Syrian prisons, mostly in Palestine Division, an interrogation headquarters of Syrian military intelligence, where he was tortured physically and psychologically, forced to

Material from this chapter is reprinted with permission from Taleghani, R. Shareah, "The Cocoons of Language: Torture, Voice, Event," in *Human Rights, Suffering, and Aesthetics in Political Prison Literature*, ed. Yenna Wu and Simona Livescu (Lanham, MD: Lexington Books, 2011), 117–38.

sign a false confession, and eventually released on October 5, 2003, after the Syrian Supreme State Security Court found no evidence of a connection between Arar and al-Qaeda.

The narrative of *Arar v. Ashcroft* details the detainee's initial experience at Palestine Division in numbered passages typical of the standardized format of a legal document:

> 51. For the first 12 days of his detention in Syria, Mr. Arar was interrogated for 18 hours per day. He was also subjected to physical and psychological torture. Syrian security officers regularly beat him on the palms, the hips, and lower back, using a two-inch thick electric cable. They also regularly struck Mr. Arar in the stomach, face, and back of the neck with their fists. The pain was excruciating. Mr. Arar pleaded with them to stop, to no avail.
>
> 52. Syrian security officers continued also subjected [*sic*] Mr. Arar to severe psychological torture. They place him in a room where he could hear the screams of other detainees being tortured. They also repeatedly threatened to place him in the spine-breaking "chair," hang him upside down in a "tyre" and beat him, and give him electric shocks.
>
> 53. To minimize the torture, Mr. Arar falsely confessed, among other things, to having trained with terrorists in Afghanistan. In fact, Mr. Arar has never been to Afghanistan and has never been involved in terrorist activity.[2]

Three brief sections retrospectively account for Arar's first twelve days at Palestine Division. Considered relevant for the purpose of documentation are the specific duration of interrogation (eighteen hours), the abbreviated details of his physical and psychological torture (the parts of the body where he was beaten is presented in list form; being forced to listen to the sounds of other prisoners being tortured is noted), and the material instruments used (the two-inch width of the cable, the threats of the "spine-breaking 'chair,'" the tire, and electric shock). Almost as an addendum, the complaint reminds its readers directly that "the pain was excruciating" and that Arar pleaded with his torturers to stop.

Arar's indifferently termed removal or rendition to Syria and his subsequent torture and imprisonment in one of the more infamous sites of

Syria's carceral archipelago is but one example of the well-documented, systematic, long-standing, and internationally condemned US policy of outsourcing the torture of detainees both prior to and during the war on terrorism.[3] "Maher's Story," as it was titled on his official website, belongs to the annals and corpus of the punitive practices and prison literatures of both the United States and Syria. It serves as another reminder of routinized US government complicity in, exploitation of, and deployment of torture in Syria and elsewhere abroad even while the same government hypocritically condemns the Asad regime's human rights record. It provides an additional indication of the connective threads between transnational, globalized prison narratives and documentary human rights discourse. Yet it is also important to consider the ways in which "Maher's Story," especially the "excruciating" details, the facts specific to his experience of torture, are concisely rendered in this particular legal document, as well as in another rendition of the events surrounding his case.[4] Maher Arar's narratives serve as an initial point of comparison and contrast for the central focus of this chapter—the issue of torture of political detainees at the hands of agents of the Syrian state and the question of its depiction in contemporary Syrian prison literature.[5]

By examining a selection of works by Nabil Sulayman, Faraj Bayraqdar, and Hasiba 'Abd al-Rahman, I consider the various ways in which different authors represent, reify, displace, marginalize, and efface torture as an embodied and inscribed event—a recurrent event that under the normative parameters of the discourse of international law and human rights must be detailed, catalogued, and rendered rationally and visibly readable through documentary and physical evidence as well as "I-witness" testimony. The portrayals of torture in these literary works offer alternative modes of depiction, a series of aesthetic interventions through which Syrian authors echo, traverse, and problematize the narrative boundaries of reportage common to descriptions of torture in human rights discourse. A series of literary texts works to blur the line between the truth effects offered by literary representations of state-inflicted corporeal assault and the necessary truth claims made against the same political regime by those who have endured the most abject of human rights abuses.

"Maher's Story": Torture and the Narrative Imperative

"Maher's Story" articulates a series of truth claims not only about Arar's experience as a detainee in both the United States and Syria, but also about the specificities of the forms of torture he was forced to endure. It is a story that also speaks to more abstract formulations of the relationship between the literal inscription of political power wrought by torture on the bodies of detainees and the question of the voice of an incarcerated subject. In her seminal *The Body in Pain*, Elaine Scarry theorizes that torture simultaneously targets the voice and the body of the person tortured in order to convert both into a form of political power. For Scarry, torture and interrogation function to create a "fiction of power" that relies on the infliction of pain by the state. Pain, including that caused by torture, is inherently resistant to language and destroys the human capacity for speech that would normally be a "source of self-extension" for the tortured subject.[6] In an exaggerated form, torture reenacts and objectifies externally pain's ability to destroy speech.[7] Together, although they are believed to be motivated by the need for information, torture and interrogation deconstruct the victim's voice and appropriate it as the political regime's own voice.[8] In an act of torture, according to Scarry, the pain inflicted is continually amplified to the degree that it becomes objectified and becomes visible to those outside the detainee's body. Pain's "totality" becomes "separated from the sufferer and referred to power, broken off from the body and attached instead to the regime."[9] In turn, this makes the regime and its power over the detainee's body "incontestably real."[10]

The political regime that employs torture will deny its existence or use, and hence its status as the cause of pain or injury inflicted on the body. Even in the midst of this denial, however, it is to the regime's benefit to have the fact of the use of torture made known in the wider public in order to generate fear. Thus, victims who speak of torture can be enveloped in a catch-22. When they make their experiences of torture known in order to seek justice so those experiences will not be forgotten, with such testimonies they can inadvertently reinforce the power the regime gains by generating fear. That is one of the reasons narrating torture remains fraught with ambiguity.

Since the publication of *The Body in Pain*, Scarry's theorizations and conclusions about the nature of pain and torture, pain's relationship to language and self-expression, and the construction of the subject have generated numerous critiques and reevaluations.[11] Several scholars, including Ñacuñán Sáez as well as Patrice Douglass and Frank Wilderson, have rightly called into question Scarry's assumption of a preexisting subject who, before the event of torture, is autonomous and lives free from violence and vulnerability, in a state of equilibrium.[12] Elizabeth Anker argues that Scarry's analysis begins with "an individual, who prior to his or her victimization, has successfully vindicated the liberal mandate to self-master via reason and the intellect" until the trauma of torture overwhelms the "formerly integrated subject."[13] In this reading, bodily suffering under torture causes an acute level of distress because it "limits the victim's experiential universe to the body alone," cuts off "the outside world, short-circuiting the foremost indicia of the human (namely, speech and reason)," and therefore destroys subjectivity.[14] Anker accurately concludes that *The Body in Pain* ultimately "certifies the exclusionary and dualistic version of the presumptively rational human that is central to many liberal theories of selfhood and rights."[15]

Scarry's and her interlocutors' meditations on the structure and function of torture offer an indication as to why some survivors, whether through their own voices or through alternative channels, reiterate an imperative to narrate the experience of torture after its infliction. The idea that "Maher's story" must be told and then heard or read and responded to once again reaffirms the link between "human rights discourses, norms, and instruments" and "an international commitment to narratability" when it comes to the question of rights claims.[16] Above all, in order for Arar to seek justice in a court of law, his story must be simultaneously narratable, readable, and legible. But even then, there are no guarantees that justice will be achieved; in 2006, a US Federal District Court judge dismissed Arar's lawsuit on national security grounds, and eventually the US Supreme Court declined to review the case.

The passage from the legal complaint cited above is but one, albeit abbreviated, version in which Arar's voice in the first person is made absent and the narrative of his torture and interrogation is re-presented and re-framed according to the requirements of legal documentation. Just as legal formalism renders "the real human person an abstraction," and legal interpretative acts "signal and occasion the imposition of violence upon others," so too do the documentary demands of human rights claims visit a kind of narrative violence on the stories of those who have suffered from violations.[17] As a casualty of the US policy of extraordinary rendition and torture at the hands of the Syrian state, Arar provides his story as testimony that instigates a rights claim. His act of witnessing, his narrative, must then be "coded to rights' instruments" in order to be credible, and in this case the experience of the first twelve days of torture is presented in fewer than 180 words.[18] This and the other modes of telling through which the account of Arar's torture and detention unfolded demonstrate once again that the voices and genres of human rights narratives not only necessarily differ from one context to another but also inevitably reflect gaps in their representation.

The divergent forms and voices of "Maher's story" include a personal statement offered to international media on November 4, 2003, shortly after Arar's release.[19] In the following passage taken from that statement, delivered directly in the first person, Arar testifies to and describes the forms of torture he endured from the second day he spent at the interrogation division:

> Interrogations are carried out in different rooms.
>
> One tactic they use is to question prisoners for two hours, and then put them in a waiting room, so they can hear the others screaming, and then bring them back to continue the interrogation.
>
> The cable is a black electrical cable, about two inches thick. They hit me with it everywhere on my body. They mostly aimed for my palms, but sometimes missed and hit my wrists. . . . Interrogators constantly threatened me with the metal chair, tire and electric shocks.
>
> The tire is used to restrain prisoners while they torture them with beating on the sole of their feet. I guess I was lucky, because they put me in the tire, but only as a threat. I was not beaten while in the tire. They used the cable on the second and third day, and after that mostly beat me with their hands, hitting me in the stomach and on the back of my neck, and slapping me on the face.[20]

This second version of Arar's description of his torture repeats many of the same facts found in first version of the complaint. In this case, Arar does not directly mention his pain, but he reminds us of the physical effects of torture and the fear it elicits. In doing so, he emphasizes both his physical and psychological vulnerability as a detainee, and thus through selective details calls on his audience to recognize how his human rights have been violated, similar to the evocations of recognition in the narratives discussed in chapter 2.[21] For example, he notes that his wrists were "sore and red for three weeks," that "my skin turned blue for two or three weeks but there was no bleeding," and that "I was ready to confess to anything if it would stop." With the emphatic rhetorical effect of repetition, his description also focuses on the soundscape of the space of interrogation—especially the fact that he could hear "other prisoners being tortured, and screaming and screaming." Noticeable as well is Arar's oscillation between general, explicative observations on the space and instruments of torture at Palestine Division and his chronological description of his own individual experience. He feels the need to comment on both the tactics and spaces used by interrogators in general; in doing so, he speaks not only for his individual case but also for a detained human collectivity.

The forms and instruments of torture that Arar describes are familiar to Syrian detainees and have consistently appeared as the subjects of descriptions in many works of Syrian prison literature since the 1970s and even earlier. In 1983, at the height of what Middle East Watch termed the Great Repression of both Islamist and secular, leftist opposition to the regime of Hafez al-Asad, Amnesty International reported that as many as thirty-eight different forms of torture were systematically being used against political detainees.[22] Although on August 19, 2004, Syria acceded to the UN Convention against Torture, as of 2005, despite several prisoner amnesties following the death of Hafez al-Asad, torture in myriad forms was "widely reported," and it has been even more extensively documented in the wake of 2011 Revolution.[23]

Both Arar's statement and the passage cited from the legal complaint hint at only a small part of an extensive lexicon of torture produced by the punitive practices of the Syrian state: the tire (*dulāb*) and the chair (*al-kursī al-almānī*), as well as electric shock and beatings with cables.

Other accounts speak of the *falaqa* (beating on the soles of the feet) or the *bisat al-rīh* (translated as the "flying carpet": a prisoner is strapped to a flat sheet of wood and subjected to beatings and electric shock).[24] However, just as torture "lacks a stable definition," the explanation of these terms and the ways in which they are detailed vary from the testimony of one prisoner to another and from one work of prison literature to another.[25] Despite, or perhaps precisely because of, experienced and descriptive discrepancies, the imperative to narrate that exists in the telling or recounting of the story of being tortured stands as an attempt to subvert one of the primary functions of torture itself. If torture is "paradigmatic in its implementation as a tool to destroy the speaking subject," then "Maher's story," along with much of the work of human rights organizations, is emblematic of the necessity of restoring the voices of the tortured after the work of torture is finished.[26]

In many ways, particularly when it comes to the representation of torture, works of prison literature can be interpreted as narratives of witnessing that offer the same impulse to restore and render visible the voice of those who have been tortured as seen in the variations of Arar's story. Yet the modes and stylistics that authors employ when attempting to inscribe torture offer far different effects than what can be gleaned from the two passages taken from Arar's case. From social realism to poetic memoir, these authors demonstrate both the imperative to narrate and the need to question and efface the event of torture through the stories they tell.

Torture and the "Ideology of Prison"

While the issues of torture and extraordinary rendition are at the center of Maher Arar's story, in many works of contemporary Syrian prison literature, torture, physical abuse, and corporal punishment are not the primary focus of the depictions of the experiences of political prisoners. Some authors, such as Ibrahim Samu'il, marginalize or avoid entirely direct depictions of acts of torture and the immediate suffering that results from them.[27] In Samu'il's works, torture is almost entirely absent but exists as a threat to his protagonists that both disappears from the main body of his short narratives and remains hovering at the edges of the stories.[28]

Sidelining descriptions of physical torture, Samu'il's tales focus on how his characters perceive a loss of dignity and the psychological and emotional harm that is caused by the system and routine of detention as a whole.

This is not to suggest, of course, that torture is not represented in Syrian prison literature. One example of torture in Syrian prison literature appears in writer and critic Nabil Sulayman's novel *The Prison* (*al-Sijn*, 1972). A social realist text, *The Prison* tells the story of the heroic Wahab, a young man who is arrested, tortured, and imprisoned along with a large number of his colleagues who belong to an unnamed underground socialist political organization in the 1950s.[29] Sulayman's novel follows a common plot pattern of many prison narratives. It begins with Wahab being arrested after months as a fugitive. It then moves on to depict his torture and interrogation, his solitary confinement, and finally his entry into the collective, routinized life of a communal cell.

In the 1970s Sulayman's advocacy of social realism and "commitment literature" bordered on the "totalitarian."[30] *The Prison* presents a portrait of the endurance and resistance of both the individual "committed" political prisoner and a group of political detainees that fall within the parameters of what Yassin al-Haj Saleh has called the "ideology of prison."[31] Molded by this ideology, according to al-Haj Saleh, much of earlier Syrian and Arabic prison literature is shaped by the authors' perceived need to represent resistance to a political regime's oppression solely as a decidedly collective, coherent, "heroic," or heavily "mythologized" project or process.[32] In the case of Sulayman's novel, Wahab successfully endures his own torture does not give away any information, despite the fact that other characters have informed on him, and then easily adapts to prison life.

In *The Prison*, Sulayman deploys a heavily detailed, realist style of depiction that frequently evokes the narrative style of traditional human rights reportage of torture. Through Wahab's story, he serializes the forms of torture that his hero must face. Yet the protagonist never gives in to the pain inflicted on his body. Wahab is beaten, whipped, flogged in the "tire," forced to endure electric shock treatment, deprived of sleep, left in solitary confinement, exposed to sound and light torture, and finally raped by his torturers. In addition, the interrogators threaten his friends and members of his family. In one scene after another in the first part of the novel, Wahab suffers but resists, and in the end, he triumphs against the systematic torture used by the regime.

An example of Sulayman's representation of Wahab's torture and his unwavering resistance to being turned into an informer can be seen when Wahab is taken to the "inner salon" and faces torture in the "tire":

> They tossed him down on the ground, and one of them stroked his head with the edge of his shoe, unkindly. From the corner, another rolled a tire out that was propped up by the body of Wahab who had begun to feel a separation from what was around him, little by little. He wanted to watch them. They put his legs in the tire, then they rolled him up well, and pushed in his head. . . . He discovered that his flexibility was great. He began to be rolled now with the tire. The game made him laugh, just as it caused his heart to bleed. The laughter that didn't surpass his lips provoked the rage of the men. They all took up the canes, and began to try to beat out one another to get to him. In the beginning, his feet were preferred, but then his entire body began to attract them.[33]

After this session of torture in the tire, the sergeant prepares to leave, telling the rest of the men that they must get him to confess or "finish" him. Wahab lowers his eyelids, and the rest of the torture that takes place in this session is not described. The next section picks up with an interruption in the process of his torture as Wahab reflects on his situation and the need for him not to give into the torture and confess.[34]

Sulayman's portrait of resistance is replayed with each session and form of torture. In this scene, as another officer enters the room, Wahab thinks:

> He was enduring in order to keep safe all he knew of the secret hiding places and the meetings of the organization: if you scream, they'll insult you. If you cry, this is not a laudable beginning. Just gnash your teeth. Don't believe the claims of the doctors, for those teeth of the bourgeoisie are damaged by pressure. Be neutral, and with that the game will end to your advantage. . . . The pain in his back and hips increased as he sprawled out, [pain] from everything that had been caused by the canes and fists of theirs.[35]

Wahab's will to keep silent, to avoid confession, and to dodge inform-ing on his comrades remain seamlessly intact throughout the novel. *The Prison* offers no echoes of Maher Arar's false confession under torture; instead, for the leftist hero Wahab, the torturers' attempt at appropriating the voice of their victim for the power of the state appears to have failed. Yet, at the same time, the rendition of torture provided here evades the kind of questioning of the problem of describing torture that emerges in other textual examples.

The Betrayals of Silence:
Truth Claims and the Self-Interrogative

An interrogation of the problem of description, not just of torture, but of the entire experience of detention, is at the heart of Faraj Bayraqdar's poetic prison memoir, *The Betrayals of Language and Silence* (*Khiyanat al-Lugha wa-l-Samt*).[36] In the different fragments of writing that constitute this text, Bayraqdar provides numerous descriptions of the torture and cruel and unusual punishment he witnessed and suffered under during his nearly fourteen years of detention. Like Rosa Yaseen Hasan's *Negative* (*Nighatif*), the text is a hybrid, experimental narrative that appears at dif-ferent times as memoir, journal, poetry collection, eyewitness testimonial, and direct political indictment. The focus in many of these passages is not on Bayraqdar's own torture or suffering, but on the physical and psycho-logical agony experienced by his fellow prisoners.[37]

One of Bayraqdar's more extensive meditations on his own suffer-ing under physical torture comes at the beginning of the memoir. In a section entitled "On the Brink of Insight," he describes his interroga-tion at Palestine Division, the same interrogation branch where Maher Arar was held in Syria. Like Arar and like Sulayman's character Wahab, Bayraqdar includes in his description a list of the tools, techniques, and instruments of torture, yet he does so with a difference. As he attempts to recount the methods of his torture, including being "ghosted" on a lad-der (strapped to the ladder, hung upside down, and whipped), he directly questions the believability of what happened and asks his reader directly to "try to find an explanation for this terrifying, engineered madness."[38] He writes:

> What will you say to people when they ask you about that?
>
> You will be silent. Because you are sure that no one will believe a single word you say.
>
> In the best of circumstances they will consider your words simply delusions or waking nightmares; it is not proper for you to remain under their force.
>
> Can you be faithful to your duty of the necessity of exposing the entirety of the experience, from the first rattle to the last hell?[39]

Bayraqdar's depiction vacillates between his attempt to describe the instruments of torture and their effects, his direct pleas to both himself and a distant audience for an explanation of what is happening to his body, and his own recognition of the possibility that what he is describing will not be taken as truth, and thus will be seen as something beyond the realm of believability by those who might be reading or listening. Here as well as elsewhere in his memoir, and with a nod to the potential language-destroying capacity of torture, the poet reflects on the dilemma of remaining faithful to the need to expose the reality of his experiences while coping with the predicament of his perception of their potential indescribability. He is a detainee and writer who fully acknowledges "the precariousness of the possibility of narration" that "underscores the stakes of the readers' and authors' 'responsibility to the story' in conditions of extremity."[40] It is thus that he evokes his profound sense of betrayal—not just his betrayal at the hands of agents of the Syrian state, but the betrayals of the language at his disposal and of a subjugating but at times unavoidable silence.

Bayraqdar unveils his memoir as a deliberately unedited and ambivalent re-cognition of his imprisoned past. The published fragments of *The Betrayals of Language and Silence* stand as his attempt at a "recovery of something once known," a series of scenes of vulnerability that call for acknowledgment from his reading audience.[41] Yet it is a recovery that is "disquieting" for both Bayraqdar and his reader as he interrogates his own representation of the torture of his own body.[42] In a plea to the extreme limits of the imagination of his audience, he attempts to describe the other modes of torture, "the mangling" and the "German chair" that he and his fellow detainees were forced to endure. At the same time he grapples with the realization that his words, even with their conscious poetic resonance or the aid of a picture or a diagram, will never fully capture either the atrocious absurdity of his torturers' tools and methods or his psychological experience of the moment of being tortured. He writes:

> A tyrannical chair . . . deaf. . . . This chair, that they call the "German chair" is a curse. A rabid curse that takes pride in the paralysis of your hands and the crushing of your spinal cord, and that grants you, finally, if they want, the blessing of castration.
>
> You have now paused on the brink of insight, and ascertained, with sufficient depth, that *this reality is not real at all.*
>
> But . . . how do you convince people of that when you yourself are aware of the difficulty of absorbing this ambiguity, and these stark contradictions in your naive linguistic game?![43]

Here Bayraqdar's use of the second person raises an ambiguous connection between himself and his audience; is the "you" of the passage the poet addressing himself, or does it represent his bid to force his reader to recognize his vulnerable position as a tortured subject, to oblige the reader to put themselves in his place? Momentarily, through the use of the second person in this passage and elsewhere, Bayraqdar enacts a form of witnessing that is a "a call to the *other* (perhaps in both senses, as the other within the poet, and the one other whom the text addresses)."[44] The narrative attempts a description of other instruments of torture, especially the "chair," while at the same time abrading the veracity of the depiction by telling us, as readers, that this reality is not real at all.

In the same fragment, as if the description offered has somehow failed to explain the experience fully, the former political prisoner leaves an extended endnote: a numbered list of definitions of types of torture used in Syrian prisons, which is headed by the title "Simplified explanations approximating some of the means of torture."[45] This list of a specific lexicon of torture appears, at first glance, to be like those found in the reports of human rights organizations, but Bayraqdar offers it in his memoir as a marginalized addendum.[46] Despite the fact that these forms of torture have already been mentioned in the narrative, he provides redefinitions of "the ghost on the ladder," "the mangling," "the tire," "the electricity," and "the German chair" in direct, stark, and simplified language.[47] For example, the entry for "the mangling" states: "this process is implemented by stretching the prisoner out on his back, then a chair is placed in the area of the pelvis, then the legs are made to enter, after folding them and fastening them between the legs of the chair, so the legs become doubled at the knee and opened at the top."[48]

The interrogative narrative reflection in which Bayraqdar acknowledges the barriers to convincing his audience of the truth of his claims is juxtaposed with the explanatory footnotes regarding forms of torture as a last resort to dictionary orderliness. It is this element of contrast that gives an indication of the discrepancies and gaps inherent in the imperative to narrate that lies at the heart of human rights claims. Bayraqdar resorts to both poetic prose and a footnoted catalogue, and therefore alludes to the fact that his aesthetic interventions against the human rights politics of the Syrian state not only carry gaps but also cannot be confined to one genre or form of narrative.

Rescripting Torture: Hasiba 'Abd al-Rahman's Cocoons of Language

While Nabil Sulayman's novel *The Prison* serves as an example of a social realist text that presents the protagonist as heroically resisting torture in all of its graphic detail, and Faraj Bayraqdar's memoir juxtaposes a definitional catalogue of forms of torture with an interrogation of the possibility of torture's description, former political prisoner and activist Hasiba 'Abd al-Rahman offers a markedly different portrayal of torture. In 1999, eight years after her release from a prolonged period of imprisonment, 'Abd al-Rahman published her first novel, *The Cocoon (al-Sharnaqa)*. Based on diaries and other writings from her prison experience but nonetheless avowedly fictional in the author's own terms, *The Cocoon* is a landmark work not only because it is the first novel about the experience of detention in Syria written by a female former political prisoner, but also because of its fragmented, asymmetrical structure and its nonlinear, polyphonic narrative.[49] The experimental, unstable stylistics of *The Cocoon* mark a significant departure from the seemingly transparent social realism of an earlier generation of novels about political detention, such as Sulayman's *The Prison*, that formed the early corpus of Syrian prison literature.

When it first circulated in Syria, the novel caused a scandal; 'Abd al-Rahman was accused of airing the dirty laundry of the Syrian opposition. One of the primary objections to the text was that it depicted a lack of solidarity amongst political prisoners, but the author was also criticized for her implicit and explicit representations of female sexuality, the rape of female detainees, and the misogyny of Syria's political elite. *The Cocoon* represents the beginnings of a process of deconstruction of the "ideology of prison." 'Abd al-Rahman's rendering of the prison experience is far from more traditional conceptions of a *riwāyya niḍāliyya* (a novel of struggle or resistance), and she herself has observed that it is impossible to portray "heroes in the age of defeats."[50]

Yet, it is not solely the scandal of discord depicted nor the conscious experiment with form in the novel and its reception that makes the text significant. *The Cocoon* offers a distinct mode of the representation of the "pain event" of torture inflicted by agents of the state on the bodies of detainees while simultaneously connecting this act of bodily punishment and pain to other major events in twentieth-century Syrian history.[51] At the time of its original publication, the novel was one of only a few published Syrian literary works to depict, even if only briefly and allusively, the siege of the city of Hama by the Syrian military in February 1982—an event that included a declaration of open conflict against the Syrian state by Islamist oppositional forces and the subsequent massacre at the hand of government troops of an estimated five thousand to ten thousand, or even tens of thousands more people.[52] The massacre at Hama in 1982 has been selectively erased in the rhetoric of more official, state versions of recent Syrian history, and until the publication of a number of novels later in the 2000s dealing with the events, it remained one of the key "silences" of contemporary Syrian literature.[53]

In contrast to the examples above, *The Cocoon* offers a juxtaposed representation of torture and historical events through the voice of the main character, Kawthar, as a detained yet persistently speaking subject. 'Abd al-Rahman disrupts Scarry's conception of the "language-destroying" capacity of torture through her textual rendition of the interrogation experience. In this sense, the novel anticipates Steve Larocco's critical reformulation of Scarry's work, in which he views pain as a "semiosomatic force" and argues that pain is "not predominantly antagonistic to language; rather, pain insists on signifying, with language being only one of its performative media."[54] For Larocco, pain, including that inflicted by torture, is not subject-destroying, but rather is "a force in ongoing subject formation"[55] 'Abd al-Rahman also layers the crime of torture against the individual body of a female detainee upon the atrocities of other events—including the state's crime of a massacre committed against the collective body of the Syrian nation. In scripting both torture and the Hama massacre against the *longue durée*—the tedious, sometimes contentious routine of imprisonment, as a broader vision of contemporary Syrian political history—the author presents language and memory within the narrative imaginary of her characters as a cocoon. Ambiguously spun throughout and around the text and linking characters and events in an erratically constructed "inaugural" continuum, this cocoon of language is posed as a sanctuary from the physical and psychological suffering imposed on the political prisoner.[56] At the same time, the novel defers the possibility that the chrysalis of political consciousness of the characters that led them to imprisonment will result in a definitively transformative individual and collective, personal and political metamorphosis.

Divided into two parts, each with multiple chapters, *The Cocoon* begins with the arrest, solitary confinement, interrogation, and torture of Kawthar, a member of an unnamed "leftist organization" and the central but not the only narrator of the novel. This is followed by a second chapter that offers a series of her delusional "visions" during and in the aftermath of the sessions of torture she endures. The initial prison of interrogation, the two other main women's prisons, and other sites of detention in the novel are never named; nor are their precise locations ever given. Because

Kawthar has been detained before, there is a constant vacillation between the time of her current detention and her memories of her previous arrests and other moments in her personal past.

As the novel unfolds and Kawthar is transferred from the interrogation division to the first women's prison and then a second one, the narrative not only offers descriptions of the space of detention from Kawthar's point of view, but also slips into the stories of other female prisoners who are variously divided into the categories of leftist/Marxist, fundamentalist, or criminal. A cohesive sense of linear time is lost as the text layers a depiction of Kawthar's movements between communal cells and the quotidian banalities of prison life against her constantly surfacing revelries about life outside and the physical and verbal arguments between inmates over space, material objects, political convictions, and religious beliefs. Kawthar's own narrative coincides and entangles with the individual, personal histories of various characters, but she is eventually taken back to interrogation in order to face another "decisive battle" with her interrogators.[57] Following this she is brought to a different women's prison, and under the effects of the torture she endures, she suffers from nightmares, including one in which she disjointedly envisions her own rape by a soldier in a city in which a massacre has taken place—a city that can be inferred from the text to be Hama.

In the second part the text vacillates between Kawthar's voice and the voices of other characters depicted through dialogue and through the metafictional references to their diaries and other papers that are included as part of the overarching structure of the narrative. The novel dwells on both the state of interpersonal conflict between the various women, which is described in the text as a continual "state of war," and the fraught relationships within the political organizations they are involved in. Because of their lack of solidarity and the continual tension, Kawthar eventually isolates herself from the collective life of the prison and describes herself as having entered a "cocoon."[58] Kawthar's cocoon in the second half of the novel is one of imagination, memory, and fantasy that serves as a refuge not from torture and bodily pain but from the ongoing arguments between prisoners. In the end, while dozens of other prisoners have been released, it is unclear if Kawthar has been freed or if she is merely once again hallucinating in a solitary cell as she narrates the conclusion of the novel in a dreamlike state.

Throughout much of *The Cocoon* the presence of torture is indicated only briefly and in a distanced fashion. These references emerge through the direct use of the term *ta'dhīb* (torture) and its derivatives: a female prisoner is awakened by a nightmare of torture, another detainee is said to have given information about the hiding places of the organization after being tortured, the women hear that a comrade has died under torture. The description of torture figures most directly toward the end of the first chapter and in the second chapter when Kawthar endures a series of torture "sessions."[59] In these two chapters, the relationship between torture and 'Abd al-Rahman's creation of a "cocoon of language" comes prominently into play.

In the scenes of *The Cocoon* representing Kawthar's interrogation, torture's capacity to destroy language, to deconstruct the detainee's voice, and to cause the obliteration of the content of the prisoner's consciousness is seemingly demonstrated by the disintegration of linear narrative, the overwhelming presence of disconnected imagery and dialogue, as well as the fading of realist detail in the description of pain. Yet just as the fracturing of linear narrative does not occur merely under the effect of a character's torture, Kawthar's "world, self, and voice" are not entirely "lost" in the pain of torture, nor are the "objects of consciousness . . . swept away and annihilated."[60] Despite their fragmented nature, Kawthar's streaming meditations, memories, and hallucinations confront the function of torture as outlined by Scarry, though these confrontations are fragmented and contingent. They reflect, even if in mutated form, how pain, especially as it intensifies, in Larocco's words, "disarticulates and rearticulates subjectivity, refashioning interrelations between the body, subjectivity, others, and culture."[61] In *The Cocoon*, the representation of the pain of torture reflects a "craving for voice"; Kawthar's pain "wants to speak, to exert non-subjective agency, to intrude itself into a world and upon others beyond the subject's corporeal boundary, to provide information that affects, that distresses, that disturbs."[62]

Kawthar's voice, intertwined with the voices of others, stands as an indirect "denunciation" of the pain being inflicted on her body.[63] Though her occasional cries of pain and her voice are ignored by her torturers, their textual presence within the novel reveals that the process of torture and interrogation has not completely erased her capacity for speech. Rather, in depicting the desubjectifying experience of Kawthar's torture and the "bi-directional pull of pain—towards one's own embodiment and towards intersubjective expression," 'Abd al-Rahman offers a surplus, an excess, of articulation.[64] Kawthar's reflections surface to interrupt and temporarily efface the presence of the interrogator and the advent and event of torture. Thus, her textually rendered speech acts literally flood the narrative and serve to "occup[y] a space much larger than the body," her body in pain.[65] In this sense, unlike the silenced subject of Scarry's analysis, whose recourse to expression comes only after the infliction of corporeal pain, 'Abd al-Rahman's tortured subject always remains in the process of speaking-the-self, a self that is not isolated.[66] Kawthar does not have to wait for the structures of traditional human rights reportage to perform and articulate a disruptive and necessarily distorted but nonetheless generative act of witnessing.

In the first chapter, while she is forced to wait in solitary, Kawthar's recollections move backward and forward in time; her story vacillates between the "enchanted world" of her childhood, her family's poverty, her teenage love of literature, references to coups d'état and war, her growing political awareness as a secondary student, and her first sexual relationship at the age of nineteen. She is abruptly brought back to the present time of the novel by the sound of bowls clanging in the hall (a sign of the quotidian routines and soundscapes of incarceration), and eventually the voice of the prison guard reintrudes on her musings. Kawthar is confronted with the interrogator's questions, and the narrative begins to focus on other sounds and voices, as well as her memories of her grandfather. As the physical torture begins, what actually happens to her body under torture is not precisely described; rather, the "atrocious" acts committed by the interrogator are referred to as "the bats of night," which "twittered in the sky, jumped over my body, tore me to pieces."[67]

While the voices of her torturers occasionally surface in Kawthar's narrative, her voice, in the first person, reflects on her relationship with her grandfather, his ghostly presence in her memory providing a kind of intersubjective mediation between the cruelty of her interrogators and her pain. This imagined presence of her grandfather is linked to the protective amulet he had given her, which still remains in her possession at the moment of her torture. Although the voices of those inflicting pain punctuate the text, the actions of the torturers are referenced in a figural rather than literal sense, not only through the image of bats attacking her body, but also through references to entering a vaguely defined swamp. While the bodily event of torture and its resulting pain are acknowledged and represented in the text, their presence becomes subsumed, undermined, and momentarily expunged through the character's voice and her memories and awareness of others not physically present during the event of her interrogation.

As Kawthar is left to recover from the session of torture, she does not contemplate the pain of her injuries; instead, her self-expression focuses on her encounters with her political comrades and her last meeting with her lover. Only occasionally does the reality of detention intrude on her thoughts, reflected through the mention of the coughs of men and women in adjacent cells. Yet, in the midst of her reflections on her lover, the narrative shifts back to the present when the interrogator tells her to enter another room. Here, however, the chapter does not end with a description of the torture she endures, but with Kawthar entering into another zone of hallucinations and dreams that will serve as the framing structure of the next chapter.

The second chapter opens with Kawthar's "first vision"; she offers a deluge of narrative imagery in the form of delusions, dreams, and nightmares that, despite their sometimes jarring and frightening imagery, initially displace the description of actual torture: "A towering mountain, the ghosts of dogs pursuing me, I run alone, I search for a point of balance, gravity flees, I search for it, I tumble . . . the soil of the earth seizes me without guidance . . . awe . . . fear . . . I scream: this is my bed, in its place, the jar of water is just as it was . . . I drink . . . I go back to sleep again."[68] The next vision begins with a scene of war and then shifts back to images of Kawthar's childhood and the interpretation of her dreams, previous and present, as she begins to enter a state of "waking dreams."[69] Briefly moving beyond the boundaries of her current place in prison, her mind returns to the present in anticipation of the return of the interrogator and the forms of torture she will endure.

When another session begins, the description of the means of torture is more elaborate and is interspersed, yet again, with the voices of the interrogators. As Kawthar faces a series of questions, her external silence is mediated by her brief interiorized descriptions of what she perceives. She refuses to provide the information requested even when tortured by electric shock. Silent in providing answers to her interrogators' questions though she may be, she is not represented as mute in the text:

> I run . . . hop, jump like a skillful athlete . . . Sports are useful amongst torturers, and the lashes follow me . . .
> "Skin her (alive) . . . Your goal is resistance?! . . . Take this."
> "Oh God . . . Oh Muhammad, but . . ."
> The damned rag . . . smothers my voice . . . oxygen . . . air. . . . the damned rag wasn't there . . . I was screaming. . . . breathing but now, damn.
> "She fainted . . ."
> "The electricity will wake her up . . ."
> Alone I scream . . . voices in every direction . . . I conceal myself . . . I hide . . . but I don't know where!!![70]

In this passage, the reality of Kawthar's torture reemerges to the surface of the narrative as the instruments of torture—electricity, scissors, "the chair"—are directly named. Yet Kawthar seeks to hide or conceal herself, and she chooses to do so in a cocoon of expression. Just as she begins to descriptively articulate her experience of torture without recourse to alternative symbolic imagery, her focus shifts and she begins to create her own fiction of power. In a scene reflecting metafictional resonances in many other works of prison literature, an interrogator gives Kawthar a piece of paper and orders her to write her personal information and a confession. After initially writing her real name, she starts to compose a fake story about her identity.

The narrative then disintegrates into a series of loose associations of voices and images in which her torturers as literal figures are rendered more and more absent, and Kawthar experiences a disconnected series of flashbacks of past conversations: conversations with her mother and discussions with her comrades about their organization's activities. The few acts of torture referenced in the narrative are referred to figuratively such as: "the sting of scorpions . . . poured . . . over my ear."[71]

Several more sessions of interrogation and requisite respites from torture occur as she recollects conversations from her childhood and her more recent past, attempts to recall her lover's face, condemns the sexism of both her torturers and the male members of her political organization, and ruminates on human nature and the breadth of human history, of which her detention, her torture, and other events are a part. Her ruminations are framed as feverish delusion, and it is not always clear if this continual reel of unconnected fragments is a creation of her imagination or if it is part of her past reality. But throughout this jumbled excess of imagery, these reflections emanating through Kawthar's own voice dominate the narrative and serve as a cocoon-like refuge while the act and effect of torture fades into the background and emerges only through an occasional reference to pain or the voice of the interrogator.

In *The Cocoon*, the torture of Kawthar is but one event among many at different textual levels in the novel—a reference to the Battle of Karbala, to a coup d'état, to a wave of mass detentions and arbitrary executions, to an attempted assassination, to the Gulf War of 1991 is layered over by the discovery and disclosure of a prisoner's diaries, a failed hunger strike, the birth of a child in prison, a battle over space or an old army blanket in a communal cell, the arrival in prison of an Egyptian actress accused of smuggling drugs. 'Abd al-Rahman positions and occasionally privileges the more everyday happenings, past and present, in the individual lives of imprisoned characters against, through, and within a simultaneous chronicling of political-historical events that might mark a timeline of larger Syrian, Arab, Islamic, and global history.

Through such juxtapositions, the text disturbs the idea that "only certain events have the power to interpellate witnesses."[72] Each event in the novel, be it quotidian or geopolitical, "testifies not so much to what it represents as to what it reveals, not so much to what it is as to what it unleashes."[73] Throughout the narrative, each event "is subsumed by its (own) reverberations," and because of this, the "constellations" of events that 'Abd al-Rahman presents momentarily appear "without theoretical limits and boundaries," and "different levels of meaning overlap" to such a degree that the reader can become lost in a textual labyrinth.[74] The reader, like the historian and like the characters represented in the novel, is thus compelled to attempt to "distinguish among events, to differentiate the networks and levels to which they belong, and to reconstitute the lines along which they are connected and engender one another."[75]

While a sense of linearity dissolves with the depiction of the effects of the bodily event of torture in the second chapter, Kawthar's "attacks of the imagination," her dreams, and her hallucinations also extend to the cryptic portrayal of a siege of a city. 'Abd al-Rahman never directly names the cities she describes in her narrative, but the reference here provides an allusion to Hama and the resistance of its residents to French rule during the Mandate period in Syria.[76] In one section, Kawthar is shown moving around this same city, which is now surrounded and occupied by unnamed military forces. With the narrative structure echoing the same fragmentation and sense of disjointedness as the scenes depicting torture, as she wanders the streets, she is "pursued" by the sound of stray bullets, witnesses "streets of dead without burial or prayer" alongside "parts of children dangling," and hears the "wails of the women."[77]

The city Hama is not named, and no reference is made to the date of 1982; yet it appears that Kawthar is envisioning the military occupation and destruction of the city and the massacre of a civilian population. Although the lack of specific dates and proper names in the portrayal of the event, as well as Kawthar's delusional state, places any confirmation of its reality in doubt, the passage is situated in conjunction with and thereby is linked to her torture. The injuries suffered by Kawthar are thus mapped onto the injuries afflicted on a collective population by the military forces occupying the city.

Later in the novel, after Kawthar is tortured once again and has returned to a communal cell of the women's prison, she suffers from nightmares. In the midst of these nightmares, echoing the previous portrayal of a massacre and directly intertwining it with images of detention, Kawthar remembers the same images of corpses, death, and bullets as she is pursued by an individual soldier. She cries out for her mother as the soldier attempts to rape her, although the actual rape is not depicted in the narrative. As the passage continues, it is revealed that Kawthar is dreaming as the other prisoners discuss what might have happened to her or what she had seen. As she fades in and out of her nightmarish state, the narrative abruptly shifts, and Kawthar senses her own "inner fear"—not of being killed or of being raped but that her lover will soon be detained.[78]

Throughout *The Cocoon*, brief references are made to the occupation, destruction, and mass death of the "closed city," the epithet that 'Abd al-Rahman uses to indicate Hama. In the examples cited here, Kawthar's individual torture, along with the possible detention and torture of others, is mapped onto the representations of another event, a crime against a collectivity of bodies—the corpses lining the streets of the city. Additionally, in the second passage the atrocity of mass killings is dislodged onto an act of sexual violence against Kawthar as an individual through the brief inscription of rape. The same surplus of language that is an inherent characteristic of Kawthar's nightmarish states and that provides a cocoon of refuge from torture produces another moment of uneasy witnessing of yet another event. In *The Cocoon*, the siege of the city of Hama, like the torture of Kawthar, is scripted as an event that appears to be beyond the realm of what can be grasped by one's imagination. Yet, torture, siege, massacre, and other events unfold, interconnect, and are inscribed in the precarious continuum of the narrative.

Through the destabilizing stories of her characters in *The Cocoon*, through their own reflections, 'Abd al-Rahman offers the uneven fabrication of a cocoon of language, of speech and voice against the silencing produced by torture and other events. Transgressing official Syrian state discourse, the author's modes of representing such events serve as a reminder that "every event, among speakers, is tied to an excess of speech . . . an appropriation 'outside the truth' of the speech of the other . . . that makes it signify differently."[79] Kawthar is depicted as spinning portions of her own cocoon as a possible sanctuary and type of vindication in and through the act of speaking and narrating, even if such an act comes in fragmented form. Yet in the context of the ambiguous end of the novel, where it is not immediately clear when or if she has been or will be released from prison, this cocoon can also only be seen as the unfulfilled potential of transformative liberation. There is, in the end, no obvious metamorphosis for Kawthar, and the novel provides indications that her cocoon of language could perhaps become another mode of detention.

4

On Forms of Life
Countermapping and Emotional Geographies

In the second essay of his 2012 collection, *At Last, Boys!* (*Bi-l-Khalas, Ya Shabab!*), Yassin al-Haj Saleh poses the question, "Can prison be a form of life?"[1] He writes:

> It truly could be. Thousands of people, even tens of thousands of people have lived in our country's prisons. They didn't choose this life, but they lived it. They lived it because they didn't have any other choice—because they didn't know what to do in prison other than to stay alive. They lived to the extent that they could even while this life was stolen from them just as their jailors wished or even while their bodies abandoned them. It is the bodies upon which authority has recorded the epic of its clear victory, and it is also upon them that it has drawn the lines of its power and violent but vacant tyranny.[2]

The experience of prison, as al-Haj Saleh insists, is a way or form of life, but it is a mandatory existence, one that is spent in restricted spaces imposed on the detainee by the state. In inscribing his own memories and observations of prison, al-Haj Saleh makes his readers well aware of the ability of the state to record, or write, its authority on the incarcerated body of the political prisoner. Even while he argues for the necessity of viewing his own experience of detention as a form of life, he recognizes that for others, prison can be lethal. The prisoner may be abandoned by his or her own body. Through a series of deprivations or abuses, through torture, denial of medical care, and summary executions, the body of the prisoner of conscience is stolen by the state, scarred, wounded, and all too frequently made lifeless.

Readers of media and human rights reports about tens of thousands of deaths in detention in Syria, especially in the wake of the 2011 Revolution, may find it difficult to assimilate or reconcile al-Haj Saleh's steadfast assertion that prison can be a form of life.[3] And like their counterparts across the world, multiple authors of Syrian prison literature frequently refer to prison as a living or social death.[4] Yet al-Haj Saleh is recounting not just his own perspective but also other detainees' will to survive and live through the experience of imprisonment. His reflections on prison life are imbued with an effort to combine a description of his own personal experience while speaking for others whose stories have not been told. Like Mansour Omari, he articulates the need to fulfill a deeply felt obligation to speak for those who have been forever silenced, those who can no longer speak for themselves.[5] For him, political detention has become an all-too-common national or collective form of life in Syria.[6]

Even while recognizing the limitations of any attempt at classification, in the same essay al-Haj Saleh designates two categories of prisoners: those who resort to "killing time" and those who focus on "buying time."[7] The former seek any available forms of entertainment and refuse to "recognize" or "reconcile" with prison. For these detainees, prison is "time lost, squandered" because the prisoner endures time negatively and focuses on the moment of liberation.[8] The latter type of prisoners attempt to tame or keep time "on their side" by gaining or learning something new while detained and avoiding focusing on the moment of their release. Noting that detainees of Tadmur Military Prison and Islamist prisoners in general are exceptions to his own personal definitions of these categories, al-Haj Saleh posits that in order to survive and live in prison, the detainee must "buy" or "gain" rather than "kill" time by granting the experience of detention special meaning and including it in his or her life plan.[9] Specifying just how detainees go about buying time by reading, studying, and writing, he poses the mastery of the temporal as a potential means of life. For al-Haj Saleh, even when the period of incarceration is cruelly indefinite or arbitrary, time—and the many ways it can be functionally utilized, conceived of, and bought, gained, or tamed—remains the essential measure of life.[10]

Yet, strikingly, in this particular essay on prison life al-Haj Saleh has little to say in descriptive terms about the physical spaces of his confinement. Primarily he names the well-known sites of detention in Syria where he spent sixteen years of his life: al-Musallamiyya, 'Adra, and Saydnaya, as well as Tadmur Military Prison, that always unsurpassable nadir and "indelible shame," as he calls it, of all of the prisons in Syria.[11] By noting the name of one prison or interrogation center after another, the reader can map the forced itinerary of his detention—an itinerary that is also clearly indicated in the timeline he presents after the introduction to *At Last, Boys!* Al-Haj Saleh's reflections on his physical surroundings come primarily in a separate chapter titled "Faces of the Years and Places."

In almost all of the other essays and interviews in the collection, the physical, material structures of detention centers are only briefly described—prison as a physical, as opposed to lived, space is rendered static, immutable, and obligatory. It briefly surfaces as a foregone conclusion that cannot be changed or altered by the detainee, appearing to confirm Michael Fiddler's observation that prisons "by definition . . . have a rigid architectural determinism built into their fabric."[12] Yet, as Fiddler also has noted, the space of prison, despite all of its limitations, can still be transformed by the detainee who articulates other experiences of prison life. For al-Haj Saleh and for others, prisoners who focus on buying time can reach a state of *istiḥbās*, a neologism created by Syrian detainees that can be roughly understood as the process of acclimating to or settling into prison, or reconciling or resigning oneself to indefinite detention.[13] This lack of emphasis on physical surroundings, on the architectural environment of being "behind bars," indicates how modern prisons are structured to increase the visibility of detainees for the purposes of surveillance while impeding their ability to fully observe their own surroundings.[14] Yet deemphasizing prison's material spaces can also reflect a prisoner's ability to forget his or her own confinement by constructing the means to mentally, emotionally, spiritually, and intellectually escape beyond the walls of the prison.

In contrast to the minimal description of material prison spaces in some of al-Haj Saleh's writings and his reflections on prison as a form of life, the reports of human rights organizations on prisons and treatment of detainees describe in meticulously documented detail the physical environments, conditions, and durations of incarceration that detainees endure. In their effort to combat the state's deliberate and steadfast denial of human rights abuses and as part of the imperative to narrate, such texts forensically reconstruct the locations and features of prisons with the logical and laudable intent of making such physical conditions known as sites of human suffering. In effect, against those states, organizations, or individuals that perpetrate crimes, human rights reports deploy a strategy of narrative and visual countermapping, highlighting and explicitly exposing the sites of human rights violations, including hidden interrogation centers and the interior spaces of prisons that are rarely, if ever, seen by the public.[15] By naming and describing sites where human rights interventions should or must occur, such countermapping strategies attempt to "upset power relations," confront and potentially overcome "predominant power hierarchies," and combat injustice.[16] At times, however, the focus on countermapping and visibility can inadvertently efface or exclude the detainees' voices and their lived experience of detention, particularly their modes of survival, negotiation, resistance, and buying time. This can lead to silencing the voice of the prisoner of conscience as a speaking subject, inadvertently muting the individuals who live through the conditions of detention.[17]

Parallel and alternative modes of countermapping appear in works of Syrian prison literature such as Heba Dabbagh's memoir *Just Five Minutes* (*Khams Daqa'iq wa Hasab*, 2007) and Bara Sarraj's *From Tadmur to Harvard* (*Min Tadmur ila Harvard*, 2016). Both authors present descriptions of prison from their personal experience, and their works highlight how detainees "reclaim and protect" the functions and meanings of prison space, reveal modes of "counter-conduct" in opposition to the disciplinary regimes of the prison, map their emotional experiences of buying or taming time, and document the creation of forms of life, reconciliation, and resistance in prison.[18] Other works, such as Faraj Bayraqdar's poetry collection *Dove in Free Flight* (*Hamama Mutlaqat al-Jinahayn*, 1997), present a constant reflective vacillation between the physical realities of detention and people and places outside the prison walls. Even if only temporarily or imaginatively, these texts also present alternative geographies of detention, emotional geographies of the carceral through which readers can begin to understand the varying forms of life for political detainees "experientially and conceptually—in terms of socio-spatial mediation" rather than merely "entirely interiorized subjective mental states."[19] These works of prison literature remind us that the "articulation of emotion" is nearly always "spatially mediated," and they reflect how prisoners emotionally efface or transgress the confines of the physical barriers that surround them.[20]

Visibility and Countermapping in Human Rights Reportage

According to Amnesty International's founder, Peter Benenson, the organization's well-known emblem of a candle surrounded by barbed wire suggests that the group's human rights work illuminates that which is concealed. The candle symbolizes the effort to provide hope to political detainees, evoking the Chinese proverb that "it is better to light a light than to curse the darkness."[21] The emblem communicates to prisoners of conscience that they will never be forgotten, that the organization works to make visible hidden human rights abuses so they can be prosecuted and prevented in the future. In line with this notion of illuminating human rights abuses, organizations such as Amnesty International, Human Rights Watch, the Syrian Observatory for Human Rights, and the Syrian Human Rights Committee must account in systematic narrative fashion for both the spatial and temporal dimensions of imprisonment when conditions violate detainees' rights.

Such forms of narrative visibility have their own descriptive, generic, disciplinary logic. In particular, human rights reportage endeavors to map, measure, enumerate, and render visible the geographical sites in which human rights violations have occurred or are presently taking place. In its 1991 publication *Syria Unmasked*, Middle East Watch (now Human Rights Watch) presents an entire chapter dedicated to prisons and torture in Syria that follows the conventional pattern of human rights reports.[22] The same sites catalogued in this chapter and others are directly and indirectly referenced in the poetry, plays, short stories, novels, and memoirs that make up the corpus of Syrian prison literature. Written nearly three decades ago, when it was estimated that there were more than a hundred prisons, interrogation centers, and other places of detention in Syria, the chapter includes a "directory of Syrian prisons." This list provides descriptions of the prisons and detention centers at al-Mezzeh (al-Mazza) and the Salah al-Din Citadel in Damascus (both now closed), as well as Tadmur, 'Adra, Saydnaya, Kafar Suseh (Kafr Susa), and Qatana, the main women's detention center at the time of the report.

In their directory of Syrian prisons, the anonymous authors of the Middle East Watch report shape their narrative by emphasizing distances, dimensions, and demographics. They provide charts estimating the prison population at the time of the report in each detention facility and identify the types of prisoners by political affiliation, ethnicity, and nationality.[23] The report offers specific descriptions of each major prison or interrogation center in an attempt to make the facilities visible by narrative means. For example, Saydnaya Prison, the largest detention center in Syria and one that has continued to operate through the Syrian Revolution, is described as follows:

> Saydnaya Civilian Prison, a large facility completed in 1987, is located in the Christian village of Saydnaya, in the mountains north of Damascus. The building is four stories high and has three wings joined at the center like spokes on a wheel. Each wing contains twenty communal cells per floor, measuring 6 meters × 8 meters; on the first floor there are an estimated one hundred smaller cells. Each communal cell presently holds 20 or fewer persons. In 1989, the prison was said to hold about 2,400 inmates, with a regular capacity of up to 5,000, and a potential (with crowding) for up to 10,000.[24]

As in the reports issued by Amnesty International, the Syrian Observatory for Human Rights, and the Syrian Human Rights Committee, Middle East Watch provides a brief overview of the architectural spaces of the prison. This includes cataloguing the number of communal or dormitory cells (the *mahja'* or *mahāji'*) and the number of prisoners detained in them, as well as detailing the approximate measurements of the cells of the prison.[25] Notably absent in this section of the report are the individual voices of the prisoners themselves.

More recently, coinciding with the rampant human rights violations and crimes against humanity committed by the Asad regime since the beginning of the 2011 Syrian Revolution, human rights reports have begun mapping precise places of torture and detention by using digital graphics and Google satellite imagery.[26] In some reports quotations from anonymous detainees are included. At other times, such as on Human Rights Watch's initial map published in its 2012 report on Syrian interrogation centers, detainees are not mentioned at all, most likely in an effort to protect the identity of those former prisoners who have provided information on their torture and treatment. However, an unintended consequence of this effort to conceal the identity of witnesses is that only the forms of torture used at each location are listed, detached from the individuals who suffered from such abuses.[27]

Another, more recent example, Amnesty International's report "Saydnaya: Inside a Syrian Torture Prison," uses digital graphics based on research conducted by the agency Forensic Architecture to reconstruct Saydnaya prison.[28] This particular interactive report includes effects recreating some of the sounds of the prison as well as illustrations of some of the interior spaces of the prison as remembered and described by former detainees. The viewer-reader is invited to explore and learn more about the prison by clicking on various links that include the prisoners' testimonies in the first and third person. This new form of digital, interactive human rights report allows for the greater incorporation of the prisoner as an individual speaking subject, even if necessarily anonymous or under a pseudonym. Both visually and aurally, the report acknowledges and depicts how detainees perceive prison spaces in a manner that differs greatly from the point of view of outside observers or prison guards.

Alongside the depiction of sites of incarceration, human rights reports calculate and effectively render visual the weeks, months, years, and decades that detainees are incarcerated, held without trial, tortured, and deprived of visitation. These chronological and cartographic constructions have become the standard forensic means of documenting evidence of human rights abuses and verifying claims made by survivors and witnesses of ongoing violations even when such violations are steadfastly denied by those individuals, groups, institutions, or states that perpetrate them.

Like descriptions of torture in human rights reportage, such mapping endeavors to reconstruct and represent prison spaces as precisely, accurately, and wholly rendered visual entities. All of this is done to serve the primary goal of human rights groups—that of ending human rights abuses. Yet the emphasis on visibility in human rights reports also has its limitations. The coherently rendered visual reconstructions of prison spaces are often necessarily generated from multiple testimonies, an indication that detainees themselves often experience prison space from different subjective standpoints. The necessary focus on abuses and violations, on measurability and enumeration, and on mapping and visibility as a way of providing legal evidence leads to certain exclusions and gaps. The detainee as a speaking subject can be inadvertently forgotten or silenced, rendered into an object to be counted, surveyed, and observed, or made entirely invisible in reports on human rights violations, particularly when the forensic mode of providing evidence of abuses works to further "dehumanise the landscape" of the prison system.[29] This narrative mode can replicate the exclusionary power structures, including some of the surveillance mechanisms, of political detention itself.

As Barbara Harlow and many other scholars have noted, Michel Foucault, in his 1975 study *Discipline and Punish: The Birth of the Prison*, drew many of his conclusions from the writings of early modern planners, reformers, observers, and administrators of prisons, but not from the perspectives of those imprisoned.[30] Discussing Jeremy Bentham's theorized but never fully realized panopticon model, Foucault notes that the prison is structured so the prisoner is "seen, but he does not see; he is the object of information, never a subject in communication."[31] While Foucault acknowledges that such forms of disciplinary power are productive, generating resistance and struggle, rather than strictly negative, he has been well-critiqued for his failure to account for human agency or the way resistance to disciplinary power works on the ground.[32] Additionally, as Lisa Wedeen points out, Syria is not an exact replica of the carceral society that Foucault theorizes, and the Syrian system of detention, as reflected in the accounts of multiple detainees, is far from a replica of the panopticon model, especially given that arbitrariness is a key element of the experience of arrest, torture, and imprisonment in Syria.[33] Thus works of prison literature offer alternative perspectives to both the prevailing Foucauldian theories of punitive "compulsory visibility" and the "documentary and coherent visibility" of space characteristic of human rights reportage.[34]

A Journey beyond Time: Heba Dabbagh's *Just Five Minutes*

In May 2011 Heba Dabbagh appeared as one of the featured speakers at an antiregime protest organized by the Syrian community in Windsor, Canada. Like Yassin al-Haj Saleh and others of the generation that came of political age in the 1970s and 1980s, Dabbagh was motivated by the advent of the Syrian Revolution to publicly speak out against the Asad regime. In a speech read in Arabic and then read by another participant in English translation, she stated: "I did not think that I would live to see the horror of what has reappeared on the soil of my beloved Syria. . . . It's as if we are reliving the 1980s, under the oppressive rule that prevented [one's] breath from being exhaled without permission and prevents the last breath of the dying from reaching those closest to them."[35] Now living in exile in Canada, Dabbagh connects human rights violations committed by the regime against her and others in the 1980s to the current abuses and atrocities committed by the state not just against all Syrians, but specifically against "the pure and dignified women." Establishing a link between Syria then and Syria now, she cautions her audience that this is not the first time the regime has implemented a strategy of collective punishment against its own citizenry, including and especially women.[36] In addition to recounting the forms of torture that she, like so many others, endured, she also reminds the crowd that all people detained are abruptly removed, emotionally and physically, from their usual environment and forced to contend with a new and hostile space.

Dabbagh was arrested in 1980 and spent the next nine years forcibly disappeared as a hostage detainee—a family member or loved one arrested by the regime in order to force a political fugitive to come out of hiding. Dabbagh's 1995 book *Just Five Minutes: Nine Years in the Prisons of Syria* (Khams Daqa'iq wa *Hasb: Tis' Sanawat fi Sujun Suriya*) is notable as the only full-length prison memoir written by a former Syrian female detainee, and until very recently it was one of the few works of Syrian prison literature translated into English.[37] Accessible as a PDF file in Arabic and in English, *Just Five Minutes* has circulated widely, bringing Dabbagh's story to the attention of other political prisoners around the world, including former Guantanamo Bay detainee Moazzam Begg, whose organization, CAGE, interviewed Dabbagh in the wake of the Syrian Revolution.[38]

Heba Dabbagh's story begins on the last day of 1980. While at university in Damascus, she and her roommate were arrested by security agents. Her mother was also detained. At the time, the security apparatus was seeking to arrest her brother Safwan, an alleged member of the Muslim Brotherhood. Dabbagh's arrest, along with the imprisonment of other relatives, was clearly intended as both a form of collective punishment—the persecution of an entire family for the dissident activities of one member—and a means to force Safwan to return to Syria and surrender himself to authorities. Originally from Hama, and hailing from a large family with twelve siblings, Heba Dabbagh would be one of the few members of her nuclear family to survive the early 1980s. Ten of her fourteen family members were killed by the regime; most of them were killed in the siege and massacre of Hama in 1982.[39]

In many ways *Just Five Minutes* follows the typical pattern of a prison memoir by retaining "certain classical conventions of tripartite plot construction: arrest—imprisonment—release."[40] The author uses simple and direct language, retains an overarching chronological structure, and describes her imprisonment in the first person. Like Hasiba 'Abd al-Rahman's *The Cocoon* (*Al-Sharnaqa*) and Rosa Yaseen Hasan's *Negative* (*Nighatif*), the memoir provides a representation of a specifically female experience of Syrian political detention. The text provides a mapping of prison space and time in addition to portraying emotional geographies of prison that differ from the accounts of the male prisoners who make up the majority of Syrian political detainees and who have written the majority of texts of Syrian prison literature. This is not solely due to the fact that some of the detention facilities where Dabbagh was held, such as Duma, were women-only prisons. The memoir's special character is also attributable to the specific ways in which Dabbagh and her fellow female detainees inhabited those carceral times and spaces.

The title of Dabbagh's memoir, *Just Five Minutes*, recalls a common expression found in the arrest scenes of many works of Syrian prison literature; security agents claim that the detainee will be gone for only a few minutes, but then the detainee is forcibly disappeared for an indefinite, arbitrary period of time. In stark contrast to al-Haj Saleh's assertion that prison can be a form of life, Dabbagh consistently defines her detention as a "slow" or "living" death. Her use of expressions such as "a journey beyond time" throughout the text reminds her reader that for the long-term prisoner in detention, "the unreality of time" can become "palpable."[41] The phrase "just five minutes" has no meaning in a system of arbitrary arrest and indefinite detention, and a "journey beyond time" evokes the idea that detainees can appear to exist in a kind of temporal suspension, where distinctions between past, present, and future become increasingly difficult to discern. Dabbagh states that detention makes the prisoner "forget the feel of freedom and give[s] you nothing to look forward to, so when you think about the future all you envision is . . . more pain and suffering."[42] Yet she also asserts and demonstrates throughout the narrative that the detainees "had no choice but to adapt and survive."[43] Whenever she and other prisoners felt the "walls closing in," they "sought new ways to vent, to breathe, and to keep alive."[44]

For Dabbagh, just five minutes turned into nearly a decade of adaptation and survival; her detention lasted from December 1980 to December 1989. The structure of her narrative is already apparent from the table of contents, with chapter divisions reflecting distinct periods of her life, and Dabbagh offers her reader a clear, linear chronotopic mapping of her detention and of her subjective experience of time spent in Syria's prisons. She explicitly names the sites of her detention and the years and months she spent in each space: Kafar Suseh Prison (January 1981–October 1982), Qatana Prison (October 1982–November 1985), Military Interrogation Prison (August 1985–October 1985), and Duma Prison (November 1985–October 1989).[45] In an effort to make visible the spaces of the Syrian detention system, she also provides a narrative, blueprint-like description of some of these prisons that is similar in some respects to human rights reportage: she precisely details the facades and exterior architecture, the measurements and lighting of interior rooms and cells, and the abject conditions of the facilities where she was held.[46] Strikingly, though, and following a pattern common in other memoirs, the later period of her imprisonment, and particularly the period spent in Duma, is narrated in a temporally compressed and abbreviated manner.

Just Five Minutes also demonstrates how prisoners perceive time and space when their field of vision is restricted. Dabbagh's narrative testifies to a prisoner's experience of a wide range of emotions, from extreme fear, anxiety, vulnerability, boredom, loss, and grief to brief moments of defiance, camaraderie, joy, gratitude, and hope. The text highlights the prison soundscape, the "acoustic environment," as an essential factor in a detainee's perceptions and emotional experience of carceral space.[47] The memoir also reflects how meditations on prison space and time are often eclipsed by other narrative priorities. In particular, *Just Five Minutes* documents the arrest tales and life stories of a multitude of other female detainees, and this emphasis on the collective experience of detention in Syria serves as a reminder that in prison narratives, "the autobiographical is inextricably linked to the communal."[48] Readers learn the stories of Hajja Madiha, 'A'isha, Umm Shayma, and the other women who survived in dormitory cells with Dabbagh.

Dabbagh explains that prisoners sustain themselves by finding ways of "marking out the passage of days."[49] She describes the different activities undertaken by the women in the prison that "break the monotonous routine of prison life."[50] In effect, Dabbagh shows that Syrian prisoners, much like the South African prisoners described by Teresa Dirsuweit, respond to the "hegemonic constructions of space" and time of detention by creating "new spaces" through generating meaningful activities for themselves.[51] In Qatana, for example, these activities included finding small joys in making sculptures and prayer beads with "dough art" (made from water and the inside of old bread), knitting, inventing games, and, most important for the author, studying the Quran and praying. Dabbagh remarks, "We tried to organize our time, to schedule time for reading and memorizing the Quran, time for reciting and memorizing special suppli-cations, and time for night prayers."[52]

The omnipresence of descriptions of soundscapes in *Just Five Minutes* demonstrates how prisons are structured to increase the surveillance of each prisoner while decreasing the prisoner's field of vision. The detainee's reliance on the aural rather than the visual reveals a "sonics of both suf-fering . . . and survival in prisons."[53] As Dabbagh's text and other prison memoirs indicate, sound, especially during periods of interrogation, can be manipulated as a form of torture to increase a prisoner's suffering, as prisoners are literally "captive audiences" with no means of escaping the sonic environment of the prison.[54] Dabbagh makes clear that during the initial period of her detention, while waiting for her own interrogation, she was tortured and terrified by the sounds of other prisoners being inter-rogated. She emphasizes the sound of torture, in contrast to the minimal visual description of the space where she is made to wait. The narrative's focus is on what she hears, rather than the visible features of the space of her confinement: "I wished I could sleep but fear kept me awake. The sounds coming from Majida in the interrogation room down the hall kept me awake. They clawed at my heart. I heard her cries, but I could not hear her words."[55] The construction of a series of terrifying "sound images" provokes the narrator's worst fears, and Dabbagh acts as an "earwitness" rather than an "eyewitness" to the torture her friend and fellow detainee, Majida, endures.[56]

At the same time, *Just Five Minutes* makes clear that prisoners are not always entirely deprived of "acoustical agency."[57] The "spatial impressions" of prisoners that are evoked via soundscapes also reveal some weaknesses in the disciplinary regime's authoritarian control, as prisoners manage to gain a sense of their surroundings even in an environment that is built for sensory deprivation.[58] Because it "enlarges one's spatial awareness to include areas behind the head that cannot be seen" and "dramatizes spa-tial experience," sound can expand or alter a prisoner's sense of space.[59] Particularly when it is linked to the ability to communicate clandestinely with other prisoners, sound also allows for a broadened construction or imagining of the prison environment. Though forbidden to speak to one another, prisoners frequently devised various means to communicate, including whispering through holes in the walls of the prison cells and creating a system of knocking on the walls that allowed them to share news.[60] These forbidden forms of communication show not only how certain aspects of the prison soundscape fall outside the control of prison authorities, but also how detainees create "spaces of solace" by devising transgressive ways to speak to one another.[61]

A poignant example of the coalescence of a prisoner's emotional and aural geographies in *Just Five Minutes* occurs early in the narrative when Dabbagh is shocked by her first encounter with her own mother in prison. After describing herself as terrified but defiant during one of several interrogation sessions, Dabbagh is led to a solitary cell in Kafar Suseh Prison. Initially, she notes that the cell is one square meter in size, a "chicken coop" where at first she sees "darkness and nothing else."[62] But as an officer attempts to force her into the cell, she hears a voice coming from nearby, a voice she immediately recognizes as her own mother's, lambasting the guard for his treatment of the prisoners. Viewing this as a source of comfort, Dabbagh recalls, "my heart jumped at the sound of her voice," and she attempts to run toward it, toward the cell where her mother is being detained.[63] The sound of her mother's voice, her mother's vocal condemnation of the guards, gives her hope and bolsters her defiance, despite the fact that the confines of the solitary cell fill her with "anxiety and fear" every time she returns there from interrogation.[64] Although her mother's voice is soon subsumed by the sounds of the guards yelling during their drunken celebration of New Year's, Dabbagh is momentarily connected with her fellow inmate and family member and has a greater knowledge of the presence of other prisoners, even without seeing them.

In *Just Five Minutes*, Dabbagh also produces a kind of human mosaic of prison life, a portraiture of her fellow inmates that allows the text to appear not just as a memoir that speaks for her individual experience of torture and detention but also as a collective document expressing the experiences of dozens of women held in Syrian prisons. Throughout the memoir the author's continual recounting of other women's stories temporarily disrupts the construction of a prison chronotope; the narrative flashes back to times and places outside of prison with descriptions of how each woman came to be detained and the suffering each endured at the hands of security agents. One such description occurs at the beginning of the section in which Dabbagh recounts her entry into a communal cell at Kafar Suseh Prison after eight days of solitary confinement. She remarks, "We spent many days together in that cell, enough days for each of us to tell her story, to relay every detail of injustice, frustration and pain."[65] In the text an ordinary measure of prison time (the "many days together in the cell") becomes a time measured by consecutive acts of narration. One after another, we hear how Hajja Madiha, 'A'isha, Umm Shayma, Fawziya, and others came be arrested, interrogated, and eventually held at Kafar Suseh, usually after the killing of male relatives by security authorities. With each arrival of a new detainee comes a new story.[66] They represent an embedded series of prison stories within the author's own framing story.

Dabbagh also devotes a portion of her narrative to describing how most of her immediate family members, including her parents, were killed during the massacre in Hama in 1982 while she was being held in detention.[67] The author did not know of the fate of her family while she remained in Kafar Suseh Prison; her mother was released, but she was not. Having been isolated from outside news, she discovered what happened much later while a prisoner at Qatana, and she relates to her reader the horrifying tale of the murder of her family members. Dabbagh ends her memoir not with a description of her last stay in prison, but with a vision of the devastated city of Hama as she views it from a vehicle:

> As we drove across Hama, I gazed out the window at the unfamiliar scenes we passed. The seven-year-long destruction of the city cast a dark shadow. The empty streets reflected empty hearts. The hum of the water-wheels' spinning arms had been silenced.
>
> Below the waterwheels, the Assey River had run dry and the trees and fields around its banks had withered and died. Everything I knew of the city was gone; the unfamiliar scenes seemed lifeless and alien. But one thing remained unchanged. Mukhabarat vehicles still lurked at every street corner, their headlights peeking out of narrow roads, observing, watching, maybe even over the dreams of those sound asleep.[68]

She concludes her memoir in a symmetrical fashion by juxtaposing her vision of Hama with a recollection of the night she was arrested. The jubilation that initially accompanied her sense of freedom at leaving the confines of the interrogation center evaporates at the recognition that her home city, with the exception of the presence of the *mukhābarāt*, is now a lifeless, unfamiliar, and alien place. Like the conclusion of Mustafa Khalifa's *The Shell*, the end of *Just Five Minutes* leaves the impression that the spaces inside and outside of prison have become indistinguishable.

Bara Sarraj: Mapping the Journey from Tadmur to Harvard

In February 2011 Syrian-American immunologist Bara Sarraj created a Twitter account to follow the events of the Egyptian Revolution.[69] Under the handle Tadmor_Harvard, he then began actively tweeting in support of the Syrian Revolution and criticizing the lack of international media coverage of the brutal crackdown on demonstrations across Syria. Like Heba Dabbagh, he repeatedly denounced the Asad regime, not just on Twitter but on Facebook.[70] In a series of tweets in both Arabic and English, Sarraj also began to share with his growing number of followers his story of arrest, torture, and detention in Tadmur Military Prison and elsewhere. Nearly fifteen years after his release, like many other former political detainees of his generation, including Heba Dabbagh, he was inspired by the uprising to publicly condemn the regime and support the protestors. Using details he had recorded years earlier, he began writing a memoir of his time in prison, short glimpses of which he would offer daily via Twitter and on his Facebook page. He ultimately completed his first book manuscript, titled *From Tadmur to Harvard*, in June 2011, and disseminated the publication as a PDF file. Over the course of the next four years, Sarraj would expand on this initial manuscript, eventually self-publishing on Amazon a longer, printed version with the same title in February 2016.[71]

Though originally from Hama, Sarraj's family moved to the Syrian capital, and in 1983 he began studying electrical engineering at the University of Damascus. March 5, 1984, began as a day just like any other. Just twenty-one years old, Sarraj arrived at the university as security agents were ordering students to stand in two lines, then subjecting them to questioning and searching before allowing them to enter the building. According to Sarraj's description of that day, the students' fear and tension was palpable; everyone knew someone was about to be arrested, a common, if not daily, occurrence in the 1980s during the Great Repression, when the security apparatus ruthlessly pursued and persecuted anyone even remotely suspected of opposing the Syrian state. Men between the ages of twenty and forty, especially university students who had not become members of the Ba'th Party, were prone to being arrested for the slightest reason, or sometimes for no reason at all.

Sarraj was completely unprepared for what was about to happen. When he saw plainclothes security agents taking students' identity cards, he wondered if the time had come for new cards to be issued.[72] Worried about being late, he went to the head of the line and handed over his ID card so he could enter the building quickly and get to class. To his shock, one of the agents ordered Sarraj to come with him, saying, just as in the arrest of Dabbagh, that it would take "just five minutes." In Sarraj's case, five minutes turned into twelve years; he was imprisoned from 1984 until 1995. Initially he had no idea why he was arrested. Over time, he would learn that he had been at the wrong mosque at the wrong time while a high school student, and that he was "under suspicion" due to one of his uncles obtaining a leadership position in the Muslim Brotherhood. Dozens of young men who had attended the same mosque were arrested also; the regime accused them all of being members of the Muslim Brotherhood or offshoot parties, and affiliation with the Brotherhood was, according to Syrian Law 49, a capital crime. A pious young man who enjoyed engaging in religious studies, Bara Sarraj, whose first name means "innocent" or "guiltless" in Arabic, was never a member of the Brotherhood, but that made little difference once he was arrested.

Like *Just Five Minutes*, *From Tadmur to Harvard* follows the conventional pattern of a prison memoir: it begins with Sarraj's initial arrest and ends with his release and his eventual decision to join his family in the United States to start his education all over again. In the United States, he ultimately completed a postdoctoral fellowship in immunology at Harvard. The former detainee provides his readers with a straightforward, chronological, linear account written in direct, clear, descriptive language. As noted by Amal Hanano in her profile of Sarraj, the author is meticulous and thorough in documenting his twelve years in Syrian prisons.[73] Each chapter begins with the name and location of the detention centers where he was held, as well as the specific dates of his incarceration. Each chapter also contains dated subheadings, followed by Sarraj's description of events or occurrences on specific dates; entries range in length from several paragraphs to a single sentence.

Toward the end of the memoir Sarraj includes an appendix of documents and pictures, in some cases scanned in color. These include personal photos from before his arrest and after his release; copies of correspondence between his relatives, the United Nations, the Syrian ambassador in Washington, DC, and US politicians, including senators Paul Simon, Edward Kennedy, and John Kerry, inquiring and expressing concern about his case; and multiple documents from the Ministry of the Interior detailing both his sentence and his request for a passport and exit visa in order to leave the country after his release from prison in 1995. He also includes a page of his dissertation, dedicated not just to his family members but to "the twelve thousand best educated of Syria, who were executed in Tadmor at the hands of Hafez Assad and his regime, just for yearning for a better future of freedom and life of dignity."[74]

In addition to these documents, Sarraj creatively engages in "distinctly public and citizen oriented mapmaking efforts"; he uses Google Earth satellite maps in his memoir even more extensively than recent human rights reports do.[75] In fact, he credits Google Earth with providing him with the means to see the prisons where he was held because, as a detainee, he was often blindfolded or forbidden to look up or around him.[76] At the beginning of each chapter, he presents a satellite image of the detention center or area where he was detained, labeling the images himself. In the case of larger prisons, such as Tadmur and Saydnaya, he includes the numbers prison authorities gave to each communal cell and courtyard (figure 1).

Additional photos of prison interiors taken from social media, as well as diagrams drawn by Sarraj himself, are included alongside the text. By using Google Earth so consistently, Sarraj presents his own digitized countermapping for his readers. In doing so he exposes and breaks the political and "cartographic silences" represented by unlabeled satellite imagery.[77] In words as well as through Google maps he depicts each space where he

سجن تدمر :أرقام الباحات بالأسود وأرقام المهاجع التي مكثت بها بالأحمر
مهجع 13: 6 حزيران 1984
مهجع 15: 28 تشرين الثاني 1985
مهجع 4: 27 آب 1988
مهجع 6 على 2: 28 نيسان 1991

1. An example of Bara Sarraj's use of Google Earth imagery. This image of Tadmur Military Prison reflects his labeling of the various courtyards and dormitory cells. Reproduced with permission of Bara Sarraj.

was forcibly detained, confirming the prisons' existence in visual terms and prompting his readers to recognize the buildings for what they are. This is especially significant because many of the interrogation centers in Syria, though known to local residents, are not visibly indicated or labeled as such by signs or gates. Many of the "dungeons" or "basements" (al-qabū or al-aqbiyya) where detainees are tortured and interrogated are underground, so the buildings of which they are a part do not always appear to reflect the typical external architecture of a modern prison. Additionally, very few confirmed photos of the interior spaces of Syrian prisons have circulated publicly, so the prisons are known but not known, visible but not visible by and to the larger Syrian public.[78]

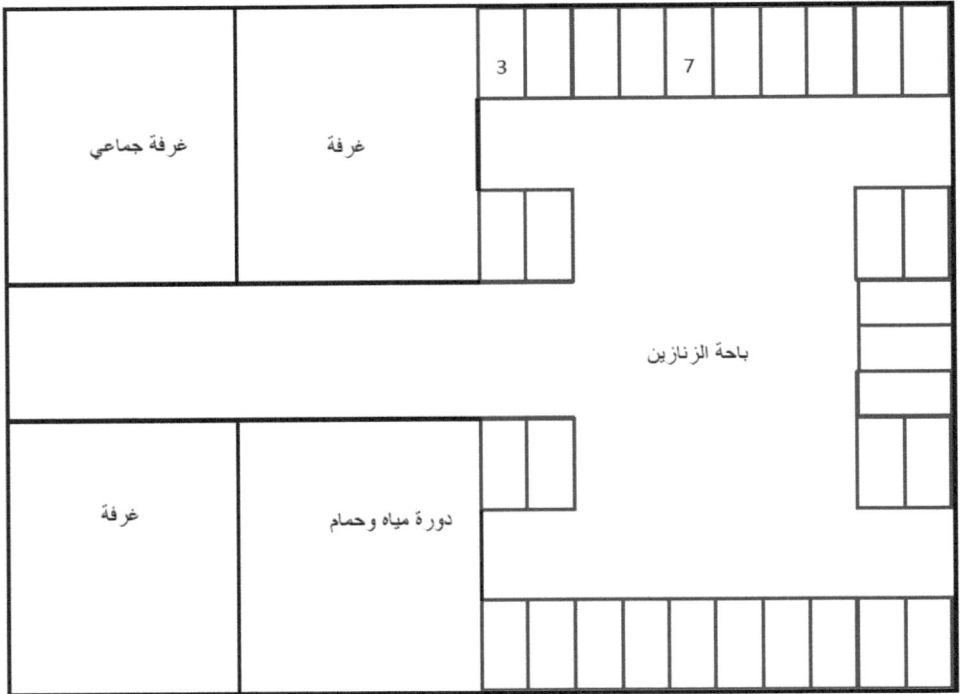

2. Bara Sarraj's diagram of the Military Intelligence Interrogation Center in Hama. Reproduced with permission of Bara Sarraj.

Sarraj's cartographic tracing of all the detention centers where he was held is coupled with his narrative documentation of the physical appearance, dimensions, and structures of the solitary and communal cells where he endeavored to survive (figure 2). For example, in describing his initial detention at the Hama Military Security Branch, he writes,

> Many stairs descending to a basement (*qabū*); Your name? . . . Your mother's? . . . They undid the cuffs and took off the blindfold and made me stand with my face to a wall in a corridor for a long period. . . . I listen to the sounds of food being distributed, a threat once in awhile, until the jailer led me to Cell Number 3 and closed the door.
>
> I couldn't see even see my hands. . . . I threw myself down, exhausted . . . two meters by less than a meter and a ventilation opening

in the ceiling that would only be moved by someone in power. The ceiling was less than my height of 180 centimeters. A nasty toilet near the door and a hateful odor of mold and humidity.[79]

In recounting his initial imprisonment at Tadmur, after providing a diagram as well as maps indicating the location of his cell within the prison, he describes communal cell number 13:

> The cell was crammed with people, among them those who were with us at the Damascus Branch. Two small rooms, between them a door opening, each of them four by four meters. One bathroom with no ceiling that allowed the smells of excrement to spread to the corners of the cell that was crowded with fifty-nine people. The floor was cement and the walls were dirty, nearly black. One of the interior walls was cracked up to the ceiling; perhaps the result of the bombs that were thrown at prisoners during the massacre on June 27, 1980.[80]

Similar passages are offered for each of the prison spaces recounted in his memoir. Equal in importance is the fact that Sarraj tracks his own and other prisoners' dates of entry and exit from particular cells. Horrifyingly, his entries on Tadmur prison include lists of the numbers and some of the names of prisoners who were executed on a weekly, and sometimes daily, basis. In some cases, the list of those executed is the only description offered for particular dates, in a single bleak sentence.

Like al-Haj Saleh and Dabbagh, Sarraj inscribes prison as a collective experience, always including the names, places of origin, and professions of prisoners he knew in his descriptions of just how he and others endured the spaces they were forced to inhabit. Despite some gaps in dates, particularly toward the end of the narrative, Sarraj's memoir also depicts the daily activities and routines of prison life, describing in detail how he and other prisoners created their own forms of community, modes of survival and solidarity, and means of resistance in prison spaces. He reflects on the lives of prisoners, including key moments of "emotional disclosure" in which he and others "exposed their vulnerabilities," and he traces common patterns of fear, terror, despair, depression, joy, and

resilience that are inherent in the experience of indefinite political detention in Syria.[81]

Despite regional, ideological, and theological differences among the
prisoners in his first communal cell in Tadmur, he recalls how he and his
fellow detainees established their own "internal regime" in an attempt to
combat the authoritarian regime's desire to impose not only an ordering
of prison space but also an "ordering of relations" between the detainees in
the prison cells.[82] Through devising their own internal regime, individual
prisoners took on different roles to maintain order and dignity in such an
overcrowded space.[83] Individual detainees were appointed to be responsible for each of the following needs: health, food, control of sound, laundry,
and the bathroom. Lack of medical care, food, and sanitary supplies made
this type of system essential to the prisoners' potential survival, especially
in Tadmur, where death was a daily occurrence.[84]

At night, while prisoners were forced to sleep "sword-style" (*sayyafa/
tasyīf*), one prisoner stayed awake to watch out for the guards peering
from the window in the roof because if they caught anyone moving, the
prisoner would be punished.[85] Sarraj himself was appointed for a period of
time as the *amīr al-mahja'* (literally, "the prince of the cell"); his responsibility was to mediate in disputes between detainees, and he also created
a collection box for prisoners who could not afford medicine.[86] Despite
the exceedingly dangerous and harsh conditions of Tadmur and the fact
that the prisoners were indefinitely detained by an authoritarian regime,
Sarraj comments that the men in his communal cell managed to create
"an internal system for a true democracy" by establishing a voting system
for all major decisions.[87] According Sarraj, the prisoners had an endless
struggle or "campaign" to establish order against the "chaos" imposed by
the officers, especially during inspections.[88]

Sarraj also recounts the myriad ways in which prisoners creatively
improvised when deprived of food, clothing, shoes, healthcare, medicine, and means of occupying their time. Prisoners would make prayer
beads out of olive pits and threads unraveled from worn, dirty blan-
kets; they created plastic thread from bags; they used the old newspapers wrapped around food in order to create their own form of news;
and they grew fungus on old bread to consume in an attempt to combat

vitamin deficiencies.[89] He recalls how one prisoner in particular became well-known for helping prisoners deprived of dental care, pulling teeth when necessary.[90] Each communal cell, according to Sarraj, also had a "comedy team" that, even in moments of intense anxiety and fear, would make "you laugh in spite of yourself."[91] Finally, he notes how frequently prisoners sacrificed themselves for each other, often by volunteering to put themselves in harm's way by making themselves more visible to the guards and officers; many prisoners volunteered repeatedly to protect their more vulnerable comrades—the sick, the elderly, and the already severely wounded.[92]

Like other religiously inclined detainees, Sarraj consistently emphasizes how his faith became his primary refuge and resource for survival. He frequently comments on how hearing the call to prayer (*adhān*) coming from outside the prison walls gave him tremendous comfort.[93] In multiple entries, he reminds his reader that the Quran was the main reason he was able to survive in prison; he wouldn't have "endured psychologically" without it, and he views the holy text as a "weapon to confront adversity."[94] He describes moments of gratitude toward God when the recitation of particular chapters or verses spared him or others from torture or death, and documents how collective recitation of certain chapters or verses provided prisoners with a feeling of security, even as they waited for more torture to come during the next roll call. He also details how he and other prisoners worked to memorize different suras of the holy book by learning from each other, and he expresses his fears at the time that those who had mastered the Quran would be transferred or executed before he had a chance to learn from them.[95] He also recalls how he and others reserved lessons or places in learning circles with specific prisoners, including elders such as Shaykh Hashim, a Shaf'i religious scholar.[96]

In some of the entries, Sarraj includes poetry and hymns (*anāshīd*) that he and other detainees memorized and recited, which became part of the soundscape of their prison experience. Prisoners composed spiritual, elegiac, nostalgic, and overtly political poetry, with verses directly or allegorically condemning the oppressive regime of Hafez al-Asad.[97] One such hymn (*nashīd*), which Sarraj asserts was the most famous in the cells of Tadmur, reflects the comfort he and other prisoners found in their faith

in God and their belief that, despite all odds, the regime will one day face
its own reckoning:

> How we sought refuge while injustice kept us from sleeping
> How our hope plead to us from the depths
> How we sought protection in the Lord of people and dawn
> How much we recited, toward the Benevolent, 'Ya Sin'
> How many nights and sighs pain us
> With the shackle of wounds nearly destroying us
> The throne of tyrants and rule of injustice will be crushed
> Be joyous my brother, for indeed, God protects us,
> Be joyous my brother, prison will become an epic
> Like the myths told over our bygone days[98]

Some of the lines, such as "The throne of tyrants and rule of injustice will
be crushed," reflect opposition to the regime that would have automatically been censored in public. Yet Sarraj depicts how it was recited quietly
in prison cells and yards, and passed on from prisoner to prisoner, in spite
of the despair and deprivation that incarceration in such spaces brings.
The inclusion of such hymns in the text indicates how detainees can view
music as "emotionally mobilising," eliciting "feelings of belonging and
struggle" that create "spaces of inclusion and solidarity."[99]

Other examples of the poetry or hymns in *From Tadmur to Harvard*
reflect prisoners' emotional states, particularly their sense of loss at being
exiled from their families, homes, and the lives that they once lived. Such
poems stress the prisoners' longing for the outside world:

> And the complaint continues, so when is the return?
> And when will the rendezvous after the absence be?
> And when will I see my mother who lives in torment?
> My mother, who tended childhood and youth,
> This question moves me; is there an answer?
>
> And if the wind of the barren desert rages
> And the clouds of thundering darkness gather

And if the terrors of life assail you like an evil spirit
Set out on the path of eternity and repeat:
After the darkness, the dew-filled dawn will break[100]

In this case, the poet expresses his desire for a long-awaited return to his old life, especially to see his mother. The missing or absent mother figure is a painfully frequent trope in the poetry of political detainees. The prisoner is depicted as being trapped in a desert storm, a clear reference to Tadmur, with only the hope of death as a release and a marker of a new dawn.

In another poem recollected by Sarraj, the poet envisions his return home upon release:

While our home has come to the point of ruin,
    it has remained in my heart as a place to wander
I'm sure that I will return one day
    to it I will cover the distance eagerly
I will set out on the path of our alley as my heart
    desires whenever it becomes closer
Jumping, racing, the two hands of my heart
    Knocking, in yearning longing, on the door
The house says, "Welcome, my dear,
    My child, you have been absent from me too long,
For you left as a boy,
    And today your hair, my son, has gone gray."
And my tongue is unable to speak to her
    So the tears flow as an answer
I kiss every handspan of her edifice
    And my mouth and saliva are perfumed from it[101]

This poem clearly expresses both the prisoner's longing to return home and see his family as he imagines the day of his release, and his excitement and bittersweet joy at the prospect of regaining his freedom. The verses also allude to the prisoner's ability to engage in the powerful effects and influence of memories as a kind of alternative to the harsh regimes and spaces of the prison.

A Vaster Blue: Faraj Bayraqdar's *Dove in Free Flight*

Three years after Bara Sarraj was arrested, Faraj Bayraqdar would face a similar fate. In 1987 Syrian military intelligence agents detained Bayraqdar for his involvement in the Syrian Communist Action Party. He had been arrested for his political activities before, but this time his detention would last fourteen years and include incarceration, solitary confinement, and torture under interrogation at numerous sites in the complex system of detention centers in Syria. Eventually, in the 1990s, the poet's plight would inspire an international campaign for his release by PEN International, Amnesty International, and Human Rights Watch, as well as local Syrian rights organizations. Coinciding with the campaign, a group of his friends and comrades painstakingly gathered and edited a collection of poems he had composed while in prison. Finally published in 1997, this collection, *Dove in Free Flight*, would garner Bayraqdar international recognition as both a poet and a prisoner of conscience.[102]

The story of the composition, eventual publication, and circulation of *Dove in Free Flight* has its own fraught but mappable itinerary, from Syria to Europe to other parts of the Arab world, including Lebanon, where for several decades many Syrian dissidents have published their writings despite the Syrian military occupation that lasted from 1976 until 2005. Throughout his detention, Bayraqdar clandestinely composed various poems. When he could find the means to do so, he recorded his poems in written form, sometimes on cigarette paper or onion peels when he did not have access to paper, and at times with ink made from tea or whatever materials he and other prisoners could find. However, like other detainees in Syria and elsewhere around the world, when deprived of the tools of writing, the poet also honed his skills of oral composition and memorization. Additionally, Bayraqdar relied on his fellow prisoners to commit his poems to memory so they could be written down later. Prior to his release, the poems that would make up *Dove in Free Flight* were smuggled out of prison and taken to members of his family in Homs. Though he enjoined his friends and family not to publish any of his writings while he was still in prison, out of fear that authorities would deprive him of visitations, friends eventually carried the papers that would become *Dove in Free Flight* to Beirut and then all the way to Paris.

Assembled in Paris by a group of friends in exile, the collection was edited by a close friend of Bayraqdar's. Also living in Paris, Syrian artist Youssef Abdelke (Yusif ʿAbdalki), who had been imprisoned from 1978 to 1980 for his membership in the same banned party as Bayraqdar, provided illustrations for the manuscript.[103] Finally the text was published in Beirut in 1997 despite fears that the Syrian security apparatus would seek some form of retaliation, not just against the still-incarcerated poet or his family but against those involved in the collection's publication. Playwright and poet Abdellatif Laâbi (Abd al-Latif Laʿbi), who has written about his own experience of political detention during the Years of Lead in Morocco, would publish a translation of Bayraqdar's collection in French, thus extending the journey of the text and adding further weight to the international campaign for Bayraqdar's release.[104] Bayraqdar finally gained his freedom in 2000 following the death of Hafez al-Asad, as part of the amnesty granted to hundreds of political prisoners in that all-too-brief period known as the Damascus Spring.

The story of how *Dove in Free Flight* came to be composed, compiled, and eventually published, even if in unfinished or imperfect form, has at times garnered as much attention as the power and the poignancy of the poems it contains.[105] Perhaps this is the case because the journey of the text constitutes a testimony in and of itself—a testimony to the strong sense of solidarity between detainees, to their modes of creativity, and to the all-too-often fraught itineraries of globalized and transnational literatures. But just as one can map the travels of the text within and beyond Syria's borders and trace its composition and transmission, one can also read the collection of poetry as a literal mapping of Syria's prison system as experienced by one particular political detainee, in a manner similar to the memoirs previously discussed in this chapter. Readers may likewise view the collection as an affective cartography of the experience of political detention—that is, a literary, often allusive tracing of the multiple ways in which the state security apparatus affects and attempts to control the body of the detainee in the spaces of detention.

This same collection of poetry also enacts spaces of potential liberation for the political prisoner—what can be interpreted, in Edward Soja's
term, as Thirdspace, which provides the "conditions of possibility for creative practice."[106] Thirdspace speaks to "moments of rupture when the user
of a space can enact 'new possibilities'" and the reader's attention "moves
beyond architecture and how people passively inhabit buildings to that
creative 'performance' of place."[107] Thirdspace is part of the sensory experience of the detainee and is imbued with a variety of emotions, including mourning, anger, defiance, longing, and love, which surface as acts of
resistance. In the poetry, images of natural elements and female figures
contrast with the harsh realities and the sometimes indescribable intensi-
ties of the prison experience, but they can also, even if only temporarily,
combat or overwrite the lexicon of detention and expand the space of the
detainee's imagination well beyond the confines of the prison cell.

Though Bayraqdar has expressed ambivalence over whether his
poetry actually belongs to the genre of prison literature and he considers
Dove in Free Flight to be a collection of poetry first, the poems in it are
replete with both direct and indirect references to prison space and to the
years the poet spent in detention.[108] Although the original Arabic edition
and the newer reedited manuscript version do not present the poems in
the chronological order of their creation, many of them conclude by indicating the year and the location of composition. These spatial and temporal markers trace the poet's enforced journey through Syrian prisons and
suggest a partial mapping of the detention system as the poet personally
experienced it. Many of the poems conclude with the words "Palestine
Division 1987" (also known as Division 235, the interrogation headquarters of military intelligence discussed in chapter 3), "Tadmur Prison 1991"
and "1992," and "Saydnaya Prison 1993." Along with naming and inscribing the sites and years of his detention, a few of the poem titles directly
reference torture and the prison experience while also suggesting a range
of meanings; these include the poems "Howl," "Groans," "Hunger Strike,"
and "A Visit."

In *Dove in Free Flight*, allusions to prison spaces and the tangible ways
in which the state and its security apparatus affect political prisoners often

appear in the form of oblique references to captivity, prison cells and their inadequate size, walls, bars, chains, guards, torture and torturers, bodies, corpses, or death. For example, in the poem "Vision" (Palestine Division 1987), the opening section reads:

> I imagined myself part of the deep night
> My friend Malik Bin al-Rayyib
> Greeted me and gave me sanctuary
> I was neither alive
> Nor dead so I made room for him
> Oh how the tightness of the space shamed me

Here, near death himself after enduring torture, the poet makes reference to using his imagination to envision himself as part of "the deep night." Night and darkness can allude to death and despair, but in this case Bayraqdar is given momentary sanctuary by the ghostly apparition of a classical poet who reportedly composed his own elegy before dying of illness on his way back from a pilgrimage.[109] Reminded of the narrowness of the space of his prison cell, Bayraqdar momentarily forgets his own pain and suffering and instead expresses shame at the lack of hospitality he is able to provide the "guest" who gave him refuge.

In the poem titled "Story" (also Palestine Division 1987), the poet takes a much more defiant tone. The second section reads:

> And if despair knocks the door
>   Upon you
> Rise up
>   And write on the wall
> Without explanation or detail:
> Oh, Master of Despair,
>   Tell your Lord the Sultan
> That the cell is no narrower
>   Than his grave
> That the cell is no shorter
>   Than his life

In this case Bayraqdar incites his comrades to defy the despondency, sense of defeat, and oppression that makes them feel even more confined than they already are in their cells. He calls for them to instead remain defiant—writing on the prison walls to remake them and take possession of them, and ordering the warden or torturer ("Master of Despair") to inform Hafez al-Asad (the "Sultan") that his death is impending, comparing al-Asad's life and his soon-to-be grave to the size of the detainees' prison cells. The poet reminds his audience that prisoners are, as Fiddler notes, "users" of prison spaces; even if only via their imaginations, detainees "can write their meaning, graffiti-like, onto what is there" and use "the spaces of the building in new and unintended ways" that allow them to temporarily "break free."[110]

At the same time, this lexicon of the prison experience and prison spaces that represents and inspires a range of emotions is consistently juxtaposed with aspects of the natural landscape and animal figures outside the prison (including birds, wolves, horses, gazelles, mountains, trees, the wind, the river, stars, the shore, and the sky), as well as haunting and haunted female figures (referred to simply as "a woman," or as sister, mother, or daughter). In particular poems Bayraqdar's references to nature or natural phenomena, often drawing on the heritage of pre-Islamic odes and classical Arabic poetry, contrast the prison interiors with the potentially unlimited spaces of the world outside the detention center. Like other texts, in some poems Bayraqdar emphasizes the soundscape of prison. The poem "Cooing" (Palestine Division 1987) provides a striking example of the stress on sound:

> Your cooing wears me out at night—
>   so wear me out.
> Like wine in the odes, you go on cooing
> and leave me what moves horses
>   to tears,
> what burdens the birds with wings
> what singing follows . . .
>
> Is the tree of the heart made of our blood,
>   or a mirage?

A question seduces me, shooting star by shooting star
    a flower a flower or two
numb upon my arm
    as dawn steals blue
to bathe the dew
    so I see it.
And for this question, the gazelle,
    and what binds us
in the nets of the answer
—and so the sky will not be confined—
I'll release a flock of fledgling doves
and open the towers of my spirit for
    the day to come . . .

The image of the poet listening to a dove who is able to fly away at will from the prison stands in contrast to Bayraqdar's own state of confinement; Bayraqdar's poetic imagery reflects how prisoners "break beyond these pre-ordained barriers of prison" and "impose their own meaning on a given space."[111] The preponderance of localized sounds and the reference to night surrounding the poet while he is imprisoned provide an introduction that frames the space of the poem as prison. As opposed to the prisoner's surroundings, the space of the sky is presented as as the space where freedom can be gained. At the same time, the "towers" (a reference to prison architecture) of the "spirit" of the detainee will be opened; there is still hope for the spirit to be free in the future ("the day to come").

The poem "The Ode of Sorrow" (Tadmur 1992) articulates a variety of spatial images and equates the images of female figures (lover or wife, mother, and daughter) with life outside of prison. In the verses, the allusion to the space of prison in which even the stars weep is subsequently juxtaposed to a female beloved ("my woman") for whom the poet longs:

The silence of my woman is salt on
    my voice, bearing the meaning
of the wound, and the name of the river,
And her hands are my two shores.
    Her silence is the foot of a turquoise mountain

Momentarily, the woman's silence not only conveys meaning but also becomes another measure of the space of the outside world (here cast as "the foot of a turquoise mountain"). In addition, the woman's hands and her embrace are posited as shores, again recalling a feature of a landscape far from the prisoner's visual point of view, as well as indicating the poet's and other detainees' hope to find a potential refuge from the harsh prison regime. Alternatively, the link between the female figure and shores, a mountain, and a river can reference the poet and political detainee's attempt to find refuge in his own memories, since "through memory, conscious and unconscious, psychic and somatic—we all carry traces of past geographies, in that there are always emotionally coloured hues ranging from pale to vivid."[112]

In a later section, the poem returns to another female figure—this time his daughter—as a figure of hope:

> My daughter's two eyes echo the
> trilling cries of joy at evening.
> And a sash of the recitation of clouds—
> she can awaken vision
> and tears in the eyes of the blind.
> She lowers eyelashes more savory
> than slumber stealing the bird from
> between its wings,
> and a heart from the hands of my mother,
> and shackles from my hands

The image of the daughter is linked to both sounds of joy and clouds outside the prison. However, the idea of a daughter being able to remove the shackles from her father's hands, thus releasing him from the pain of his imprisonment, is disrupted by the return of references to the poet's continued detention in the next stanza. The expression of longing and affection for his daughter is nevertheless retained, serving as a reminder that though emotions might be viewed as "contained in psycho-social and material boundaries . . . such boundaries are never impermeable or entirely secure."[113]

One of the longer poems in the collection, "Alphabetical Formation" (Saydnaya 1993/1999), can be analyzed in a number of ways. To depict language and writing as a form of refuge, the last stanzas evoke the power of memory and imagination in creating spaces of liberation for the detainee. The stanza, titled "Nun," reads:

A gift is my rib
And my spirit a brown horse
And memory is my pavilion
For to whom do I entrust my belongings
And to whom do I entrust my desire
For a mirage that doesn't betray its master
One day as the capitols
Have betrayed their people.

The poem refers to the spirit of the poet-narrator as a "brown horse," a figure of strength and potential freedom of movement, and the power to remember is cast as a place of sanctuary, refuge, or even celebration removed from the space of prison. At the same time, in typical self-questioning form, the poet asks if there is anyone left to whom he can leave what few material items he possesses.

The final stanza of the poem, titled "Ya," alludes to the idea that the composition of poetry produces spaces outside of the poet's prison cell, imagined spaces that allow the prisoner to persist and defy the odds despite all the struggles he endures. Composing poetry ultimately represents the means through which one can leave the confines of the cell walls and "embark" to another "shore" to experience a "vaster blue":

Has he finished . . . ?
No . . .
He doesn't know this verb,
and doesn't accept its conjugations,
it embarks within us
and if he arrives to the shore,
he says: Apologize to it for me.

Around me is a vaster blue
out of your dreams

Bayraqdar concludes "Alphabetical Formation" on a note of hope, reminding his audience that the poet and his poetry must persevere despite the oppression and obstacles they face: "And as for the poetry/We say: No . . . And we say: we will try."

5

On "The Kingdom of Death and Madness"

Sousveillance and Surrealism in Tadmur Military Prison

On May 13, 2015, the Islamic State of Iraq and Syria (ISIS/Daʻish) launched an offensive to take over the central Syrian city of Tadmur, or Palmyra as it's known in English. Within eight days, the Syrian state army had withdrawn completely from the city and its environs, which, at the time, gave ISIS control over 50 percent of Syrian territory.[1] According to rumors on social media, regime forces also prevented some civilians from evacuating to the west, abandoning the city's remaining residents to an unknown fate at the lethal hands of the militant group. In a little over a week, Daʻish achieved its goal of taking over both modern Tadmur and the ruins of its ancient city in the Homs desert, once a popular tourist destination and one of six UNESCO world heritage sites in Syria. ISIS had long undertaken a scorched-earth policy and an extensive, coordinated campaign of "spectacles of violence," that included systematically destroying sites of cultural and religious heritage in Iraq and Syria.[2]

Several English-language news outlets, including CNN, focused their televised coverage on the potential destruction of ancient Palmyra, particularly the Temple of Baal, now under Daʻish control.[3] This media attention to a major site of antiquity and former hub of the Silk Road triggered yet another people-versus-monuments debate stemming from the wars in Iraq and Syria. As one Tadmur resident stated, "the world doesn't care about us . . . all they are interested in is the stones of ancient Palmyra."[4]

125

Despite their extremist stance against visual "idolatry," Daʿish, without any acknowledgement of the irony, followed their usual protocol of disseminating forms of heavily choreographed media to augment their own visibility. They released a series of videos to celebrate their self-proclaimed "glorious" conquest of the city. A number of their clips used Palmyra's ancient ruins as a stage.[5] Initially at least, spokesmen for ISIS declared they would not destroy any of the structures or artifacts of the site, and instead they used various locales within the ruins, including its amphitheater, for their already-ubiquitous theatrics of bloodshed.[6]

But in addition to fears for the remaining civilian population of Tadmur and, of course, the world heritage site, there was another locus of concern in the small city. Much more prominently than their English-language counterparts, in their early coverage Arabic news networks emphasized another site: Tadmur Military Prison, that other Palmyra, well-known only by reputation to most Syrians and well-established as a source of paralyzing dread and terror for anyone who has opposed the Asad regime since the late 1970s.

Originally built by French Mandate authorities as a military outpost in the 1930s, Tadmur was converted into a prison for soldiers convicted of nonpolitical, "ordinary" crimes sometime after Syrian independence in 1946.[7] According to some sources, beginning in the late 1960s, the Syrian government began sending political prisoners there.[8] Under Hafez al-Asad, Tadmur's function as a political prison expanded greatly, with new buildings added to the compound and with a minimum of twenty thousand political prisoners passing through its overcrowded cells between 1980 and 1990. The vast majority of the prisoners in the 1980s and 1990s were members of or accused of affiliation with the banned Muslim Brotherhood.[9] But some detainees from banned secular, leftist, or Marxist parties were also sent there as a form of additional punishment for refusing to confess, renounce their political activities, or sign loyalty oaths to the regime, even after their original sentences had expired. In a 2001 report Amnesty International presented Tadmur prison as "synonymous with brutality, despair, and dehumanization," where, according to an anonymous prisoner, "death can come about at any moment."[10] Widely referred to in Syrian literature by the moniker "the desert prison," Tadmur has been crowned "the kingdom of death and madness" by now-exiled poet Faraj Bayraqdar, and defined as the "absolute prison" by Yassin al-Haj Saleh.[11]

In the first few weeks of the ISIS takeover, Tadmur Military Prison featured in the broadcasts of the staunchly anti–Asad regime Al Jazeera network, as well as a number of other Arabic-language news organizations. Only briefly mentioned in early articles by the *Guardian*, the BBC, and the *New York Times*, this most infamous detention center in the Syrian carceral archipelago immediately became the subject of a number of special interviews and programs on the Arabic news channels as ISIS took control of the city.[12] Former detainees reappeared on talk shows and interview segments to denounce both ISIS and the Asad regime, and documentary films on Tadmur Prison and Syrian prison literature re-aired.

Well aware of Tadmur Military Prison's notoriety and its symbolic capital as one of the deadliest sites of human rights violations perpetrated by the Syrian state in the past forty years, members of Daʿish immediately claimed to have liberated the detention center and those imprisoned there. This assertion came, once again, with no acknowledgment that the militant group itself is guilty of detaining, torturing, raping, enslaving, and executing thousands of Syrians and Iraqis for political, religious, and ethnic reasons, and sometimes for no reason at all.[13] Their claim of releasing the prisoners was an attempt to co-opt the suffering of Syrian regime detainees for their own ideological agenda and propaganda. But in addition, the declaration that they had liberated Tadmur and other rumors that ISIS had released the detainees held in the prison caused an enormous amount of turmoil for families of political prisoners held in Syria.

Outside the walls of this and other detention centers, many expected, hoped, and prayed that their loved ones would finally be able to come home if, in the wake of the destructive trajectory of the war in Syria, their homes remained intact. For weeks families and friends waited for any news of the prisoners and carefully scrutinized every Daʿish video and social media message for clues to the whereabouts of the missing. It was not just the families of Syrian detainees who were in tortuous limbo, but also the families of Palestinian, Jordanian, and Lebanese prisoners. This included Lebanese citizens who had been arrested during Syria's thirty-year military occupation of Lebanon, and who are believed to still be alive today. Tragically, at the time of the writing of this chapter, the fate of those political prisoners believed to be in Tadmur in May 2015, most of them unnamed and their numbers unaccounted for, remains unknown— much like the fates of thousands of the detained and forcibly disappeared throughout Syria since the beginning of the 2011 Revolution.

With no acknowledgment of the agony of those in waiting, members of ISIS produced and circulated a video and photographs of the dusty grey and brown exterior and interiors of the prison, now unlocked, ungated, pillaged, and deserted. At the entrance, the black and white banner of ISIS was staked into the head of a crumbling statue of Hafez al-Asad. On the walls of inner yards one could see a series of still-visible murals: the familiar Baʻth party slogan of "unity, freedom, socialism," two-starred Syrian regime flags, and fading, dusty paintings of that unholy trinity—Bashar al-Asad and his late brother and father, all three garbed in fatigues, berets, and sunglasses, suitably outfitted for both the desert and a military prison. The video also surveyed the dark solitary cells and the long-stained cement walls and floors of the now bare and empty communal cells of the prison, with their heavy steel doors and small, single-grated ceiling aperture. In one of the communal cells, one could read and ponder the words "to preserve the dignity of the citizen" painted on the wall. One could also peer into an abandoned administrative office with a few scattered files and a dusty and faded photograph of al-Asad the father precariously hanging on a wall.

These interior images of Tadmur Prison were, to my knowledge, the first ever to be circulated internationally, spread rapidly on social media by human rights activists and former detainees, and were soon picked up by major news networks around the world, with their original provenance often erased. Prisoners, the rare visitor (usually having paid a very costly bribe), military police and officers of a range of ranks, security agents, those who served as guards, torturers, field trial judges, executioners, and administrators had, of course, viewed the interiors of the prison. However, the larger public had never seen inside the prison prior to the Daʻish takeover of the city. There was much to take in from these newly circulating images, but those much-anticipated, supposedly newly freed political

3. Google satellite image of Tadmur Military Prison tweeted by Bara Sarraj (@Tadmor_Harvard) on Twitter on May 13, 2013. Reproduced with permission of Bara Sarraj.

detainees were nowhere to be seen in the Daʿish-produced video about their self-vaunted liberation of Tadmur Military Prison.

Although there are Google aerial shots of the exterior (figure 3) and maps, sketches, and diagrams drawn by former detainees, no pictures of the inside of the prison while it was still in use as a detention facility were widely available to the public prior to May 2015.[14] The sole possible exception to this is a single unverified, grainy black and white photograph of the shroud-wrapped bodies of some of those killed during the state's 1980 massacre of at least one thousand prisoners charged with being members of the Muslim Brotherhood.[15] Yet even this photo appears to have been taken outside of the prison. Hala Mohammad's daring documentary *A Journey into Memory* (*Rihla ila al-Dhakira*, 2006), the first full-length documentary film about Tadmur prison, features only slightly blurry, brief

4. Still from Hala Mohammad's *A Journey to Memory*, featuring former political prisoners Yassin al-Haj Saleh, (foreground), Ghassan al-Jaba'i (background left), and Faraj Bayraqdar (background right). Reproduced with permission of Hala Mohammad, Yassin al-Haj Saleh, Ghassan al-Jaba'i, and Faraj Bayraqdar.

takes of an exterior wall that presumably is part of the prison's compound. The shots of the wall appear to have been taken clandestinely through the window of a speeding car or van. Almost all of Mohammad's film consists of a conversation between three former detainees, Yassin al-Haj Saleh, Ghassan al-Jaba'i, and Faraj Bayraqdar, recalling their experiences of Tadmur. Throughout the film the three men are pictured sitting in a vehicle as they speak, with an occasional shot of a road sign or a landscape scene on the desert highway heading northeast from Damascus. The conclusion of the film shows the three former detainees wandering the ancient ruins of Palmyra (figures 4 and 5).[16]

Prior to May 2015, oral testimonies, writings, and drawings by prisoners as well as human rights reports have constituted the primary sources of everything envisioned about Tadmur by larger publics both in and outside Syria. In stark contrast to Da'ish's effort to make its temporary control of the prison so visible, for decades the Syrian regime has attempted to render the same site unseen through its steadfast denial that political

5. Still from Hala Mohammad's *A Journey to Memory*, featuring Yassin al-Haj Saleh, Ghassan al-Jaba'i, and Faraj Bayraqdar, in the ancient ruins of Palmyra. Reproduced with permission of Hala Mohammad, Yassin al-Haj Saleh, Ghassan al-Jaba'i, and Faraj Bayraqdar.

prisoners were held there and that any human rights abuses, let alone the outright murder and massacres of prisoners, were ever perpetrated within Tadmur's walls. According to the state, it was a military prison—nothing more—and the inmates detained there, if not soldiers who had committed crimes, were "terrorists." This denial was belied when, in 2001, in an effort to improve its international image with respect human rights issues, the Syrian government countered critics of its human rights record by claiming that the prison had been closed, with all detainees previously held there transferred to detention centers with supposedly less harsh conditions.[17]

Several organizations, from Human Rights Watch to the Syrian Human Rights Committee, have made Tadmur Military Prison the subject of special reports since the early 1990s.[18] These reports follow the conventional patterns of the human rights reportage. Using as much verifiable detail as possible, drawn from mostly (and necessarily) anonymous witnesses, these reports document, chart, measure, and map the total number of prisoners held, their names and ideological or party affiliations when available, and the official length of their sentences. They also describe the measurable structures and architecture of the prison; the size and specific numbers of detainees crammed into overcrowded communal cells, where prisoners are forced to take turns standing, sitting, or sleeping sword-style due to lack of space; the lack of food to the point of starvation; the horrendous conditions prisoners live under, including poor sanitation and freezing and blisteringly hot temperatures; the rapid and deadly spread of communicable diseases such as tuberculosis and cholera; the myriad forms of daily torture improvised by guards; and the number of prisoners killed in a given time period—whether arbitrarily through torture or by execution. Most of these conditions have existed at other prisons in Syria, but at Tadmur they were more frequent, more systematic, more intense, and more lethal than at any other prison until its reported closure in 2001. Now, after the 2011 Revolution, Tadmur Military Prison's notoriety has been surpassed by that of Saydnaya and other detention centers.

In the same way that it has been the distinctive concern of human rights organizations, Tadmur Military Prison occupies a haunting, nearly mythical position in Syrian prison literature, much like that of Abu Ghrayb in Iraqi prison literature.[19] Tadmur's infamy is highlighted by the common saying: "The one who enters it dies, and the one who leaves it is reborn." As al-Haj Saleh writes: "Let us imagine a prison without visits, without books and pens, without means of entertainment and without 'tools of production' of any sort, without domestic facilities—kitchen fixtures, stoves—without hot water . . . just a closed place that doesn't open up except for food and . . . punishment. That is Tadmur prison: the Syrian shame that is indelible. In this prison, time does not pass. It accumulates over the prisoners and suffocates them."[20]

Other former detainees echo al-Haj Saleh in the numerous memoirs composed about the prison, in addition to essays, novels, short stories, plays, and poetry. They continue to publish works even now, with some who were detained there in the 1980s and 1990s being motivated to tell or publicly circulate their stories since the 2011 Revolution.[21] Though much of the writing produced about Tadmur shares traits in content and form with texts about other prisons in Syria and the Arab world, the literature about the prison is unique not only in its emphasis on the level of the state's grotesque acts of depravity perpetrated against detainees there, but also in its reflections on the incomprehensibility of, absurdity of, and difficulty of describing of such acts.[22] Authors of such works are generating a body of testimonial literature and producing a collectively written, mosaic-like history of the prison. They are also making Tadmur Military Prison and the forms of suffering they endured there visible to their reading publics, an act and process that have become even more imperative in light of the prison's alleged destruction by Da'ish and the fact that the Asad regime has retaken the city of Tadmur and remains firmly entrenched in power.

But how, then, do former detainees make Tadmur visible? How do they reconstruct and revisualize their experiences of surviving the prison? In writing of their own and others' survival in detention, how do they see the prison and how do they make it seen for their audiences? These questions are complicated by the fact that in Tadmur, as in other prisons, making oneself visible meant making oneself vulnerable, with often lethal consequences. Prisoners were under constant surveillance and threat of torture and death, in addition to being confined in the same dark, usually windowless cells for years. They were often forced to wear blindfolds or hoods, including when they slept. When in the yards, they were also consistently ordered to keep their heads bowed in a display of abject submission and humility, including when they were forced into stress positions for hours at a time. Guards forbade them to glance around their environment or to look up unless specifically ordered to. For prisoners to dare to meet the eyes of their jailers and torturers, to peer around them, or to stand out in any way meant risking becoming marked (*mu 'allam*) for additional brutal punishments by the guards. Being marked would result in, at the very least, some form of degrading or excruciating physical torture and, at the very worst, being tortured to death. As Bayraqdar notes of his experiences at Tadmur, "To raise your eyes would be to raise your own casket and prepare to march at the front of the funeral."[23]

In some prisoners' descriptions of their inability to see and their constant awareness of being under the guards' unending visual and aural scrutiny, the system of discipline and punishment at Tadmur enacts a kind of panopticism, albeit with variations, especially the incorporation of the daily physical torture inflicted on prisoners. Under persistent threat of death, Tadmur prisoners were ordered not to look in certain directions and not to speak, and such commands would diminish the detainees' agency and subjectivity, especially considering the fact that vision is of "central importance for an inmate's attempt to 'make space' within the prison environment."[24]

Despite all of the limitations on prisoners' field of vision, most authors describe the physical structures of the prison, or at least the parts of the prison they encounter in visual terms during their detention. Especially in nonfiction works, authors such as Muhammad Salim Hammad, Bara Sarraj, Ali Abou Dehn ('Ali Abu Dahn), and Khalid Fadil describe the spaces they are forced to dwell in with minute detail and exact measurements, much like the documentary style of human rights reports. Yet once writers have described the physical attributes of the parts of the compound they have seen, usually upon their entry, the material, architectural spaces of Tadmur Military Prison are effaced, except for brief references. Authors of the prison literature about Tadmur document everything from obscene acts of torture, to the names and numbers of those executed, to the consistent, often minute forms of resistance they enact. They describe the emotional ties they establish with one another, and the multiple ways prisoners created to survive despite the harsh regime of the prison indicating "how people cope, how they carve out spaces for themselves in the space of the prison," even in a site of extreme deprivation and violence, like the desert prison.[25] For other writers, making Tadmur visible for their audience means inaugurating and inscribing a mode of countersurveillance or sousveillance, like the "hidden observer" protagonist of Mustafa Khalifa's novel *The Shell* (*al-Qawqa'a*, 2008). At the same time, there are those, such as Bayraqdar in his memoir, *The Betrayals of Language and Silence* (*Khiyanat al-Lugha wa-l-Samt*, 2006) who make Tadmur visible by interrogating the possibility of ever fully capturing what he and others experienced there.

Witnessing Tadmur

In his 1998 memoir, *Tadmur: Witness and Witnessed* (*Tadmur: Shahid wa Mashhud*), Palestinian-Jordanian Muhammad Salim Hammad details his arrest and his detention at the prison. Born in Iraq in 1960 and raised in Jordan, Hammad became acquainted with the teachings of the Muslim Brotherhood while a high school student. He eventually became the head of the student branch of the Muslim Brotherhood at his high school because the organization was not banned in Jordan at that time. He later was accepted to the University of Damascus to pursue a degree in engineering, and while a student there he continued his work for the Muslim Brotherhood, including carrying messages from leaders of the organization in Jordan to members in Syria, where the Brotherhood was banned. He was arrested in August of 1980, tortured and interrogated, and eventually sent to Tadmur. He would not be released until 1991.

The subtitle title of Hammad's memoir, "Witness and Witnessed" highlights the function of the text as a visceral testimonial of what prisoners endured in Tadmur Military Prison, particularly in the 1980s. In recalling both daily and exceptional events of his and other prisoners' suffering, the former detainee strives to make starkly visible the regime's atrocities against its own citizens, including the 1980 massacre of detainees at the prison. Like Sarraj and several other writers, Hammad includes in his text constant references to prisoners who were killed, "martyred," while detained at Tadmur—those murdered arbitrarily by the guards or executed on the orders of the judges of the tribunals routinely conducted in the prison.

Unconventionally, Hammad begins his memoir not with the story of his arrest, but with the day of his transfer out of Tadmur Military Prison. Describing himself waiting in a "red Toyota bus" as he was transferred to another facility just before his release, he notes his shock at seeing the outside world for the first time in eleven years:

> It was a cold morning in the last days of the year 1991 and life in the desert city of Tadmur was carrying on normally. Early in the morning the children walked toward their schools. Their mothers, after having sent their men off to work and cleared the house of any disturbances, were at home engaged in conversation with their neighbors. The *dakakeen* in the city welcomed its wide array of visitors, greeting a blend of women and men, civilians and soldiers. The streets opened their paths for those walking and those on animals and in cars.[26]

Along with his fellow detainees, Hammad experienced a strong sense of alienation and defamiliarization upon witnessing what should be ordinary, everyday scenes beyond the prison's walls. Having endured indefinite detention for eleven years, never knowing when he would be released or if he would be executed, he was startled by these initial sites of the outside world. He notes that the bus transporting the prisoners "drew no special attention from those around it as it meant nothing to anyone—except its passengers inside."[27] Describing how he and the other passengers simply sat, starred, and gazed, Hammad reflects: "We were like babies who had just entered the world from the wombs of our mothers, or like visitors from another planet in their first experience on Earth."[28] Later, toward the end of the memoir, Hammad tells his readers how he realized that it was only on the day of his transfer for eventual release that he finally really saw the prison and the faces of the guards who had tormented him.[29]

The opening of Hammad's memoir moves from the day of his transfer out of the prison, back in time to recount how he came to be involved in the Muslim Brotherhood, how he eventually moved to Syria to begin his studies, and how he was initially held and tortured in a military interrogation center. Most of the memoir, however, details his and others' experiences at Tadmur. In a way similar to the accounts of Ali Abou Dehn and Bara Sarraj, he recounts his transfer, blindfolded, disoriented, and sitting in a cramped vehicle for hours. He and his fellow detainees could only guess by the length of the trip that "the much feared Tadmur must be our destination."[30] His worst fears were realized. He describes his first glimpse of the prison just before dawn:

> A nervous chill traveled through my body as I descended the car and was struck by the bitter, icy air of the desert before sunrise. The officers removed our blindfolds and unchained the restraints around our arms and legs and threw them into the back of the truck. Through the darkness of the night, there shone upon us bright lights from the prison and I was able to see military police moving around us as they completed the technicalities of prisoner exchange. I gathered that it was a military prison as well. All the factors combined brought me to the unfortunate certainty that we had, without a doubt, reached Tadmur.[31]

Describing his initial arrival at the prison, Hammad indicates just how limited a prisoner's field of vision is. In this case, the bright searchlights prevented the detainees from seeing much around them and filled them with an even greater sense of foreboding. Their vision was even further restricted when they were ordered to keep their eyes closed in anticipation of the "reception party" (*haflat al-istaqbāl*) of torture they would receive. Hammad's reception included being struck in the eye with a metal whip, and he notes "here, we were not allowed the assistance of a cloth to cover our eyes, but were forced to simply keep our eyes shut at all times."[32] During the reception and intake, Hammad recalls, he became marked by one of the guards by virtue of the fact that he is a Jordanian citizen, but fortunately for him, that guard was transferred to another section.

Hammad recounts just how restricted the prisoners' field of vision was and also describes the state of being under constant surveillance by prison guards. In contrast to the prisoners' awareness of always being under the eyes of the guards, the author also tells of incidents in which prisoners relied on the prison soundscape for information while being under constant threat if they dared to look around.[33] In recalling the space of the first communal or dormitory cell he and the other new prisoners were herded into, Hammad notes that at the top of the cell walls were "open windows with metal bars," but they were too high for prisoners to reach in order to look outside.[34] In addition, he describes two barred vents in the ceilings; through these vents, the officers who stood at guard twenty-four hours a day could "watch everything that we were doing below."[35]

Cataloguing the routines of life in Tadmur, Hammad recollects the daily, tortuous process of roll call and the "breather" or "break" (*tanaffus*) in the courtyard that the prisoners were forced to endure when torture and beatings by the guards were all part of a systematic routine. After one session of roll call, he notes: "The guards left and each of us returned to his mat, head lowered, heart shattered. Our devastated nerves made us jump and stand at attention at every sound we heard in the hall or from above us. And if anyone even thought to lift an eyelid and take a look at what was around him, he remembered the fate of our brother Saleh who

glanced upwards during the first announcement."³⁶ However, the prisoners' fear of opening their eyes or glancing around them did not prevent
them from sensing and at times seeing the events happening around them.
They also managed to devise ways of circumventing the guards' surveillance in order to take part in activities that were otherwise prohibited in
the prison. When they perceived that they were "even the lightest bit isolated from the watchful eye of the officers," Hammad and others would
take part in activities, such as prayer, reciting the Quran, and religious
study, that "nourished our souls and comforted our hearts."³⁷

Hammad also dedicates a good portion of his narrative to his witnessing of the "grossly unfair court trials" and executions of his fellow
Muslim Brotherhood members.³⁸ Noting one such occasion, he writes:
"More than ten brothers left the hall that morning. As they walked out,
it was as if they were different men than the brothers we had known all
this time. They were calm and composed, with traces of happiness on
their faces. They were content with the path that was chosen for them and
looked forward to meeting their Creator."³⁹ Like other Islamist authors
of prison literature, Hammad emphasizes these prisoners' readiness to
become martyrs, though he also recounts the depression and despair he
and others faced due to the constant threat of death. On this particular
day, he sees the executions take place through a crack in the door of the
cell, and he recounts how "the scene—particularly the pitiful equipment
being used" for the executions was a "gross violation of even the basic provisions a hanging field should present."⁴⁰

Along with witnessing and making visible the summary executions
that took place in the prison, Hammad inscribes his and others' grief and
mourning at the loss and brutal deaths of so many. Commenting that those
who remained alive "possessed only prayer and faith in God to maintain
our sanity," Hammad recalls: "These men had become our true brothers
though the darkest times. . . . They left this world, and we would never see
them again until the end of time when all will be called for Judgment."⁴¹
The memoir concludes with a "roster of martyrs"—an endeavor to record
and preserve the names and memory of those detainees killed in Tadmur,
a reminder that the term *shahīd*, drawn from the same trilateral root as
the words in the memoir's subtitle, also means "witness."

Sousveillance in Mustafa Khalifa's *The Shell*

In 2008 Mustafa Khalifa published his debut novel, *The Shell*, the first novel to focus entirely on Tadmur Military Prison. Though he was never officially a member of any Syrian oppositional political parties, Khalifa was imprisoned from 1982 to 1994 in both Tadmur and Saydnaya prisons. In *The Shell*, Khalifa presents the semiautobiographical story of a seemingly apolitical protagonist named Musa, who returns to his homeland after studying filmmaking in France. Musa is arbitrarily arrested at the airport, brutally tortured at an interrogation center by military intelligence agents, mistakenly identified as a member of the Muslim Brotherhood, and sent to the "desert prison."[42] He does not learn of his alleged crime until just before his release: while he was in Paris, an informer, a fellow student, had filed a report stating that he had verbally criticized the ruling regime at a party.

Like many detainees, Musa masters the skill of oral composition and memorization, what he calls "mental writing"—an art that allows prisoners to resist the silence imposed within the prison walls, where they are deprived of basic writing tools and frequently barred from speaking to each other.[43] Deeming himself a "tape recorder," Musa retains each diary entry in his memory. Eventually, once he is released, he is able to record some of the entries on paper.[44] Except for the initial section, the novel is composed of these dated entries, narrated in spare, simple language. Some entries are just a day or two apart, and some are separated by several months, as if the protagonist is temporarily silenced or has no desire to speak. At the beginning of the novel Musa admits that it would be impossible to produce a complete account of his experiences: "I cannot write and say everything. That would require an act of confession, and confession has its conditions. Objective circumstances and another party."[45] Many of the entries contains parenthetical observations—italicized editorial comments seemingly made at a later time, as if the narrator has returned to the composition again and again to add more of his thoughts or observations.

The subtitle of the novel is "Diary of a Hidden Observer" or "Memoir of a Hidden Observer (*yawmiyāt mutalaṣṣiṣ*)." The word *mutalaṣṣiṣ* can also be translated as "peeping Tom" or "voyeur," but Khalifa, despite acknowledging this connotation in the narrative, does not deploy the term in the traditional sexualized sense. The term alludes to the idea of prisoners internalizing the surveillance mechanisms of detention, including the possibilities of prisoners spying and informing on each other, a false charge that is continually leveled at Musa by his antagonistic fellow prisoners. So intense are the mechanisms of constant control and punishment that at certain points Khalifa's protagonist and his cellmates seem to be enacting a form of autosurveillance, the apex of panopticism, whereby detainees have completely internalized the observational role of the prison guards.[46] Additionally, the word makes a slight dig at the regime's surveillance and censorship of the Syrian population as a whole by implying that regime intelligence agents who spy on citizens are voyeurs.

Yet the main character naming himself a *mutalaṣṣiṣ* also reflects his agency. It reveals the potential of the detainee to turn the tables on regime authorities, even if only under severely limited and dangerous circumstances, and to generate forms of countersurveillance or sousveillance ("watching from below") to make what happens in the Syrian prison system visible to those reading his diary-as-novel.[47] If surveillance is "associated with monitoring and control as key elements of the exercise of power," then Musa exercises a minute form of self-empowerment against the state and the extremists in his cell by becoming a *mutalaṣṣiṣ*.[48] Even before he is transferred to Tadmur, Musa draws on his training in film and attempts to "neutrally" observe his surroundings and fellow inmates. In one particular incident, he sees other prisoners fighting over a rarely available small piece of meat: "My professional and artistic sensibility was crouching in a far-off corner, watching, but not intervening—a sensibility that remained beyond the domain of pain and anxiety, awake and neutral, observing and recording however great my own psychological and physical pain."[49]

In a lengthy entry dated April 24, Musa describes his arrival at Tadmur. Initially he takes note of both his physical surroundings and those around him, jailers and prisoners. He sees dozens of military police officers in front of the prison and a stone plaque over the main door with the Quranic verse "In retaliation there is life for you, men possessed of minds."[50] As he and other prisoners are led off the truck, he is surprised to find that the guards accompanying them during transfer are now treating

them with pity. With a lexicon familiar to readers of Syrian prison literature and similar to the descriptions found in memoirs by Hammad and
others, he also describes in detail the "reception party" given to prisoners
as soon as they arrive at the prison. Musa surveys the military police waiting to meet them, commenting on their faces, "How had they been flayed?
Why? Where? I didn't know. But I could see that these false faces weren't
like the faces of the rest of humanity, not like our families' or friends'
faces. They had an inhuman sheen to them."[51] The proximity of so many
guards and the perception of their inhumanity causes the prisoners to
cling closely to one another.

Musa is also struck by the posture prisoners automatically assume
when they are faced with threats of imminent violence. His description
indicates how prisoners attempted to avoid confrontations provoked by
looking too directly: "More than a hundred military policemen swarmed
around us. All the prisoners avoided looking directly at any of them. Our
heads were slightly bowed and our shoulders flopped. It was an attitude of
deference, humiliation, and subservience. How was it that all the prisoners had agreed on this way of standing, as if we had been used to standing like that before? I don't know. Each one of us seemed to be trying to
hide inside himself."[52] He then proceeds to describe the initiation of their
reception into the prison. Each is forced to drink filthy water from a sewage drain. A demoted brigadier general is ordered to go first. He refuses
and is beaten to death. Those who drink are treated to more torture or
endless "hospitality," as the guards call it. Eventually, unable to endure
any more, Musa and others who are severely wounded lose consciousness, and they are either carried by the more able-bodied prisoners or
crawl their way to the communal cell. Six months will pass before the next
entry, perhaps an indication of the time the protagonist needed to recover
from his initial injuries.

Musa never receives a trial and, like the author, is detained for twelve
years, mostly in Tadmur. He is, however, sentenced to silence by his fellow detainees because during his initial interrogation he was overheard
telling his torturers first that he is a Christian and then that he is an atheist in an effort to convince them that he is not a member of the Muslim
Brotherhood. Labeled an atheist and a spy, he is completely ostracized

and shunned by the other inmates in his communal cell in Tadmur. As a self-protective coping mechanism, Musa describes himself as withdrawing into his shell: "As the days passed, a shell began to grow around me, made up of two walls. One wall was formed of their hatred of me. I was swimming in a sea of hatred loathing and revulsion, trying hard as I could not drown. The second wall was made up of my fear of them. I opened a window in the hard wall of the shell and began to spy on the dormitory from the inside, the only thing I could do."[53]

Having very little interaction with other inmates, the protagonist constantly peers out of his shell and watches those around him for years to come. Their cell leader orders him to sleep at the far end of the room next to an elderly prisoner who has gone mad and covers himself with a blanket. Musa then discovers a small hole in the wall that he can peer through into the courtyard and also keep concealed by stuffing a stone into it. Wanting to keep the hole a secret from his cellmates and the guards who observe the prisoners from the roof through the *sharrāqa* (a small observation aperture or hole in the cell's ceiling), he begins imitating the blanketed prisoner, creating a shell of cloth in order to conceal his ability to observe both inside and outside the cell. Rendered mute by the disciplinary mechanisms of prison and by the rejection of other detainees, he watches and listens attentively to everything and everyone around him, meticulously observing as both insider and outsider, diligently recording all that he witnesses and later giving voice to his observations through his diary.

From the beginning of his detention at Tadmur, Musa's life is threatened not only by the prison guards, who unceasingly inflict torture, humiliation, and degradation on the detainees, but also by the Islamist extremists in his cell who believe that he, as an atheist, should be executed. Rescued and then protected by the moderate, pacifist Shaykh Darwish and a physician who treated the wounds afflicted by his torture, Dr. Zahi, he nonetheless remains isolated for ten years. For ten years no one will speak to him because he is considered impure; this mimics the muting of thousands of political prisoners who passed through Tadmur and other sites and who are unable to tell their own stories, though in his case Musa is silenced not just by the regime, but also by his fellow citizens. Still, Musa speaks through his diary.

Without respite, through the entire narrative everyday activities bring arbitrary death. Musa recounts how prisoners are routinely whipped, lashed, and beaten during breaks in the yard; how prisoners are not allowed to raise their eyes toward their jailers; and how the warden randomly executes fourteen of his cellmates. He also methodically describes daily aspects of prison life—the baths; the illicit prayers; the confining, airless dimensions of the communal cell; the secret communication between prisoners using body language and Morse code; the innovative treatments prisoners devise for the wounded who are deprived of medical care.

After nearly a decade in isolation, Musa is once again confronted by an extremist calling for him to be tried and executed by the other prisoners. Finally he breaks his silence and vocally confronts his would-be executioner. From that moment, he becomes intimate friends with Nasim—an inmate who was detained as a hostage due to his brother's affiliation with the Muslim Brotherhood. Like others, Nasim will eventually suffer a breakdown. His descent into madness occurs when, using Musa's secret observation place, he witnesses three brothers being executed in the yard after their father was promised that the youngest would be spared.

Abruptly, in the twelfth year of his detention, Musa is transferred from the prison back to the military interrogation center, and the conclusion of the novel, much like the ending of Hasiba 'Abd al-Rahman's *The Cocoon* (*Al-Sharnaqa*), is far from optimistic.[54] Through the influence of a relative Musa is finally freed. After his release he returns to his family home, which he inherited from his father and where he lives with his niece and her family. Despite family pressure to marry and to work, he does neither. He isolates himself from the world around him, and he turns his "veillance" on himself. Eventually he learns that Nasim and others he was imprisoned with have been released. Nasim, however, has never recovered from his breakdown; Musa witnesses him taking his own life after a brief reunion with other cellmates.

At the end of the novel there is no sense of celebratory liberation for Musa. Instead, noting that he has never truly been released from prison—with the implication that the entire country of Syria is the larger prison—he describes himself as having lost the ability to communicate, as perceiving an insurmountable abyss between himself and all others, and as carrying a grave within himself. Rather than creep out of his shell to watch and record what is happening around him, he enacts the strictest form of isolation and autosurveillance, rendering himself incapable of contact with anyone or with the outside world. He states: "I am not consumed by curiosity to spy on anything. I try to close the smallest peephole in my shell, not wanting to look out. I close the gaps in order to focus my gaze entirely toward the inside, toward me, toward myself."[55] And yet despite this pessimistic ending and this image of Musa internalizing the surveillance mechanisms of prison to the point of self-annihilation, he still speaks and makes his experience of imprisonment in Tadmur visible through the diary-as-novel.

Of Tadmur and Guernica

In *The Betrayals of Language and Silence*, Faraj Bayraqdar devotes a number of chapters to grisly and excruciating scenes of detainees' torture that he witnessed during his detention at Tadmur Military Prison.[56] Like other authors he recalls his visit to the ancient ruins of Palmyra years before his imprisonment, and then recounts his initial arrival and "reception" at the desert prison. Yet in line with other sections of his poetic memoir, Bayraqdar's writings on Tadmur are fragmented, nonlinear, and self-interrogative. Rather than attempting to inscribe a detailed chronicle of his days and years at the military prison, he instead offers a series of juxtaposed portraits of detention there. In doing so, he problematizes the notion of providing a cohesive and complete narrative of his and others' experiences. Much like his inscription of his initial torture at Palestine Division in 1987, he calls into question the capacity and limits of language in representing the violence endured by Tadmur's detainees.[57]

In a chapter titled "Tadmuriyat: Beyond Surrealism," the poet provides seven brief, numbered vignettes or portraits that reflect his field of vision as a detainee—his experiences of seeing Tadmur and the often absurd and inhumanly cruel forms of torture that guards would devise to punish the prisoners. The first and second portraits are poetry rather than prose and are quoted in full here:

1.
High walls of stubborn, cold cement . . .
Watchtowers . . .
Minefields . . .
Barriers and checkpoints . . .
Fortifications and highly trained military units . . .
And finally . . . encircled by slogans of pure, nationalist
    terror
Oh, names of God!
Even if all of Syria fell,
It would be impossible for this prison to fall

2
Has it ever occurred to an artist
To sketch a blue, tear-filled sky
Wearing a veil of barbed wire
Anyone destined to stand in a courtyard of Tadmur
    prison
And steal a fleeting glance up above
Will see this oppressive portrait
And realize, then, what genius nurtures our reality and our dreams![58]

In these initial sections of the chapter, Bayraqdar juxtaposes elements of
what he, as a detainee, could possibly glimpse, even as his visual field was
severely circumscribed, while standing in the courtyard outside one of
the communal cells. This includes elements of prison architecture—"high
walls of stubborn, cold cement," "watch towers," and "fortifications,"
"slogans of pure, nationalist terror" painted on the walls. Calling out the
"names of God" also connects to the voices of prisoners who are calling
out as they are about to be executed. The second portrait draws readers
("anyone") into imagining themselves in the position of Bayraqdar or any
other detainee who manages to "steal a fleeting glance above," only to see
a mournful sky framed by "a veil of barbed wire." The poet raises the question of whether an artist would or could imagine or create such an image
or "oppressive portrait." Only the Asad regime, the poem implies, has the
"genius" to produce such cruel artistry.

In staccato and fragmented prose, Bayraqdar presents the subsequent grotesque and surreal portraits, numbered three to seven. Each section describes an incident of guards inflicting horrifying and unimaginable forms of torture on prisoners in a courtyard, and the walls of the courtyard frame the portrait described. In successive portraits, he recounts how a guard forces an elderly prisoner to lick his boots and then slaps him for frowning while doing so, how guards routinely whip and lash prisoners who have been forced into stress positions on top of each other, and finally, how guards treat a prisoner as a human trampoline.

At times, these portraits appear to go beyond the poet's descriptive ability and demonstrate "the tension between the need to report, to demonstrate authenticity, and to bear witness versus the literary urge to develop empathy, to coax the imagination, and to offer the catharsis of expression."[59] As the chapter progresses, the narrative includes more ellipses, indicating a pause in Bayraqdar's ability to put into words precisely what he's seeing, or perhaps an allusion to being momentarily stunned into silence. Bayraqdar increasingly articulates what he has witnessed from the point of view of a more detached or disembodied observer. For example:

> The sixth portrait has taut lines, and the strokes of a brush, cruel and enduring, to the point of ridicule.
>
> It portrays the head of a prisoner, hair and beard shaved off, with eyes closed to the peak of pain with lines of shadowing that have been etched in such a way that it appears as if they are the traces of intersecting knives. A soldier presses down on the prisoner's head with a hand, which makes the neck lean to the right, and in his other hand, pliers pressed on the prisoner's ear.
>
> It is clear that the portrait contemplates the scene of tearing off the prisoner's ear or perhaps a moment of tearing the ear with the pliers, and the rattling and splitting that accompanies it.[60]

As a narrator in a state of shock or completely numbed by all of the horrors he's seen, Bayraqdar describes the scene of torture he's witnessed almost as if he's an aficionado lecturing a novice about a portrait in a gallery, complete with reference to "taut lines" and "brush strokes." In this passage, as elsewhere, he uses the second person to draw the reader into his and other prisoners' point of view. He states, "Maybe you can see this with more than your eyes; rather, maybe you can hear what tearing off and ripping does by sounds that resemble the noises caused by the cruel removal of the roots of Bermuda grass from uncultivated earth."[61] It is not just the visual elements that make up the poet's experience of the scene before him; rather, the colors of the portrait are also generated by the sounds, smells, and movements that accompany this "lightning quick" sketch.[62]

At the end of the last portrait, after describing a guard jumping up and down on a prisoner's neck until it breaks, Bayraqdar concludes: "Echoes of heavy, suffocating silence; you don't know where it began, and where it will end."[63] With a query repeated in different variations throughout the memoir, he then asks his readers, "Do you want the truth?" His own response to the question is: "A shocking panoramic portrait. Not Guernica, nor deities, nor legends."[64] The violence and inhumanity described in each portrait surpasses even that portrayed in Pablo Picasso's 1937 mural depicting the aftermath of a German bombing campaign in the Spanish Civil War. Much like the portraits that Bayraqdar verbally paints, Picasso's world famous *Guernica* has been described as "a painting of violence rendered with violence, full of strong contrasts, sharp angles, jagged edges, broken shapes, contorted postures."[65] His language and descriptions are marked by "the trace of extremity," the extremities of Tadmur Military Prison. Bayraqdar reminds his audience that, surreal and unimaginable as such scenes may seem, what he is attempting to describe really did happen, and the seven portraits provide only an incomplete and very abridged record of all that he and others endured and witnessed in the desert prison. Any ethical reading of this text, in recognizing the forms of visibility that Bayraqdar and others construct in their writings about Tadmur, "does not inhere in assessing their truth value or efficacy as 'representation,' but rather in recognizing their evidentiary nature: here language is life-form, made by human experience."[66]

Revisualizing Tadmur

Three years before the short-lived ISIS takeover of Tadmur, Monika Borgmann and Lokman Slim began conducting research into the experiences of Lebanese citizens detained in Syria in the 1980s and 1990s. Their

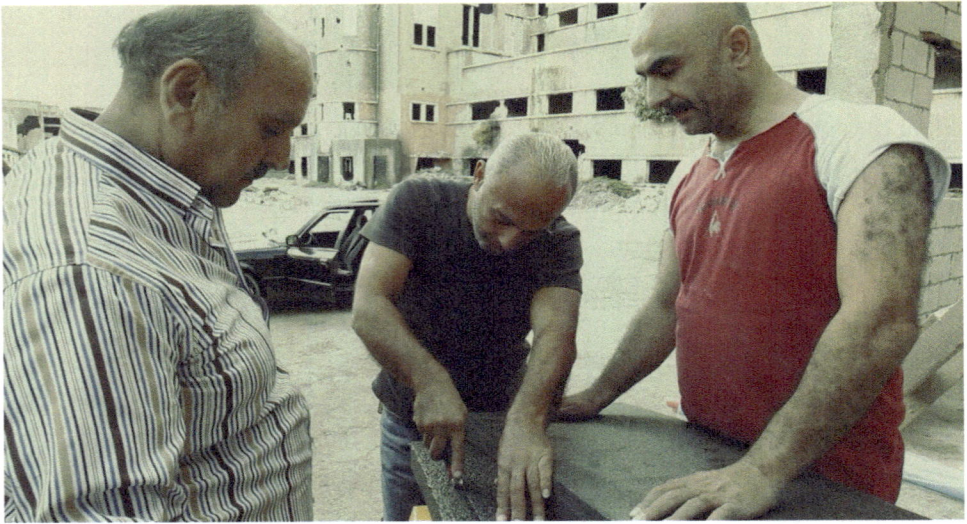

6. Still from Monika Borgmann and Lokman Slim's *Tadmor* (2016). Author 'Ali Abou Dehn (left), Moussa Saab, and Raymond Bouban fashion guards' weapons out of Styrofoam in order to reenact their prison experience. Reproduced with permission of Monika Borgmann, Lokman Slim, Ali Abou Dehn, Moussa Saab, and Raymond Bouban.

research led to the 2016 documentary titled simply *Tadmor*. A collective project, the film follows a group of former Lebanese prisoners who, motivated and moved by the 2011 Syrian uprising and the state's violent repression of protestors, come together to reenact and talk about their time in Syria's most infamous prison. In the opening of the film the men, including author Ali Abou Dehn, are shown fashioning a makeshift prison; they use a drill to make an observation hole in the ceiling of a room, reattach steel doors to thresholds, and recreate the guards' batons and other instruments of torture from foam and other materials (figures 6 and 7).

Unable to return to the original site of their imprisonment, the former detainees have come together to fashion a replica of Tadmur in an abandoned and dilapidated school complex outside of Beirut. They have done so in order to make their experiences starkly visible to a wider public. With memories of the traumatic human rights abuses that the Syrian state denies ever perpetrating, these survivors of Tadmur have taken on

7. Still from *Tadmor* (2016). The former prisoners create a *sharrāqa* (a guard's observation hole) in an abandoned classroom. Reproduced with permission of Monika Borgmann and Lokman Slim.

the burden of visually and verbally re-creating the forms of suffering they endured. After much physical and emotional preparation, the film's written narrative tells us, the men are ready to return "to the darkness of those years, and reclaim those bitter chapters from their lives." In the opening of the film we learn that the former prisoners will act in the roles not just of prisoners, but of the perpetrators—the guards and torturers of Tadmur Military Prison. Interspersed with interview segments in which the participants describe their individual experiences in full detail, the film consists of the detainees reenacting various scenes of their experiences of detention—the daily beatings during inspection and roll call, being forced to drink sewage water, the torture of the baths and the barber, being forced to stand in stress positions with faces to the wall and heads bowed down (figure 8), sleeping blindfolded side by side (figure 9), using a thread to divide a single, boiled egg among eight starving prisoners, and attempting to calm a fellow inmate who eventually loses his sanity and whose shouting will provoke the wrath of the prison guards.

Though research for the film began much earlier, *Tadmor* was produced in the same time period as the ISIS takeover of the city and prison,

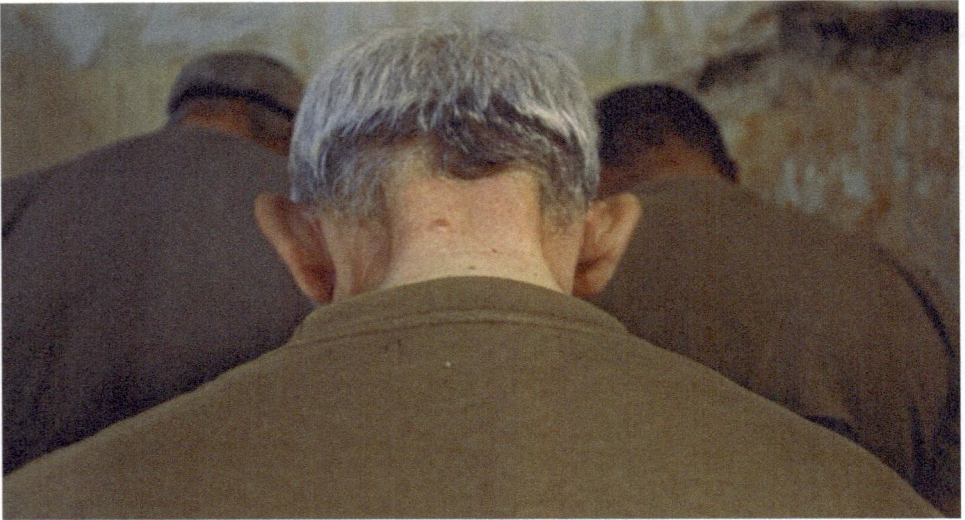

8. Still from *Tadmor* (2016). Former prisoners standing in makeshift courtyard in stress positions with heads facing down. Reproduced with permission of Monika Borgmann and Lokman Slim.

and though it has not received anywhere near the same amount of mainstream media attention as the atrocities committed by Da'ish, the documentary serves as a reminder of the dire need for a broader audience to see and listen to the forms of visibility that former Tadmur detainees have generated. Nine days after their initial conquest of the city, ISIS released yet another video, this time allegedly showcasing the detonation and demolition of Tadmur Military Prison.[67] Regardless of ideological affiliations, many former detainees, including those involved in the Free Tadmur Prisoners Association, condemned the destruction of the prison. In detonating the notorious site, ISIS not only appeared to have decimated evidence of the Asad regime's human rights violations and crimes against humanity, it also had destroyed the possibility of former detainees returning to Tadmur in order to reconcile or come to terms with their experiences there.

Whether the prison was actually razed was an open question at the time this chapter was written, but the Syrian state's present control of the city is not in doubt. It is unclear whether the regime will rebuild or reopen

9. Still from *Tadmor* (2016). Former prisoners re-creating the overcrowded, sword-style sleeping conditions of communal cells. Reproduced with permission of Monika Borgmann and Lokman Slim.

the prison, but undoubtedly more former Tadmur detainees will come forward to share their stories, to make visible their suffering, and to confront and condemn the acts of violence that the state has perpetrated against them and continues to perpetrate against others. The question remains: Will the visibility of these prisoners and their stories be enough to prevent a new generation from enduring the same?

6

The Stairwell of Solitary Days

Carceral Metafiction and Exile

My hand and my pen trembled at that moment, and worried, fearful,
the first letters emerged out into the light. For the place that I had
chosen for this event was surrounded by barbed wire and prohibi-
tions. And behind it, there were guards threatening to break both
your pen and your dreams.

Hasiba 'Abd al-Rahman[1]

In *Longing for Life* (*Tawqan ila al-Haya*, 2015), 'Abbas 'Abbas begins his
collection of prison papers and essays with the tale of one Abu Hammud,
a detainee in his late fifties who dies suddenly and quietly in his sleep
one night. The official report declares that Abu Hammud suffered a lethal
heart attack, and his body is eventually returned to his family, who has
been waiting for him for ten years. Days later his name appears on a list of
prisoners whom the authorities have designated for release. Sardonically,
the author tells us that the story of Abu Hammud "documents two prison
precedents"; first, he was released ten days before the rest of his group,
though he was no longer alive, and second, his death came without agony
and was "noble and quiet."[2] Abu Hammud's passing, 'Abbas recalls, pre-
cipitated his own existential and psychological personal crisis—a period
of profound self-questioning and doubt during his detention. He, himself,
would never desire such a merciful, but quiet and sudden death. He would
want the opportunity to say "what he wishes to say" to his loved ones and
to "the people, all of them," regardless of whether his death would hold
any meaning for them.[3]

This essay is *Longing for Life* is titled "Wasiyya," and 'Abbas uses the term a number of times throughout this and the following chapter as he reflects on his fourteen-year experience of political detention and meditates on the act of writing. He reminds his reader that *waṣiyya* carries multiple connotations; it is a bequest, legacy, disposition, directive, command, or injunction. Most poignantly and profoundly in this case, it is a last testament (*waṣiyya 'akhīra*), a testament that 'Abbas inscribes not just on behalf of Abu Hammud and other detainees, but also for himself in the form of his prison papers. As Lebanese journalist Yusif Bazzi notes, *Longing for Life* was published posthumously, three years after the author's own passing.[4]

In evoking the notion of a last testament or testimony at the beginning of his work, 'Abbas 'Abbas also questions what it means to write from the "point of view of the vanquished."[5] He finds appealing the "bitterness" of writing from the perspective of what he calls "the truth of defeat." It makes him see in his prison experience and personal history what he could not see before, and opens up, through the process of inscription, "a path to explore—tempted, obligated, and surrounded by exposed intrigues with all the requisite obscure obstacles and labyrinths."[6] For 'Abbas, writing in and about prison is a torment, a burden, and a confrontation. At times, it can feel like "nothing but an artful deceit," filled with the "hesitations of beginning."[7] Yet writing also "appears . . . as if it's a sanctioned escape toward a freedom that you coexist with on paper without fear of a censor."[8] Despite the struggles involved in inscribing his prison experiences, writing is, in the end, abundant proof of the detainee's longing for life.

'Abbas 'Abbas is not alone in his ruminations on the process, ethics, and efficacy of writing and writing prison. Like Mansour Omari in *82 Names* and other authors whose work is discussed in this book, 'Abbas is but one among many authors to express that he writes not just for himself but for a collectivity of detainees. As Heba Dabbagh informs her readers in *Just Five Minutes*:

> The duty I feel to speak out against the oppression of the Syrian regime overpowers my worries of the consequences of doing so. I feel entrusted with the task of documenting these events. As painful as it is to bring

the past to light, it seems easy in comparison to keeping the secrets of the oppressors and allowing all of our suffering to be in vain . . . The pen would tire before I could describe every detail of what took place and every pain I felt while I was imprisoned by this evil regime.[9]

Like Maher Arar's narrative imperative in recounting, again and again, his story of extraordinary rendition and torture in order to seek justice, Dabbagh asserts that she must record her experience as evidence against the human rights abuses she has suffered. Evoking the idea of writing as a means of "public legibility," she calls for her prison-memoir-as-documentary-record to be recognized as a work of resistance literature that engages "in a re-definition of the self and the individual in terms of a collective enterprise and struggle" in opposition to the Syrian regime.[10] Though aware of the necessity of asserting her right to narrate against the numerous "infringements" of her human rights, she, like so many others, acknowledges the impossibility of inscribing every detail of her experience.[11]

Nonfictional prison memoirs and papers, like those of Dabbagh and 'Abbas, are not the only venue for authors' deliberations on the testimonial, documentary efficacy and function of their writings. From Faraj Bayraqdar's poetry to Ghassan al-Jaba'i's short stories, Syrian and Arabic prison literature is replete with references to and reflections on writing.[12] While some works depict scenes of state agents forcing prisoners to write confessions or disavowals as a form of torture, authors of both fictional and nonfictional works of prison literature also privilege and problematize the desire to write while in prison and the obligation to etch on paper the prison experience as a challenge to the authority of the state and a means of documenting their experiences. In recent Syrian and Arabic prison literature, writers simultaneously sustain and sabotage the notion of writing as resistance or the view of writing as purely an act of transformative or liberating redemption. Authors' constant evocations of and reflections on the act of writing, whether through descriptions of and references to the tools, artifacts, and products of writing or in the direct self-reflexive voice of the narrator, draw their readers' attention to the constructed nature, gaps, distortions, and exclusions of their own narratives.

In representing the prison experience, works such as the short stories of Jamil Hatmal and Malik Daghastani's experimental novella *The Vertigo of Freedom* (*Duwar al-Hurriyya*) are what I call carceral metafiction—fictional texts, which present an omnipresence of writing about writing, or referencing, evoking, and interrogating the act of inscription within a fictional narrative that is tied to the representation of the experience of imprisonment.[13] In modern Arabic literature more generally, carceral metafiction has been growing since the experimental shift in the mid-1960s and has been generated directly in response to the political oppressions of postcolonial authoritarian regimes in the region.[14] Carceral metafiction in the Arabic literary field emerges from and addresses the phenomenon of detention and at the same time interrogates the relationship between imprisonment and writing, not just as an act of creativity, but also as an act of representation. A work of carceral metafiction, to borrow from Patricia Waugh, "self-consciously and systematically draws attention to its status as an artifact in order to pose questions about the relationship between fiction and reality." [15] Such metafictional tendencies also destabilize narrative truth effects and closure as well as attempts at narrative transparency that are so necessarily prevalent in human rights reportage.

Carceral Metafiction in Arabic and Syrian Literature

Two of the foundational texts of modern Arabic prison literature reflect these metafictional tendencies. In Egyptian writer Sun'allah Ibrahim's *That Smell* (*Tilka Ra'iha wa Qisas 'Ukhra, 1966*) and Saudi-Iraqi novelist 'Abd al-Rahman Munif's *East of the Mediterranean* (*Sharq al-Mutawassit, 1977*), the act of writing constantly punctuates the narratives.[16] Ibrahim's semiautobiographical novella *That Smell* is exemplary in its status as a link between Arabic literary experimentalism from the 1960s onwards and the emergence of contemporary Arabic prison literature.[17] Ibrahim's narrator, freed from an Egyptian prison and under routine surveillance, must adhere to a curfew and sign a police officer's notebook every evening. In an alienating state of captivity outside of prison, not only is he sexually impotent, he can no longer write. The recording of his name in the register of the authorities has supplanted all of his other forms of writing.[18] However, for the reader, Ibrahim offers a glimmer of hope in the very existence of the text of *That Smell* as a literary artifact. The autobiographical slippage between the narrator of the novella and the position of Ibrahim himself as a writer and former political prisoner suggests the possibility that eventually a text came to be written. Bare and stark though its narrative may be, *That Smell*, as a form of cultural production, now exists to be read and interpreted by its audience.

At the beginning of *East of the Mediterranean*, Munif's protagonist, Rajab, has been coerced into signing a confession after years of resistance. In addition, in order to be released so he can receive medical treatment outside of his unnamed country, he must also agree to work as an informer, to write reports about his compatriots while he is in Europe. Rajab eventually refuses to inform on his fellow citizens; in this case, to write would be to betray his comrades. Instead, he contemplates writing a novel about his experiences of torture and detention to expose the oppressions of the political regime under which he lives. Forced to return to his homeland when his brother-in-law is detained, Rajab is once again arrested and dies as a result of injuries caused by the torture he endures. After his death his sister gathers his papers and publishes them against his final wishes. The scattered remnants of Rajab's writing are seemingly compiled and generate the manuscript that will become the novel *East of the Mediterranean*. Like *That Smell*, Munif's novel appears to be a self-begetting one that is the published end result of the protagonist's political and poetic struggles.

Metafiction is also prevalent in Syrian writer Sami al-Jundi's novella *My Friend Elias* (*Sadiqi Ilyas*, 1969), Lebanese novelist Elias Khoury's novel *Yalu* (2002), and Iraqi novelist and poet Sinan Antoon's *I'jaam* (2004).[19] These and other texts of Arabic prison literature provide, as Waugh notes, "a critique of their own methods of construction," and in doing so, they examine the core structures of narrative fictions.[20] Although Waugh is concerned primarily with works of fiction in which the author appears to intrude on the text as a self-reflecting narrator, metafiction also includes nonreflexive references to writing, such as the use of letters, journals, and diaries, either in the content of narrative or as structural frames, as can be seen in Hatmal's short story "Abu Salih."

Distinct from Waugh, Mark Currie argues that metafiction is a "borderline discourse"—one that "places itself between fiction and criticism, which takes the border as its subject."[21] In raising the reader's awareness of the fraught "conditions of meaning-construction" in narrative, metafiction produces its own trajectory of self-critique.[22] It is this capacity for critically negotiating the dilemmas of representation and criticism that gives metafiction the unique power to expose the potential contradictions and erasures involved in written depictions of the lived experience of detention. Carceral metafiction's critical function as a borderline discourse also counters the emphasis on legibility in the narrative imperative that is fundamental to the construction of truth claims in human rights discourse.[23]

Of Metafiction and Exile

In Damascus in 1983, journalist and former political prisoner Jamil Hatmal wrote a short story titled "Infi'al Thalatha: Daraj Ayyam al-Munfarida" ("Reaction 3: The Stairwell of Solitary Days"). The third and final text of a set of interconnected tales, Hatmal's story depicts a narrator who confronts the (f)utility of the act of self-inscription: "I am the man who opens himself up as a white piece of paper with absolute naivete. For in the end, there is nothing but blackness declaring itself over the whiteness of the paper."[24] The narrator scripts himself as a blank page—a page that will soon be so encased by and inundated with words that the writing merges into one indistinguishable swath of black. Vacillating from the narrator's disjointed first-person address to the voice of an absent female figure (a recurring motif throughout the author's work, as in that of Faraj Bayraqdar and Malik Daghastani), to his abstract musings on his relationship with "the other," to his meditations on writing, "The Stairwell of Solitary Days" is indicative of Hatmal's ability to continually present a synthesis of the tropes of prison, writing, and exile in a single short narrative. The narrator speaks from an ambiguous position or location at the beginning of the story. Is he addressing his reader from a solitary prison cell, a place of banishment within his homeland, or from the solitary of exile beyond those borders? Or is he located on the tenuous, connective thread of a stairwell between, beyond, or before exile or imprisonment? The answer is revealed, but only partially, toward the story's conclusion.

"The Stairwell of Solitary Days" is indicative of the thematic triad of writing-prison-exile that surfaces again and again not just in Hatmal's short stories but in his own life history. Born in 1956 in Damascus, Hatmal began writing short stories early in his youth, later worked as a journalist, and was briefly imprisoned in 1982 for four months due to his membership in the Syrian Communist Action Party. He was released early due to a heart condition that was greatly exacerbated under the conditions of his detention. Long before the post-2011 Syrian refugee crisis, Hatmal began a life of itinerant exile, working as journalist for major Arabic newspapers and writing from Lebanon, France, Cyprus, and elsewhere. Having undergone several heart operations in Paris throughout the 1980s and early 1990s, he died in exile in a hospital in Paris in 1994.

In his introduction to Hatmal's posthumously collected stories, Munif notes that stories such as "The Stairwell of Solitary Days" and Hatmal's autobiography provide a succinct picture of the historical phase in which he lived.[25] Hatmal's life trajectory repeats and his short stories reenact an all-too-familiar pattern for those engaged in Syrian oppositional politics over the past five decades. Taken together, the author's life history and works demonstrate emphatically that prison and exile are "two sides of the experience of oppression."[26] His short fiction shows that prison literature can and, in many ways, must be understood as a literature of exile. While imprisonment can be seen in simple terms as "exile within," the "crippling sorrow of estrangement" inherent in exilic experience marks "the complex and paradoxical location of exile as a liberating space and as a prison of sorts."[27]

Paradoxically, for many writers, the experience of exile, much like imprisonment, produces complex identities that are represented through innovative narrative strategies.[28] As physical, political, and historical experiences, and in their aesthetic expressions, exile and detention, their circumstances and their effects frequently coincide, parallel, mimic, and meld into one another. In their real and metaphorical senses, prison and exile are both means of punishment in the forms of banishment, defamiliarization, and alienation. Prison *is* exile: the detainee is forcibly cast out, disappeared, and often removed from the public visual field, but not the memory of the nation. Yet the prisoner remains within its borders and is abandoned, confined, in solitary alienation. Exile can become another form of detention: expelled from or compelled to leave behind the territory of the nation space, the exilic figure can be imprisoned by eternal displacement, by the continuous deferral of the dream of return, by the absence of all that is familiar. Like the political prisoner, the exile, in Munif's words, is marked as "a person accused," but often the exact charge remains ambiguous, unnamed, or unknown in Hatmal's short stories.[29]

Munif views sorrow or melancholy as an underlying theme of Hatmal's short stories.[30] Despite the negative force of this inscribed sorrow or sadness, he also points out the potential redemptive and productive capacity of Hatmal's narratives: "Jamil considered life mud and misery, and so long as it was like that, then redemption was inevitable, and the presence of people redeeming others was inevitable because they were created for this purpose."[31] Reflecting on Hatmal's biography and its relationship to his short fiction, Munif argues that life's miseries inevitably lead people to act, to endure pain and suffering in order to make life worth living for a greater collective or community. His meditations on the redemptive potential of Hatmal's sorrow echoes the notion that exile, much like the experience of imprisonment, can provide a space for transgressive or subversive creative production despite, or perhaps because of, its physical and psychological turmoil. The exile sees "the entire world as a foreign land" and thus, much like the detainee who is removed from a familiar world, the exile has the possibility of obtaining, creating, and sustaining an "originality of vision."[32] Always aware of at least two or more worlds, the exile has a "plurality of vision" that "gives rise to an awareness of simultaneous dimensions," an awareness that is, as Edward Said reminds us, "contrapuntal."[33]

Yet, Said cautions against any wholesale celebration of the "benefits of exile as a redemptive motif"; he reminds us that we must not lose sight of the real and tragic consequences of political detention, even while honoring the aesthetic interventions of the literature of prison and exile—the idea that a form of "glamour can be attached to the figure of 'the exiled writer'" or that the glorification of "the metaphoric exile" can devalue the "reality of terror and the loss experienced by those who have fled for their lives."[34] For Nigerian writer Chris Abani, both the condition and the discourse of exile speak to an "uneasy dialectic" that is informed by two dominant binaries. There are those who "celebrate exile as redemptive" and see "exile to be a vital condition for writing, a form of alienation that produces a double-mindedness."[35] In this case, the adherents of this "positive, even optimistic, side of the debate" tend to "celebrate and romanticize the position of the exile, elevating the exilian to noble standing."[36] Even though Said warns against viewing exile as a celebratory aesthetics of humanism, he alludes to the "romantic benefit" of the exilic position given his assertion that exile is a "potent, even enriching motif of modern culture."[37] The notion that exile is an enriching motif echoes the discomforting idea that prison stories, as the protagonist of Sami al-Jundi's novella *My Friend Elias* sardonically tells us, have a special quality that renders them particularly "thrilling" or "fascinating" for their audience.[38]

Abani's discussion of the "pessimistic" side of the binary in the discourse on exile is both bleak and terse, and it serves as a reminder to acknowledge the complexities and complicities of the "redemptive" potential of prison literature and its direct connection with the historical suffering and sacrifices of those who have endured the worst possible carceral conditions. This negative side of the discourse on exile is marked by violence, death, and destruction; it can be seen in the tragic example of the suicide of the exiled South African poet Arthur Nortje and the death of Jamil Hatmal in Paris in 1994.[39] Thus, Abani cautions, we must always question the "anomie of romance" when it comes to any cultural value placed on exile.[40]

In his attempt to provide an elegiac introduction, Munif highlights the possibility of some form of consolation that resonates in the actual existence and the production and publication of Hatmal's collected works. For Munif, Hatmal's suffering, his imprisonment, and his exilic estrangement are remembered and memorialized by the very fact that he *wrote* and that his stories are being passed on, again as a literary artifact, after his death. Yet between the two poles of prison and exile, in the ambiguous spaces of his stories, Hatmal both poses and undermines the potential redemption wrought by the process and publication of his own fictional inscriptions. Hatmal scripts both exile and imprisonment as inherently intertwined with and through the act of writing, but for him such writing always reveals its own contingent nature and provides us with a caution-ary tale. The act of inscription is neither depicted solely as the narrative imperative that accompanies human rights claims, nor highlighted as a clear-cut path of mental or emotional escape or a means of resistance. Rather, writing, in and of itself, can meld into another space of banish-ment or detention where inscribing exile into being becomes a closed cir-cuit or a labyrinth with no exit.[41]

Strikingly, many of the over sixty stories in Hatmal's five collections do not directly describe the precise physical conditions, events, or circum-stances within the walls of a prison.[42] Just as Ibrahim Samu'il does not depict torture or politics directly in his fictional writings, Hatmal's prison references are often only briefly or allusively evoked in his stories.[43] Instead, what dominates his short fiction as a whole is the always self-questioning and self-doubting voice of a narrator who is reflecting on both his sense of isolation and his role as a writer, as the one telling the fractured tales offered to an anonymous addressee and to his readers. This voice and all of its skeptical metafictional refrains resurface throughout and connect the tales written or published from the late 1970s through 1994.[44]

His first collection of stories, *The Girl with the White Hat*, differs from the other collections in that the stories are marked by date only and were presumably primarily written in Damascus, and there are very few, if any, self-conscious references to the practice of writing on the part of any of his first person narrators. Yet a sense of estrangement and defamiliarization permeates the stories of this first collection and the ones to follow.[45] The characters, as if already in exile within the borders of the homeland, are presented as feeling "out of place," and have a sense of "the deprivations felt at not being with others in the communal habitation."[46] For Hatmal, the exile within of the experience of prison begins even before detention, and the alienation experienced by his characters even while they are at home anticipates their estrangement in external exile.

Additionally, in the majority of Hatmal's stories, the threat and fear of arrest on the part of the protagonists consistently frames the narratives. In the first story, "Walking with Slow Steps," exilic estrangement is presented by the narrator as both political and sexual or romantic as he learns of his comrades being arrested, while at the same time he fails to maintain an intimate dialogue with his female lover. His narrators and protagonists appear to be imprisoned by unavoidable circumstances. The reader also witnesses the alienation experienced by a frustrated political activist (as in the story "A Day That Is Not Exactly Ordinary in the Life of a Citizen Who Is Not Exactly Ordinary"), and the depiction of another failure of a romantic relationship because of a lack of harmony in the vision of political commitment of a man and a woman, and the man's subsequent absence due to his arrest (as in the "Forest of Violets").

Hatmal presents the sorrowful reflections of a young man who is on the run from the security authorities as he comes to recognize the pain he has caused his family, and then is detained before their eyes in "A Smear of Chocolate." He evokes the narrator's stark sense of alienation and life's futility in the title story "The Girl with the White Hat." In this first collection, a more direct depiction of prison appears in only three stories. In "The Room under the Stairs," Hatmal describes how a naïve young man who has recently arrived in Damascus becomes politicized after he is arrested and tortured due to his cousin's political activities. In another story, titled "The Policeman," he depicts a traffic cop imprisoned for bribery. In "Tender Green Grass in an Earthen Wall," the narrator is in a state of reminiscence, and it is not until the middle of the narrative that the reader becomes aware that he is in prison.

In his second collection, *Reactions* (which includes "The Stairwell of Solitary Days"), and in the later collections that Hatmal wrote while in exile from Syria—*When There Is No Country, Stories of Illness, Stories of Madness*, and *I Will Tell Them*—the narrators emerge again and again to indirectly depict the experience of prison-as-exile and exile-as-prison. In several stories, the depiction of these experiences is connected to reflexive reflections on writing and the questioning of the act of writing itself. The use of this reflexive form becomes increasingly prominent and increasingly complex as one reads through his oeuvre. In Hatmal's short stories, the notion of metafiction as a borderline discourse that draws attention to the uneasy relationship between fiction and reality coincides with certain conceptual views of exile; exile enacts the same borderline condition of the metafictional. If the exile exists in "the perilous territory of not-belonging," then for Jamil Hatmal, the dangers of not belonging are reflected in his own interrogation of the significance and (f)utility of the act of writing.[47]

The variations in Hatmal's metafiction are extensive; traces and reminders of writing as an act, practice, or artifact are threaded throughout the collections and surface to connect the notion of prison-as-exile and exile-as-prison through the narrator's estrangement from his own writing or narrative process or his alienation from the artifact of writing. In his first collection, writing as an act, object, or narrative frame surfaces frequently, and in two cases, the act of inscription can be linked to imprisonment. In one story a prisoner, like Rajab in *East of the Mediterranean*, is forced to sign a confession, and in another story a police officer who is arrested mourns the loss of his poetry notebooks.[48] Particularly in his later stories Hatmal presents narrators who are critically concerned that they might be telling or writing the story the wrong way or that they aren't getting the facts right for an unknown audience. They tell their stories anyway, even if the end of a story is rendered ambiguously unclear or if the narrators remain alienated from the conclusions they reach. This emphasis on how the story is told, on the formal aspects of the act of composition, alludes to a kind of privileging of form over the truth of the story's content; Hatmal's characters must speak, but they consistently call attention to the problem of accuracy and authenticity in their own stories.

In the beginning of Hatmal's second collection, *Reactions*, the first three stories, including "Reaction 3: The Stairwell of Solitary Days," are connectively narrated in a fragmented fashion, for the most part, by a first person, anonymous narrator. These three tales are especially indicative of the ways in which Hatmal juxtaposes and intertwines exile, imprisonment, and the act of writing.[49] In "Reaction 1: A Room" ("Infi'al Wahid: Ghurfa"), clearly speaking from a position outside of prison, the narrator describes his daily routine, his boredom, and his alienating sense of isolation. Emphasizing the fact that he is alone, a stranger in this city, and being truthful, he imagines himself talking to an unnamed woman he sees in a café. He tells her he will speak of "the military, the dungeons, friends who are absent or fugitives, in spite of themselves, just like me."[50]

This first story frames the narrator as speaking in geographical exile, where he is overwhelmed by a sense of estrangement and longing for home. Not only does the narrator want to speak of the politics of cruelty from which he and others have fled, he also wishes to talk to the woman (or anyone) about his love for his native city, his lover who is waiting for him there, his little sister, his books, and "the scraps of paper and news-papers scattered in them."[51] The conclusion of the story abruptly shifts to the third person; the once-narrator is described returning to a gray room alone, where he lays down on an old bed and sobs uncontrolla-bly.[52] Although the act of writing is referred to only indirectly ("scraps of paper") in this first tale, it is highlighted with greater emphasis in the two stories that follow.

The initial part of "Reaction 2: A Peephole" ("Infi'al Ithnayn: Kuwwa") is framed as a letter in which the first-person narrator addresses an absent female interlocutor. The immediate impression is that he is speaking from a distant location, perhaps a foreign city, as he asks his reader whether it is raining where she is, while mentioning the incessant rain in his current location. He goes on to describe a countryside excursion he took with a friend, expresses his longing to hear her news, and promises that he will soon visit her. Mirroring "Reaction 1: A Room," the short concluding paragraph of this story shifts to the third person. The narrator is revealed to be in prison rather than in a foreign or distant city, as he is described looking "from the peephole of the narrow prison cell."[53]

Here the narrator's experience of exile and prison meld into one expe-rience.[54] Initially at least, the story develops the expectation that the nar-rator is not in prison, but abroad. Writing as a structural device appears through the fact that the body of the story, with the exception of the final paragraph, is scripted as a letter to the narrator's beloved. But in this case the futility and frustration generated in the act writing result in the nar-rator tearing up the piece of paper on which he had been writing. Unlike the case of Abu Salih's diaries, discussed below, the narrator destroys his own writing as he comes to realize that he is imagining a lover who does not exist. The destruction or erasure of the written word is paradoxically contrasted with the actual writing of the story, which exists as part of Hat-mal's short story collections.

"Reaction 3: The Stairwell of Solitary Days" provides a tale in which, once again, the narrator's position in a prison cell or in exile outside the borders of the nation is unclear. In this story the narrator's anxious, self-conscious reflections on his vulnerable psychological state and on philosophical questions of existence are intertwined with an interrogation of the functions and purposes of act of writing. As in the preceding two stories, the tale is initially told in the first person and is framed by the narrator's attempts at addressing, in a disjointed, stream-of-consciousness fashion, an absent, unnamed female. In this case the narrator is pleading with the female figure to understand his current mental state and all that he has lived through as he describes himself in state of completely breaking down.[55] The narrator raises a number of philosophical queries regarding his relationship with the other and then turns to the issue of writing. He asks: "Do I write now rather than respond, do I write to prevent the breakdown, and when writing doesn't come to me do I run toward the outside proclaiming my scream? Or my anger? Or my suffocation?"[56] He imagines the world ignoring his scream of anguish because the world has become deaf. Writing here is posited as a means to control or avoid the narrator's emotions, to prevent a complete psychological breakdown, but it is tool that does not appear to be fully effective for the narrator. In the end he is presented as being unable to write, much like the protagonist in Sun'allah Ibrahim's *That Smell*.

Instead the narrator presents himself as "the man who sits in the stairwell of solitary days"[57] Alone, abandoned, and alienated, he compares himself to a blank piece of paper that is inundated with ink until no white space is left.[58] The image created by the narrator's self-description as one who sits alone in the "stairwell of solitary days" speaks to a permanent, irreconcilable, borderline condition. He is held captive between a state of exile and a state of detention, between remaining silent and the potential rewards and risks of self-expression through writing. For Hatmal's narrator in this story, writing is equated with a forced confession in which he would be "conceding once again, as usual, slowly to the decisions written for me."[59]

The narrator then reflects on the difficulties he faces in defining his own self—difficulties, which can be linked to his uneasy relationship with the act of writing. He states, "This is I who knows his self, but I don't know how to grasp that self. This is I . . . . and I . . . I must give priority to any work that isn't decided by anyone but me. A work that I will not be able to regret ever. . . . I must now."[60] This passage ends as if the narrator has suddenly been interrupted. The final section of the story alludes to the narrator's death and possible suicide, once again referencing the image of blank paper: "Suddenly, in the stillness of the night, a small spot of blood poured out from a head fallen over the paper."[61] The abrupt and bleak ending of the story, with the image of blood instead of words flowing onto white paper, is indicative of Hatmal's ambivalence about the use of writing as a redemptive mode of self-definition or transcendence against the political oppressions of the state or the alienation of exile. Writing itself appears to be enmeshed with death, with a capacity for self-destruction, and fails to "reassemble identity."[62] Unlike the notion of writing as a means of survival and testimony, found in the story "Abu Salih," here writing becomes a source of imprisonment. It is neither a means for the narrator to "prevent the breakdown" that he fears, nor a way for the narrator to seek relief from his sense of isolation in his "solitary days."

"Abu Salih" is a story in which prison and writing are depicted in interlocking tandem with an abject and eventually fatal execution of exilic rift. The narrative is presented as a series of separated quotations from the journals and letters of Abu Salih, a detainee who has managed to obtain a pen and paper while imprisoned. These quotations in turn are framed as being read by an anonymous narrator (perhaps Abu Salih's cellmate). Similar to "the interweaving of the narrative present with the past" in particular works of Chinese prison wall fiction, Abu Salih's own words are contrasted with the narrator's present moments (not set in quotations) of imagining or flashing back to Abu Salih's past, particularly the day of his arrest, as well as his more recent time in prison.[63] Retelling Abu Salih's story in piecemeal fashion, the narrator positions and projects himself as Abu Salih, using the second person to describe the character's actions and emotional states. In essence, as in 'Abbas 'Abbas's telling of the story of Abu Hammud, the narrator testifies in place of a now-absent prisoner, and it is never clarified in the story if the narrator is inside or outside of the prison. Yet the story is not merely a testimony of one man's suffering and death, sense of alienation, and feelings of nostalgia, loss, sorrow, and estrangement. It is a meditation on the very necessity of writing, even if writing can act only as a partial form of redemption or restoration from a painfully oppressive past.

The juxtaposition of Abu Salih's journal entries with the narrator's descriptions structurally evokes the borderline conditions of metafiction, prison, and exile.[64] The opening section abruptly begins in the middle of a passage from Abu Salih's diary; he remarks that nearly a year has passed since he was arrested and that his books were "arrested" along with him. Yet his greatest loss is that of a notebook, and it is the absence of the notebook that commands his attention. He comments: "There I placed the intertwined fusion of my heart and my head. . . . I had wanted to look at it and observe it every once in a while. Now, I've forgotten most of what I wrote over the leather of its pages. I am no longer able to remember the precise features of those days."[65] This first passage consists entirely of Abu Salih's voice in written form. From the beginning, the focus is on Abu Salih's sense of loss because he no longer has his notebook. Without his notebook, he has no proof of his own existence in writing; his recorded memories are lost, and his sense of self has been shaken. He fears that his own memory will not serve him well and that he will forget the details necessary to fully account for his past.

Delineated in the text by graphic breaks, the fragments of the short story consist, in part, of excerpts from Abu Salih's writings in his own, first-person voice as he reflects on his arrest, detention, home, longing for family and friends, unrequited love for a woman, meditations on philosophy, and emotions. These excerpts alternate with sections in which the narrator is speaking in the second person to articulate various flashbacks pertaining to Abu Salih's story.[66] The continuous vacillation between fragments of Abu Salih's writings and the narrator's projection of the memories and imaginings of the same character causes the reader to pause and question who is speaking and whether the narrator is Abu Salih himself. Additionally, the shifting back and forth between these two voices reinforces a sense of separation and distance felt by both Abu Salih and the narrator, while at the same time the narrator's use of the second person evokes the idea of the reader putting himself in the former's shoes. Abu

Salih, we will eventually learn, is no longer there to narrate his own story. But momentarily, like the portrayal of torture in Hasiba 'Abd al-Rahman's *The Cocoon*, the narrative emphasizes the act of speaking rather than the speaker or the actual content of the story.[67]

As the story progresses, the narrator's recollections of Abu Salih's past give way to Abu Salih's own personal writings about his imprisonment. The act of writing begins to emerge as a key point of Abu Salih's inscribed reflections; he recalls that at the beginning of his detention, obtaining a pencil and paper were his first priority: "The communal cell is completely quiet. Everyone is sleeping, and I am drowsy. Do you believe that the possibility of writing doesn't exist for me unless everyone goes to sleep? This is what has made me an addict of staying up all night, not because I write every day, but because I sit to remember in quiet, or daydream as I please, and live this intertwined fusion, of dreams, thoughts, and feelings as I wish. I can't do this as I please, except after everyone goes to sleep."[68] For Abu Salih, having access to the tools of writing while in prison is tantamount to reconstructing his sense of self. He also envisions writing as a form of escape that encapsulates a feeling of solitude rather than isolation. The act of inscription is intertwined with the moments he allows himself to remember, dream, think, and feel freely. He notes, "Illusions like this are very necessary for the prisoner" because "when he fantasizes, he feels precisely as if he is living with whoever he wants, saying to them what he wishes, and making them say to him what he wishes."[69] The narrator, in his turn, exhorts Abu Salih to resort to such illusions when necessary in order to remember that he is still alive and "still capable of dreaming, writing, and the possibility of love, you are still capable of life."[70]

Abu Salih's being "capable of life" is reinforced throughout the text by the presence of his writings. The narrator also indicates that it is these writings that must be read and recognized as a form of witnessing. Yet the story concludes with the narrator's final, haunting reflections, questioning whether Abu Salih is still alive: "And one morning, one morning very early one day, they came to you, woke you up, and took you out quickly. You didn't know where. You gazed around you. At the faces that woke up questioning, astonished, at the faces staying up all night that hadn't yet slept. Perhaps you also gazed at the corner where you were hiding your papers and the pen. Those papers. That pen that remained alone, alone since that cold dawn, that dawn."[71]

The narrator's last passage reveals that Abu Salih has most likely been executed; what remains of Abu Salih in the barracks are his pen and papers, which the narrator presumably has been reading as he tells Abu Salih's story. Abu Salih, in his final commentary, writes of a "vocabulary" consisting of three terms: life, death, human being. At the time of writing, he marks himself as hesitant to answer the questions formed by those three words. At the end of the story, from the narrator's perspective, Abu Salih provides an answer—by refusing to respond to the questions of the interrogators and by sacrificing his life, presumably for his comrades and a political cause that remains unknown in the story. His written record remains to be redeemed by the narrator and to stand as proof of Abu Salih's existence and suffering, but the record is irredeemably incomplete because of the absence of its author.

On the one hand, Hatmal's short stories provide a cautionary tale that reveals the fraught fictionality of his own writing and that hints at the destructive potential of the process of inscription. Yet, returning to Munif's point, the reader is left with stories that are to be read and interpreted and that incite a critical awareness that this writer/detainee/exile is in a precarious position of not-belonging. Hatmal's texts are a key example of how prison can be inscribed as exile, how exile becomes an incarceration or a suspended moment of arrest, and how, in both of these cases, writing can vacillate between the status of redemption and the space of exilic imprisonment in which redemption surfaces but then is undermined, deferred, or left for the reader to recover. Like the poetry of Mahmoud Darwish, whether alluding to the space of prisons within the nation or the locations of physical, geographical exile outside the boundaries of the native land, many of Hatmal's short stories speak to the "need to reassemble an identity out of the refractions and discontinuities of exile" and detention.[72] Locked in the reverberations of loss and longing, especially the longing for an absent or unobtainable female figure that can be read as a symbol of the lost homeland, both the author's and the narrator's identity and the impossibility of exilic return are rewritten again and again without the formulation of a fully enunciated redemptive conclusion.

Munif's introduction to Hatmal's collected works resonates with a tone of mourning for lost "progressive" dreams. He reads the stories as testimony, as Hatmal's final act of "writing on the wall of cruel time, declaring that he lived and saw, that he tried and suffered."[73] For Munif, no matter the actual content of the narrative, it is the experience of political detention, its traces, and its effects that echo in all of Hatmal's stories. Prison "emerges as one of the beasts, watching over the dreamers and the disappointed in order to annihilate them one after another, oppressively tearing them apart."[74] Whether emerging from the viewpoint of exile-as-imprisonment or imprisonment-as-exile, Hatmal's narratives provide a momentary attempt at subverting the displacement caused by an exilic rift through an assertion or repossession of language. The need to overcome the estrangement of exile and imprisonment through the act of writing appears in Hatmal's stories as emphatically "urgent" and as "an absolute precondition for dealing with the primary business of self-definition and creativity in a world devastated by a history of dispossession."[75] Yet in many of his stories the drive to reconstitute an identity or establish a stable mode of self-definition, like the homecoming of an eternal exile, remains in a state of deferral or delay. This deferral of self-definition, of homecoming, of release from real and metaphoric prisons emerges as a prediagnosed condition of "terminal loss," just as it echoes the as yet unknown fate of many political prisoners of Hatmal's generation and the generation that has witnessed the 2011 Syrian Revolution and the subsequent war and refugee crisis.[76]

Through the continual use of metafictional references, many of the stories in Hatmal's complete works reveal that the attempt to repossess language, though a productively creative act, is not always enough to redeem either the writer or the narrators from the incarcerations of the chronic sense of loss and longing that is a characteristic of the conditions of exile and imprisonment. As an alternative, what is communicated is an irredeemable displacement that appears to foreclose or forestall any resolution. Hatmal's narrators speak with a recognition that the authority of writing is suspect—it can be undermined and sabotaged, and it can detain the one attempting to write. In the end, positioned on the "stairwell of solitary days," the final potential redemption for the exiles/detainees rests in the constitution of a body of texts and in the acts of restitution performed by the audience that reads what has been written and will draw and write their own conclusions of the stories of Hatmal's complete works.

Writing as the Vertigo of Freedom

Published eighteen years after the passing of Jamil Hatmal, Malik Daghastani's landmark work *The Vertigo of Freedom* is one among several novels and novellas dealing with detention that diverge sharply from the dominance of social realism in Syrian literature from the 1950s through the 1970s—a form of social realism that is reflected in works such as Sa'id Hawraniyya's "The Fourth Barracks" (1958) and Nabil Sulayman's *The Prison (al-Sijn)* (1972), both of which emphasize the "ideology of prison" and the image of the committed intellectual heroically resisting the coercion of tyrannical political authority.[77] Daghastani's narrative also marks a departure from the plotline of the more conventional prison novel, which describes the arrest, interrogation, prison life, and then release of a protagonist in a linear fashion.

The novel is scripted as an extended daydream or fantasy, but it is also an example of a work of prison literature in which metafictional tendencies serve as the backbone of a sometimes opaque, stream-of-consciousness narrative. At his trial for an unknown political crime after being in detention for seven years, the unnamed narrator sees a woman he doesn't know. The anonymity of the narrator not only alludes to potential fears of censorship and repercussions for writing the story, but also marks him as representative of thousands of other political detainees. The narrator proceeds to compose, seemingly in written form, an elaborate and sometimes tedious fantasy of their long-term emotional and sexual relationship, addressed primarily to her in the second person. While much of the story consists of a description of an imagined outing to a garden with his fantasy lover and a reflection on their first imaginary sexual encounter, the narrator's daydream is pervasively interrupted by other, seemingly more urgent events. Throughout, his musings are disrupted and intruded on by the voices of court officials, officers, and interrogators, brief descriptions of scenes and sounds from the court and prison life as well as memories of childhood and the imagined voice of his mother. Most significantly, the text highlights the narrator's own questions and reflections about the process of writing and its relationship to sex as well as his cognizance of the purpose, or futility, of the act of storytelling.

Like 'Abbas 'Abbas reflecting on his own prison papers, Daghastani's protagonist is concerned with the adequacy of language and the question of truth in storytelling. The narrator reveals his awareness that the process of writing always carries inherent dangers, a parallel to Derrida's words, that "there is thus no insurance against the risk of writing. Writing is an initial and graceless recourse for the writer."[78] Despite its pitfalls and risks, the act of writing, of inscribing his fantasies, appears as the narrator's only means of constructing a sense of liberation as a speaking subject while he is detained. Even while grasping at the idea that writing can be equated with freedom or a form of resistance in the midst of extremely oppressive circumstances, the main character is well aware of the potential slippage, distortion, or loss in and of meaning, for his readers and himself, of what he is attempting to convey.

In *The Vertigo of Freedom*, the narrator repeatedly questions whether his own stories are ultimately believable. This self-interrogative questioning emerges in the text despite the fact that it is replete with non sequiturs and presents the narrator's acknowledgment that he is living, at least partially, in a fantasy world. Yet this dreamscape allows him to imagine himself outside the prison walls and thus expands his sense of prison space and time. In his mind he seeks recognition from both the female objects of his obsessions and his audience. He sardonically asks his imaginary lover as well as his reader, "and so that we can come closer to the truth of what happened in the garden, I say: I am speaking to you. You are most likely convinced by the truth of my story, and you are not gripped by any doubt as to its realism."[79] The narrator remains aware that as he recounts his imaginary encounters, his words approach a particular version of his truth. Ironically he asserts that his audience is "most likely convinced" that the story he is relating is real, factual, and true.

The protagonist frequently elaborates on the relationship between imprisonment, the need for mental and creative forms of escape, and the search for new forms of expression. In one such passage, he takes a brief respite from describing his encounter with the woman he is fantasizing about. He calls out to his mother, who he imagines would reprimand him for his sexual fantasies, and pleads with her by stating that he is creating such daydreams in order to mentally escape his confinement, to "change the map of this death."[80] He tells her:

> This is prison, Mother, and prison is where I listen to the rattles of my own voice and search for anyone who I might tell that I am suffocating, but I find no one.
>
> Prison . . . whoever came upon the idea to build the first prison in history was an insane criminal, no doubt. Oh Mother, it is not the devilries of a rebellious boy, but an attempt to beautify this grave with some flowers and some beats outside of the systems of stern hearts. It is the outbreak of a dream in the midst of these blended nightmares, making it so that I can breathe another extra day. It is a language to combat the death besieging the fortress of the heart surrounded by disappointments and a depressing beat.[81]

The composition of his fantasy appears to be the only means the narrator can use in order to ward off death, despair, and his near-lethal sense of isolation. He frames fantasy as a language at his disposal, and this language becomes a means of combat, a momentary mode of resistance. Yet despite this momentary vindication of the potential powers of storytelling, fantasy, and written expression, the narrator then proceeds to abruptly shift to reflect on the night he was conceived and the relationship of language to sex.

While he is seemingly being put on trial for his political activities, the narrator deliberates on the links between language, writing, sex, and sexual climax. Continuing an imaginary conversation with his mother, he describes the night of conception as a moment "when the words cease being language and a suitable means of disclosure," and as "the return to what was before languages."[82] Languages, according to this passage, are "killing the abilities of virgin expression."[83] He ponders the sexual encounter as a moment without or prior to language. For Daghastani's imprisoned protagonist, no language gives the ability to speak like "an unhurried touch."[84] Thus at times in the text, in the view of the protagonist, the physical connections between two bodies during a sexual act have the power to surpass language in all of its forms.

Eventually apologizing to his readers for diverging from the subject of his original daydream, the narrator goes back to envisioning his time in the garden with the woman he has seen in court. Nonetheless, his childhood memories, his mother's voice telling him to stop being delusional, and the sounds of his guards continue to intrude on his fantasy. Despite these interruptions, he insists on the dire necessity of storytelling-as-dream; instigated by the "loneliness of this place," the "dream story" empowers him to "push away from the emptiness of the soul."[85] Despite the fact that he is occasionally forced to recognize that "Yes. . . . Yes, I am still in prison," he continues to insist that the "elements" of the dream are "planted deeper and deeper" in his soul.[86] Eventually his description of his sexual encounter with the woman intersects with his desire to compose a poem about her as well as a childhood memory of writing.

The details of his fantasy lover's body, their imagined sexual act, and the poem become more elaborate, while simultaneously he makes repeated references to whether or not particular words are adequate or appropriate for the story he is telling.[87] Finally these different elements of the narrative converge as the protagonist offers more extensive metafictional meditations that mirror the moment of sexual climax:

> Writing is exactly like love, an act justified in and of itself. It is first, and above all, an act of freedom, and it does not need any justification outside of itself. I do not conceal my hidden lust with the twistings of the letters, nor do I imprison my temptations at the end of the lines.
>
> I write, I swim, I fly possessed with pleasure, in a daze from vertigo. The vertigo of a terminology, bare-chested, that falls and is picked up from the edge of the hip by the end of the line, making love over the bed of a poem, plucking its flower. I am dazed and dazed and I write. . . . It is the vertigo of the excess of freedom.[88]

The narrator's reflections on writing converge with the culmination of his imaginary sexual encounter. Writing, here, is offered up as a path to liberation, though that path may be confined by the limits of his imagination and may be blocked by the intrusion of the realities of his detention. It is a form of freedom structurally intertwined with a freedom of form that leaves the narrator dazed, unbalanced, and momentarily lost. And eventually, he is brought back to the present reality of his detention and trial by the sound of the guard's voice ordering the prisoners to cue up for a car to take them back to the prison.

For Daghastani's narrator, writing is the vertigo of freedom and appears temporarily as a means of subverting the power of the Syrian security authorities who have tortured, detained, and put him on trial. However, the narrator cautions the readers that writing has a material presence that has the potential to be lost, altered, or distorted despite all of the detainee's bravado: "Here. I have watched over the end of the writing of the dream and it shows me as afraid of what I have written, despite all I possess of madness and recklessness. Will I keep these papers like this, exactly as they are? Or will I tear them up and scatter this forbidden delirium, and this impossible nonsense? Will I throw the shreds of paper in front of me on the floor, then stumble with my fist on the wall, hitting, with strong, strong force?"[89] The narrator does not, in fact, protest by banging his fist on the wall; instead, he briefly attempts to return to the fantasy of the garden and the memory of his mother's voice. In the end, with the image of the protagonist's tearing up his own written words (also a fantasy), Daghastani posits writing as an effective act of rebellion. The prisoner remains in detention, but his written papers appear to us in the form of the book—*The Vertigo of Freedom*.

Coda

In 2010, just before the start of the Syrian Revolution, a group of filmmakers in Damascus came together to create what would become the world-renowned anonymous collective Abounaddara (Abu Naddara, meaning "the man with the glasses" and also the name of a satirical newspaper published by the nineteenth-century Egyptian satirist Y'aqub al-San'u). In the wake of the violent and deadly government crackdown on protests, the subsequent militarization of the conflict between the opposition and the regime, and the saturation of the mainstream media, both regional and international, with images of these events, the collective began to articulate their specific mission. Abounaddara coined the phrase *emergency cinema* to describe their productions. As a term, *emergency cinema* expresses a clear connection between their artistic endeavors and a powerful sense of urgency to speak to the moment of revolution, war, and displacement. They began to produce and distribute weekly "bullet films," which one critic describes as "short, urgent, and aimed at breaking through the visual noise associated with media coverage of war and atrocity."[1]

The collective itself has not offered a single complete definition of what constitutes emergency cinema; instead, Abounaddara has seemingly preferred to let their films speak for themselves, to let the films and the people featured in them define the various facets of what constitutes emergency cinema.[2] A few scholars and critics have attempted to glean a definition of emergency cinema from the statements of the collective as well as its spokespeople. Zainab Saleh argues that emergency cinema is "interdisciplinary," combining "visual culture and film with philosophy, history, science, sociology (and more) to provide in-depth analyses linked to visuality."[3] Unlike much of the mainstream media coverage of the Syrian war and refugee crisis, the collective avoids explicitly identifying the religious or political affiliations of the subjects of many of its films; those featured in Abounaddara's bullet films speak for themselves.[4] Having won numerous film and human rights awards, including the Vera List Center Prize for Art and Politics, the collective has produced hundreds of short videos chronicling and at times satirizing the various complex facets of the contemporary Syrian experience, with revolution, war, displacement, political oppression and censorship, resistance to religious extremism and sectarianism, and countering Western media stereotypes of Syrians, Arabs, Muslims, and refugees.

Abounaddara has consistently articulated via its official statements and through one of its spokespeople, Cherif Kizwan, a right that is not included in the Universal Declaration of Human Rights or later human rights conventions: they argue that all human beings, including Syrians, have "the right to the image," as a fundamental human right.[5] In an essay the collective posted in 2015, they observe that in circumstances of war and massive human rights violations, excessive mediatization creates "typical images of victims."[6] However, for Abounaddara, this drive to expose suffering and injustice "has taken humanity away" from people and has failed to capture the dignity of those who resist oppression.[7] Citing the saturation of images of disfigured and emaciated bodies, miserable refugee camps, and the ruins of bombarded cities, the collective calls on the media and other producers of visual culture to focus on forms of collective social, political, and cultural life that "sustain individuals in their struggle for life in dignity and peace.[8] Tying the notion of a right to the image with dignity, Abounaddara reminds its viewers that any representation of human suffering and oppression is a choice—not just an aesthetic choice, but an ethical and political one. Individuals, the collective argues, can possess their own image if they "are legally . . . empowered to speak."[9]

But, the collective asks, what about those who do not have such a power? The filmmakers' response is that people whose humanity is erased in images from the violence of war and mass human rights violations are never allowed to speak. They are not allowed to both have dignity and "be a victim."[10] In such a case, "your wounds can speak, but you cannot."[11] With a clear concern for the problematic "aesthetic instrumentalization of trauma," Abounaddara insists that international human rights law must contend with the dilemmas of the representation of people who are reduced to "bare life" through human rights abuses and war.[12] In another statement they note that ordinary Syrians citizens are represented through a "spectacle of indignity streamed almost live from Syria since 2011," while Bashar al-Asad, who used chemical weapons against his own citizens, is presented as a "gentleman defending his views to the world's media organizations."[13] For the collective, the public circulation and sensationalism of undignified images without the subjects' express permission or ability to speak for themselves is a human rights violation. Such images include the body of lifeless toddler Alan al-Kurdi, washed up on a Turkish beach, which his family requested that the media stop using; people who were tortured, maimed, starved, and killed while in detention, as in the Caesar photographs, and whose images were then displayed at the UN (to no immediate effect) and the United States Holocaust Memorial Museum; and the victims of ISIS featured in the group's infamous videos.

In all of their films the collective strives to respect this concept of the "right to the image," and a number of them address the issue of detention and torture. Many of their films follow a common format and structure; for example, a number of their videos that deal with imprisonment and interrogation feature a single person who speaks without being prompted by any questions from an unseen filmmaker.

The two-part film *The Syrian Patient* (*Al-Marid al-Suri*) features a doctor describing a detainee who is brought to the government or military clinic where he is working. The doctor's face and exact features are never shown. Rather, slowly and softly, he narrates the story with a close up of his head in silhouette against a white background; the viewer can just make out the shape of a beard. Ordered by two security agents carrying weapons to examine the patient, the doctor recalls how he observed bruises on his stomach, back, and chest. Recognizing that the patient's condition was poor and getting worse, he and the resident physician tried to get the patient admitted, but the agent refused multiple times. Finally they were allowed to admit him to intensive care, and the interviewee considered this an "achievement." Remembering how he went to visit the patient in intensive care the next day, he notes that the patient was under the watch of two guards and handcuffed to his bed. He states that he always tried to stay with "these patients" because "they were fighting for a cause" similar to his own. When he returned the next day, he was informed that the patient had died. He goes on to say that he noticed that the patient's death was not recorded in the hospital registry: "Officially, this person did not die in the hospital." There was no postmortem or death certificate, and his name was not recorded; "He died unknown."

In the second part of the film, the viewer discovers that the doctor eventually ended up in the position of his patient because he, himself, was detained—a sign that anyone might end up in prison, that anyone, anywhere in Syria is vulnerable to arrest. He describes how he entered a crowded, communal prison cell that was packed with "a mass of humans, a mass of naked pale humans" who all had the "same look" as those prisoners he had attempted to treat. Speaking in a lower voice layered with sorrow, he begins to talk about how a man died in his cell. This young man, despite being injured himself, had asked the doctor to examine his father. The father was in critical condition from acidosis. The doctor's voice becomes tearful as he recalls how he examined the father again at the youth's request, only to discover that the father had died. The body was left alone, but the son continued to insist that his father was alive. The film ends with a story of a failure of recognition—the doctor states that what affected him most was the fact that the son refused to recognize his father's death and initially had no emotional reaction to his passing.

In another film, titled *The Detainee Is Not Present* (*Al-Muʿtaqal Ghayr Mawjud*) a mother describes her search for her son once she realized he'd been arrested. Similar to the doctor in "The Syrian Patient," the narrator of this film is presented in silhouette, with much of the screen black and viewer just able to make out the lines of her head and arm as she sits in a chair. She describes how she went to an Air Force Security Division and begged the guard to reassure her that he was safe and to give him a jacket and few other items. Eventually, she tells viewers, the guard took the items and told her to come back later that night; she returned and was reassured that he was well. The next day, she returned again to find out when he would be released and why they had arrested him. A different guard told her it would be just a few days. Yet, the woman tells us, she kept returning and he was never released. After three days, she realized her son wasn't there, so she began searching for him in different interrogation centers every day. The film ends with her stating that after fifteen days, she decided to check at all the security branches in Damascus (an indication that she and her son lived in one of the outer suburbs); no one could tell her where he was. No information is provided in the film about how long after her son's arrest the film was made. The question of how long the mother has been searching and waiting for her son to come home remains unanswered.

One of Abounaddara's longer films is the seven-part video *Saydnaya Prison . . . as Narrated by the Syrian Who Wanted the Revolution* (*Sijn Saydnaya . . . Yarwihi al-Suri Alladhi Arada al-Thawra*). The seven parts of the film carry the secondary titles of "The Demonstrations," "The Reception," "The Punishment," "The Holiday," "The Hospital," "The Visit," and "The Salvation." The film features an unnamed man in his late twenties or early thirties who tells his story of participating in the peaceful protests in Aleppo and being arrested and eventually sent to Saydnaya. All seven parts of the film consist simply of scenes of the man, shown from the waist or shoulders up as he sits on a couch and tells his story. Occasionally during particularly poignant points of the film, the camera shifts to offer a close-up of his face. The lighting in the film is dim, and as he narrates, his face is mostly visible but sometimes partially hidden in shadows as he moves his head.

Though the first part of the film deals with the narrator's work in organizing and participating in protests and coordinating with the Free Syrian Army, in many ways, the film follows the typical pattern of a prison memoir. The narrator's story describes his initial experience of detention and then offers his audience a series of stories or vignettes about other inmates and himself. In the second and third part of the film, the man describes his arrival and torture at Saydnaya Prison, he and others' shock that they and other civilians were being held at the military prison, and how the prisoners who had been detained there longer were eager for news from outside about the Revolution.

He then tells the story of one Abu Fu'ad, from the neighborhood of Baba 'Amr in Homs that was the site of many protests in 2011 and, later, of clashes between regime and opposition forces. Abu Fu'ad had been a builder by trade and was not involved in the demonstrations against the regime, but he was detained because he answered "I don't know" when questioned by a regime soldier about the whereabouts of opposition fighters. Abu Fu'ad, the narrator tells us, had already been interrogated and tortured by agents from four different security branches in his home city. When he arrived at Saydnaya, he couldn't move his fingers and hands, and he suffered from multiple other injuries. Later, his cellmates learn that Abu Fu'ad had a strong constitution and withstood the initial rounds of torture. He refused to confess to something he didn't do, and because of this, he was hung by his wrists in a solitary cell for three days and given no food or water. He finally signed a false confession, and then was transferred from one interrogation center to another. He arrived at Saydnaya ten to fifteen days later, and according to the narrator, he and his cellmates tried to help him recover. He was taken for a two-minute trial and severely tortured again, with the result that swelling appeared throughout different parts of his body. He was eventually taken to the hospital twice, where he said he was used as a "lab rat." He died under the watch of the narrator. Though the narrator mentions that he had a close relationship with Abu Fa'ud, he tells his story in a matter-of-fact tone, with his emotions mainly registered in his eyes.

The story of Abu Fu'ad is followed in part four by the narrator's account of how prisoners were viciously tortured on all of the 'īd days (feast days or holidays), especially by the most notorious guard, whom they called 'Abdu. As he speaks, the narrator becomes slightly agitated and slightly more emotional as he repeatedly reaches up to rub his forehead or adjust his glasses. One "unbelievable" torture session occurred on Valentine's Day. The prisoners referred to it as the "Valentine's Day massacre" because guards, including 'Abdu, used a new, heavier type of baton and systematically beat a number of prisoners from each communal cell to death. At first, the narrator states, they thought the killings had occurred only in their wing, but later they learned that it had happened in every wing of the prison. They realized that an order must have come down from the top of the prison's administration because at least two hundred prisoners were killed that day.

In the fifth and sixth parts of the film, the narrator describes a trip to a military hospital when two of the detainees in very bad condition were left untreated overnight in a cold outer building. Though near death, they were still alive when an orderly came. The narrator recalls how the orderly refused to believe that they are alive and forced the other detainees to put them in body bags even though they kept trying to tell the orderly they are not dead. Later the prisoners are ordered to load the two supposed corpses onto a makeshift ambulance, only to discover that there were at least twenty-two other bodies of prisoners there.

In the next part of the film, the narrator describes how his transfer to a different communal cell marked a deterioration in his health in May 2014. His cellmate and friend Muhammad had died, and he had started to experience similar symptoms. He had severe, rapid weight loss, couldn't focus, and faced difficulty walking. He knew he had a visit on June 1, and he was worried that he wouldn't be able to make it to the visitation room and didn't want his parents to see him in such a poor state. The day of the visit came, and he couldn't get up, so a guard forced him to stand and begin the agonizing process of walking to the visitation room, but he collapsed. Propped up by the guards and taken to visitation room on warden's orders, he tried to hide his condition from his parents, but they knew something was wrong, and the guards cut the visit short. The process of getting back to the cell was pure torment as the guards kicked and beat him. For the next twelve days, he tells his viewers, he couldn't walk.

The final part of the film, ironically called "The Salvation," is much shorter than the other parts, lasting just two minutes and forty-seven seconds. The term used for salvation, *khalās*, appears to allude to the young man's eventual release from prison. But instead, the narrator describes how they only received superficial news of what was happening outside the prison when new prisoners arrived. Eventually they are shocked and angry to learn about the creation of oppositional militias who were independent of and in conflict with the Free Syrian Army. He states, "In prison, our expectations are as great as the suffering we endure. There are many in prison who dream that the Free Army will come and liberate us. That was many people's dream. Even me. It was my dream." For the narrator, the militias "only aggravated the detainee's suffering." At the end of the film, he states: "No one can feel what the detainees go through. Those in Saydnaya truly wished they were dead. Even me, I wished that. If they wanted to do us a favor, they should make the prison collapse on top of us. We want to die. Death is easier than life here."

Each of these three Abounaddara films feature a single person telling their story, and each of the stories reflects several parallels to the works of prison literature discussed throughout this book. Much like the short stories of Ibrahim Samu'il and Ghassan al-Jaba'i, these films encapsulate the same core themes of recognition, vulnerability, unknowable endings, and uncertain futures. The videos speak to the imperative to narrate the experience of detention and torture, but also reflect the inevitable silences and gaps that occur when former detainees recall and navigate their own and others' experiences of the trauma of violence inflicted by the Syrian state. They depict acts of solidarity between detainees as well as the agonies of those waiting for them outside the prison walls.

Yet despite the utterly horrific events and scenes of depravity and suffering they describe, the subjects of the films present themselves and are featured in a way that avoids sensationalizing their experiences or turning their unstated pain into a spectacle. The picture of a person speaking, whether in complete silhouette or with their face shown, stands in contrast to the horrors they are describing in the context of a revolution and war that has been hypersaturated with images. For the filmmaking collective, this is part of what constitutes emergency cinema, and the subjects of the films, even when never fully seen by the audience, have retained their rights to their own images and stories.

Animating Revolution and Detention

Like Abounaddara's *Saydnaya Prison*, Jalal Maghout's short animated documentary *Suleima* (2014) offers a portrait of a participant in the peaceful demonstrations that marked the early part of the Syrian Revolution. Like the unnamed narrators in the Abounaddara films, the titular character and narrator, who is a Palestinian woman from one of the suburbs of Damascus, is also detained. Despite this, Maghout's film offers a much more optimistic vision of the Revolution. Based on a true story, the film opens with Suleima's participation in a small antiregime protest that breaks up suddenly when the *mukhbārāt* appear. During her interrogation, which is only briefly shown, she begins to flash back to different moments of her childhood, teenage years, and young adulthood, including her initial involvement in the uprising. The memories of her past include her encounter with official Syrian state discourse and various forms of oppression. She recalls, for example, walking with her father and seeing a teenage boy being beaten up by two men, also *mukhbārāt* agents. When she asks her father about it, he refuses to reply. With depictions of constant surveillance and security agents everywhere, she flashes back to a moment in school when she was frustrated with the official curriculum and the constant evocations of proregime propaganda. She said out loud, "I hate Hafez al-Asad!," and was reprimanded by school officials. Once she returned home, she was warned that "they would have taken your father" because of what she had said.

As part of the flashbacks, the film shows how Suleima first became involved in the demonstrations early on in the Revolution when she joined the funeral procession of a protester killed in Ghouta. She was the only woman in the procession. Later she became more involved in the revolutionary movement, and she began to work as a medic and nurse for people who are shot or otherwise injured by regime forces during demonstrations. Her husband feared for her safety and also reproached her for spending so much time away from home, and eventually he left, taking their son and daughter with him. The painful memory of the absence of her children returns Suleima back to the present with her interrogator. She is released, but she is arrested again after a protest against the massacre of civilians in Houla in 2012, perpetrated by proregime militias. In a prison cell, she comments that hearing the torture of others is worse than being tortured herself. She continues to reflect that although she has lost everything, she is happy because she is with her people. The film concludes with her commenting that she is not afraid for her children, and that she is mother to them all (the children and all those supporting the Revolution).

The pseudonym Suleima is a diminutive name derived from the more common name Salma, meaning pacifist. Both are derived from same root as the word *salām*, or peace. When the demonstrations are portrayed in the film, they include people holding signs with the word "peaceful" (*silmiyya*) as well as "stop the killing" (*awqifu al-qatl*) and "dignity" (*karāma*). Maghout tells Suleima's story through black and white hand-drawn animation, with a mix of animated-in after effects and stop-motion illustration.[14] The black, white, and gray colors are occasionally broken up with the use of yellow to depict light or to highlight moments of hope, including the end of the film. The security agents, interrogators, and other government official in the film are always depicted in black suits or darker clothes. The members of the *mukhabārāt* and the interrogators, especially, appear as large, menacing, lurching, boxlike male figures, while Suleima and the other activists and protesters are represented in shades of grey or white.

Her interrogation is only briefly depicted. Though the film implies that she is tortured, her torture is not directly shown. Instead, her recollections of her childhood and her memories of the early protest movement fill the screen, much like the way the character Kawthar, in Hasiba 'Abd al-Rahman's *The Cocoon* (*Al-Sharnaqa*), effaces the presence of her torturers by speaking her memories and delusions. The term *human rights* is never specifically mentioned in Maghout's film; rather, the focus of the protesters is on the notions of freedom and dignity, and Suleima's final message is one of solidarity, unity, and hope for the future.

Of Ladders and Dreams

One of Syria's most prominent filmmakers, Muhammad Malas, managed to navigate the mechanisms of censorship and silencing by the Syrian state for decades without being detained. However, in March 2014 he was arrested at the Syrian-Lebanese border. He had been planning to fly from Beirut to Geneva to attend the International Film Festival and Forum on Human Rights and screen his most recent film, *Ladder to Damascus* (*Sullam ila Dimashq*). Released the same day, he was prevented from leaving Syria, but *Ladder to Damascus* has still been screened at various festivals around the world and is available on a number of websites.

Shot in secret in Damascus without official state permission and, not surprisingly, banned in Syria, the film tells the story of two young people, a would-be filmmaker named Fu'ad (otherwise known by his nickname,

"Cinema") and an actress named Ghalya. Like parts of *Suleima*, *Ladder to Damascus* takes place during the first years of the uprising and the early onset of armed conflict between regime and oppositional forces. Neither Ghalya nor Fu'ad are involved directly in the protests or armed battles, but the uprising and the growing danger from military conflict is evoked constantly in the background of the film, including through its sound-scape. While Fu'ad is obsessed with filmmaking, Ghalya is obsessed with a woman named Zayna and her story. Zayna was a young woman from Tartous whose father was detained. Unable to bear the thought of his absence and his being in prison, she decided to commit suicide the day her father was arrested by walking into the sea and drowning herself. Throughout the film Ghalya attempts to inhabit Zayna's story. She reenacts elements of Zayna's life; she ventriloquizes Zayna's story and speaks from her perspective. Ghalya does this, seemingly, in an effort to understand why she took her own life. Her sense of being becomes so intertwined with Zayna's story that at times she loses her grip on reality and her own sense of self.

Having become enchanted with Ghalya after seeing her act out part of Zayna's story (either in a play audition or in rehearsal), Fu'ad approaches her, and eventually the two become close. She convinces him to make a film out of Zayna's life story in which she portrays the protagonist. Though presented in fragmented and nonchronological form, part of *Ladder to Damascus*'s narrative consists of clips of Fu'ad's film about Zayna shown in the background while other action is taking place in the narrative. This includes interviews with Zayna's once imprisoned father, who is played by writer and playwright Ghassan al-Jaba'i, and who is shown speaking about the experience of detention throughout the film and questioning the government's need to detain tens of thousands of people.

The other major part of the film depicts the lives and interactions of the artistically inclined residents of a large, traditional house in the Old City where Fu'ad and later Ghalya live. The residents, Fu'ad and Ghalya included, are of different religions, come from various regions of Syria, and represent a microcosm of Syrian society as they interact with and encounter each other on a daily basis. None of them directly advocates for the use of violence to overthrow the Asad government, and they appear to hope for a peaceful resolution between the protesters and the regime.

However, many of the residents are directly affected by the growing conflict; various characters, including Fu'ad, receive calls throughout the film from or regarding relatives escaping dangerous events in other cities of the country.

The threat of being detained by the security apparatus is always present, and one of the residents eventually gets arrested. At one point, their elderly landlady, who is a practicing Muslim, witnesses government forces shooting protesters after she attends prayers at the Umayyad mosque. The final scene depicts one of the residents, Husayn, reacting to bad news about events in Homs. He becomes agitated and makes his way to the roof of the house. Concerned by his behavior, all of the residents follow him. He takes a long, blue ladder and attempts to stabilize it while climbing it, but he can't do it by himself. Not quite understanding what he was trying to do, all of the members of the household come together to hold the ladder as he climbs to the top. The film closes with both with an image of Husayn reaching the top of the ladder and shouting the word "freedom" ("*ḥurriyya*") at the top of his lungs, and a message about solidarity and unity.

Ladder to Damascus is not Malas's only film to touch on the experience of detention in Syria. One of his first films, titled *Everything Is in Its Place and All Is in Order, Officer* (*al-Kullu fi Makanihi wa Kullu Shay' 'ala Ma Ya Ram Sidi al-Dabit*), was produced in 1974 at the Moscow Film Institute, where Malas was studying.[15] The film's script was written by both Malas and Egyptian novelist Sun'allah Ibrahim, and directly links the defeat of 1967 to political oppression by following the reaction of a group of prisoners to news of the war. Many years later, as part of Amnesty International's celebration of the fiftieth anniversary of the Universal Declaration of Human Rights in 1998, Malas produced and directed the film *Over the Sand, Under the Sun* (*Fawq al-Raml, Taht al-Shams*). In a fragmented fashion, this film depicts the tragedy of the experience of political prison from the point of view of prisoners' families, the prisoners themselves, and recently released political prisoners. Many of the actors in the film, such as journalist and writer 'Ali al-Kurdi, are former detainees themselves. Additionally, detention figures as part of the backstory to the film *Passion* (*Bab al-Maqam*), in which the character Rashid's imprisonment sparks tension among family members who mourn his absence; prisonlike images, such as gates and barred windows, appear throughout the film.

Yet *Ladder to Damascus*, particularly with the presence of former political prisoner al-Jaba'i—from an earlier generation of those who opposed the Syrian state—playing the role of a detainee critiquing the state's use of detention as a form of systematic collective punishment, connects the suppression of earlier opposition movements in the 1980s and 1990s to the more recent Revolution. Once again the Syrian regime has deployed a strategy of mass incarceration, torture, and extrajudicial execution as one tactic among many to avoid losing its grip on power. Though *Ladder to Damascus*, like *Suleima*, does not expressly mention the term *human rights*, it does reflect on issues of freedom, dignity, and diversity, particularly in its presentation of a household of different ages, regional backgrounds, religions, ideologies, and ethnicities. In the end of the film, despite all of their differences, the household comes together to support the free expression and the desire for freedom of one of its members.

The films of Abounaddara, in particular the ambivalent and ambiguous end of *Saydnaya Prison: As Narrated by the Syrian Who Wanted the Revolution*, may serve as a reminder of the abject failures of the international human rights regime to prevent, intervene in, or end the violations, abuses, and atrocities of the Asad regime both before and after 2011. Though the film's subject is released from prison, there appears to be no salvation for him, due to the near-death of his dream of a new and free Syria. Yet the film collective still keeps a degree of faith in an aspirational concept of human rights that is flexible enough to accommodate new and alternative formulations of what those rights can be. They view the right to the image as "complex and multilayered"; it is inherently connected to "individual choice and the dignity of the human person," as well as the "right of a people to freely determine the terms of their political association including issues related to the expression of cultural identity."[16]

Abounaddara urges a shift in thinking of what constitutes a human right in the international community. The collective's advocacy of the right to the image highlights palpable gaps in international human rights law. While scholarly critiques of human rights in the English-language academy have pointed to such gaps, to the "end" or "end times" of human rights, and have challenged the efficacy of the very notion of legal rights and examined how legal fictions produce the "civil death" of particular populations and sustain systematic racialized state violence in the US and elsewhere, it remains unclear what alternative can be formulated in lieu of rights, human and otherwise. Where does this leave those who continue to fight for their rights? This impasse appears especially acute when, across the world, people who are generating political movements against oppression and forms of violence explicitly engage the language of rights in all of its variety in their struggles for justice.[17]

The urgency of Abounaddara's right to the image suggests that "against realists, pragmatists and the ideologues of power," the "energy" necessary for any protection, expansion, and reformulation of human rights must come from "those whose lives have been blighted by oppression or exploitation and who have not been offered or have not accepted the blandishments and rewards of political apathy."[18] Perhaps if we attend to the ways in which rights are reevaluated and reformulated by collectives such as Abounaddara and listen to and look for critical and alternative voices and modes of expression of those confronting injustice, we can begin to formulate a new concept and diverse practices of global human rights that would result in a future where the foundations and bases for imperialism, war, and authoritarianism would never come into being.

Notes

Arabic Bibliography

English Bibliography

Index

Notes

Introduction

1. Omari's arrest was highlighted in an Amnesty International video in honor of the Day of the Disappeared in 2013. See Amnesty International Ireland, "Amnesty International, Day of the Disappeared 2013," filmed September 2013, YouTube video, 6:05, posted September 2013, www.youtube.com/watch?v=uwRsc11_vtA, accessed November 22, 2018.

2. For coverage of the thousands of extrajudicial killings perpetrated by the Asad regime in Saydnaya Prison alone, see John Davison and Stefanie Nebehay, "Amnesty Says Syria Executes, Tortures Thousands at Prison; Government Denies," Reuters, February 6, 2017, accessed November 10, 2018, www.reuters.com/article/us-mideast-crisis-syria -amnesty-idUSKBN15M00F. See also Amnesty International, "Human Slaughterhouse: Mass Hangings and Extermination at Saydnaya Prison Syria," Amnesty International, February 7, 2017, accessed August 9, 2018, www.amnesty.org/en/documents/mde24/5415 /2017/en/,/. As of August 2016 Amnesty conservatively estimated that almost 18,000 people had been killed in regime prisons. See Al Jazeera, "Almost 18,000 Died in Syria's Prisons: Amnesty," Al Jazeera, August 18, 2016, accessed October 5, 2018 www.aljazeera.com /news/2016/08/18000-died-syria-prisons-amnesty-160818051435301.html. As of 2018 the Syrian Network for Human Rights had estimated that over 14,000 have been killed since 2011 under torture in regime detention centers, with 98.99 percent of those killings perpetrated by the Asad regime. See Syrian Network for Human Rights, "Toll of Deaths Due to Torture," Syrian Network for Human Rights, n.d., accessed December 1, 2018, sn4hr .org/blog/2018/09/24/toll-of-deaths-due-to-torture/.

3. After appearing on an episode of *The Daily Show*, Bahari was arrested while reporting for *Newsweek* on the 2009 elections and protests in Iran and held in Evin Prison for 118 days beginning in June 2009. The story of his arrest is recounted in the film *Rosewater* (2014) and in his memoir: Maziar Bahari, *Then They Came for Me: A Story of Injustice and Survival in Iran's Most Notorious Prison* (London: Oneworld, 2013).

4. Upendra Baxi, *The Future of Human Rights? Theory and Practice in an International Context* (New Delhi: Oxford Univ. Press, 2002), 18.

5. For a description of the exhibit, see the US Holocaust Memorial Museum's web-site: www.ushmm.org/information/exhibitions/museum-exhibitions/syria-please-dont-forget-us. This exhibit and the museum's exhibit on the Caesar photographs have been criticized for equating the atrocities and war crimes of the Asad regime with the Holocaust as well as for the fact that the museum highlights human rights abuses perpetrated by the Syrian and other states but fails to acknowledge the Israeli state's systematic human rights abuses of Palestinians.

6. See the bibliography for works depicting the experience of detention post-2011. See also the website of The Creative Memory of the Syrian Revolution, an extremely important resource, for several video testimonies of detention, especially under keyword searches of "detainment" and "torture": creativememory.org/en/.

7. miriam cooke, "The Cell Story: Syrian Prison Stories after Hafiz Asad," *Middle East Critique* 20, no. 2 (2011): 169–87.

8. For an overview of the history of human rights movements in the Arab world, see Anthony Chase, "Introduction: Human Rights and Agency in the Arab World," in *Human Rights in the Arab World: Independent Voices*, ed. Anthony Chase and Amr Hamzawy (Philadelphia: Univ. of Pennsylvania Press, 2006), 1–17. Chase cites the early 1980s as the period marking the rise of human rights movements, but it is clear at least in the Syrian case that both formal and informal human rights associations existed earlier.

9. While more works have been translated into French, Italian, and German, the few works available in English at the time of writing include Heba Dabbagh, *Just Five Minutes: Nine Years in the Prisons of Syria*, trans. Bayan Khatib (Toronto: n.p., 2007); Mustafa Khalifa, *The Shell*, trans. Paul Starkey (Northampton, MA: Interlink, 2017); and Muhammad Saleem Hammad, *Tadmur: Witnessed and Observed*, trans. Syrian Human Rights Committee (n.p.: Syrian Human Rights Committee, n.d.), accessed December 20, 2017, www.shrc.org/en/wp-content/uploads/2017/02/Tadmur-Witnessed-and-Observed-Final-1.pdf. A collection of Faraj Bayraqdar's poetry that he composed while in prison has also been published in English: Faraj Bayrakdar, *Mirrors of Absence*, trans. John Asfour (Toronto: Guernica, 2015). For a concise overview of the causes, including economic, of the 2011 Revolution, see Paul Gabriel Hilu Pinto, "Syria," in *Dispatches from the Arab Spring: Understanding the New Middle East*, ed. Paul Amar and Vijay Prashad (Minneapolis: Univ. of Minnesota Press, 2013), Kindle. For more on the revolution and war, among many other texts, see Yassin al-Haj Saleh, *The Impossible Revolution: Making Sense of the Syrian Tragedy*, trans. Ibtihal Mahmood (London: C. Hurst and Co., 2017); Robin Yassin-Kassab and Leila al-Shami, *Burning Country: Syrians in Revolution and War* (London: Pluto, 2016), Kindle; Ziad Majed (Ziyad Majid), *Suriya: al-Thawra al-Yatima* (Beirut: Sharq al-Kitab, 2014); and Nikolaos van Dam, *Destroying a Nation: The Civil War in Syria* (London: I. B. Tauris, 2017).

10. For an analysis of three prison novels produced after 2005 as part of the political geography that informed the Syrian Revolution, see Rita Sakr, *"Anticipating" the 2011*

Arab Uprisings: Revolutionary Literatures and Political Geographies (New York: Palgrave Macmillan, 2013), Kindle. For an examination of the Syrian state's use of violence, including detention, and its role in informing the political subjectivities of Syrians, see Salwa Ismail, *The Rule of Violence: Subjectivity, Memory, and Government in Syria* (Cambridge, UK: Cambridge Univ. Press, 2018).

11. I am borrowing the term *speaking subject* from Joseph Slaughter and Kelly Oliver. See Joseph Slaughter, "A Question of Narration: The Voice in International Human Rights Law," *Human Rights Quarterly* 19, no. 2 (1997): 407, and Kelly Oliver, *Witnessing: Beyond Recognition* (Minneapolis: Univ. of Minnesota Press, 2001), 7. For Oliver, "through the process of bearing witness to oppression and subordination, those othered can begin to repair damaged subjectivity by taking up a position as speaking subjects. What we learn from beginning with the subject position of those othered is that the speaking subject is a subject by virtue of address-ability and response-ability." Drawing primarily on Michel Foucault, the term *discourse* here refers to "the general domain of statements, sometimes as an individualizable group of statements, and sometimes as a regulated practice that accounts for a number of statements," that varyingly construct the field of knowledge that constitutes human rights. Foucault, *The Archaeology of Knowledge and the Discourse of Language* (New York: Pantheon, 1972), 80. Inherent in this use of the term *discourse* are both the notion of exclusion and the problematic of how human rights truths claims are bounded through discursive constraints. In focusing on the notion of human rights as a discursive formation, Upendra Baxi's pertinently warns: "Discourse theorists often maintain that discursive practice constitutes social reality; there are no violators, violated, and violations outside discourse. However, such discourse theory ignores or obscures non-discursive or material practices of power and resistance. This way of talk *disembodies human suffering here and now,* for future ameliorative/redemptive purposes, whose status (at least from the standpoint of those that suffer) is *very obscure, indeed to a point of cruelty of theory.* The non-discursive order of reality, the materiality of human violation, is just as important, if not more so, from the standpoint of the violated." Baxi, *Future of Human Rights*, 14, emphasis in the original. In focusing on narrative representations of the detention experience as they relate to human rights discourse, I do not mean in any way to deny the real and objective suffering of detainees in Syria.

12. For more on the meanings and definitions of the terms *truth effects* and *truth claims*, see chapter 1. In using the term *human rights regime* I draw on Michael Freeman's discussion of the term in *Human Rights: An Interdisciplinary Approach* (Malden, MA: Polity, 2013). Tracing the term to scholarship on international relations and the work of Jack Donnelly, Freeman notes that "international regimes consist of rules and institutions to which states commit themselves. International human rights constitute such a regime, though the implementation of the regime is relatively weak. . . . The international human-rights regime not only implements human rights to some extent itself, but also provides the basis for human-rights actions by both governments and non-governmental

organizations (NGOs)" (156). See also Jack Donnelly, *Universal Human Rights in Theory and Practice* (Ithaca, NY: Cornell Univ. Press, 2003), 128–54. It is also obviously not my intention in using the term *human rights regime* to equate the atrocities perpetrated by the Asad regime with the successes and failures of the international human rights regime as inaugurated by the Universal Declaration of Human Rights. Rather, I want to draw attention to the internationalization of the concept of human rights and the institutional and narrative practices that are connected to it.

13. Jonathan Culler, *Literary Theory: A Very Short Introduction* (Oxford: Oxford Univ. Press, 2011), 62, Kindle. Culler notes that poetics "starts with attested meanings" of a given literary work and "asks how they are achieved," in distinction to hermeneutics, which "starts with texts and asks what they mean, seeking to discover new and better interpretation" (61–62). Though emphasis is placed on poetics in several of the close readings of literary texts that follow in this study, my analyses, like much literary criticism, again as noted by Culler, often combine hermeneutics and poetics.

14. For more detailed examinations of the history of modern Syria, the emergence of the Ba'th Party, and the rise to power of Hafez al-Asad, see Derek Hopwood, *Syria 1945–1986: Politics and Society* (London: Unwin Hyman, 1988); Hanna Batatu, *Syria's Peasantry, the Descendants of Its Lesser Rural Notables, and Their Politics* (Princeton, NJ: Princeton Univ. Press, 1999); Raymond Hinnebusch, *Syria: Revolution from Above* (London: Routledge, 2001); and John McHugo, *Syria: A Recent History* (London: Saqi, 2014). For a journalistic account of Syria before, during, and immediately after the Damascus Spring, see Alan George, *Syria: Neither Bread nor Freedom* (London: Zed, 2003). For an analysis of key intellectual and political debates in Syria in the 1990s and 2000s, see Elizabeth Suzanne Kassab, *Enlightenment on the Eve of the Revolution: The Egyptian and Syrian Debates* (New York: Columbia Univ. Press, 2019). For an account of Syria from 2000 through the 2011 Revolution, see Cartson Wieland, *Syria—A Decade of Lost Chances: Repression and Revolution from Damascus Spring to Arab Spring* (N.p.: Cune Press, 2012). While I acknowledge that the time frame of texts examined in this study may work to reify the official state version of Syrian history under the Asad regime, I would argue that focusing on works published from 1970 to 2015 also highlights the history of heightened political oppression and human rights atrocities as well as political opposition and dissent under the same authoritarian system.

15. Giorgio Agamben, *Homo Sacer: Sovereign Power and Bare Life*, trans. Daniel Heller-Roazen (Stanford, CA: Stanford Univ. Press, 1998).

16. For a detailed overview of human rights abuses under the Asad regime in the 1980s, see Middle East Watch, *Syria Unmasked: The Suppression of Human Rights by the Asad Regime* (New Haven, CT: Yale Univ. Press, 1991). For more on the history of the suppression of the Muslim Brotherhood, see Umar F. 'Abd-allah, *The Islamic Struggle in Syria* (Berkeley, CA: Mizan, 1983); Raphaël Lefèvre, *Ashes of Hama: The Muslim Brotherhood in Syria* (New York: Oxford Univ. Press, 2013), Kindle; Naomí Ramírez Díaz, *The*

Muslim Brotherhood in Syria: The Democratic Option of Islamism (New York: Routledge 2018), Kindle.

17. Human Rights Watch, "No Room to Breathe: State Repression of Human Rights Activists in Syria," Human Rights Watch, October 16, 1997, accessed September 10, 2007, www.hrw.org/en/reports/2007/10/16/no-room-breathe-0. Between 1978 and 1980, the Union and its Community for Human Rights called for lifting the state of emergency, the abolition of special courts, and the safeguarding of the independence of the judiciary. After the Union called for a one-day strike in 1980, the government dismissed the leaders of the Union, dissolved the Committee for Human Rights, and arrested several of its members. For more on the persecution of human rights activists in the 1980s and 1990s in Syria and in the Middle East generally, see Amnesty International, "Challenging Repression: Human Rights Defenders in the Middle East and North Africa," Amnesty International, March 11, 2009, accessed April 10, 2009, www.amnesty.org/en/library/info/MDE01/001/2009/en.

18. Sophia A. McClennan and Alexandra Schultheis Moore, "Introduction: Aporia and Affirmative Critique: Mapping the Landscape of Literary Approaches to Human Rights," in *The Routledge Companion to Literature and Human Rights*, ed. Sophia A. Mc-Clennan and Alexandra Schultheis Moore (New York: Routledge, 2016), Kindle. As McClennan and Moore note, Samuel Moyn heavily highlights 1977 as a "breakthrough" year in popular usage and currency of the term *human rights* in English-language contexts and by the American public. See Samuel Moyn, *The Last Utopia: Human Rights in History* (Cambridge, MA: Belknap, 2010), Kindle.

19. A number of films related to detention were also produced in the same time period. For example, a documentary film titled *Ibn al-ʿAmm*, about the head of the Communist Party Political Bureau, Riyad Turk, was produced and directed by Muhammad ʿAli al-Atassi and screened in Beirut in 2001.

20. Additionally, after the events at Qamishli in 2004 three Kurdish human rights organizations were formed when government forces killed at least three hundred people. According to Human Rights Watch, Kurdish activists formed their own organizations because they thought the other Syrian organizations were not adequately addressing the rights of the Kurdish minority in Syria.

21. See, for example, the website of the Syrian Human Rights Committee, which provides, in addition to testimonials and more current reports, links to the prison memoirs of Heba Dabbagh and Muhammad Salim Hammad, among others. www.shrc.org/en/.

22. Nabil Sulayman, "Nahwa Adab al-Sujun" ("Toward Prison Literature"), *al-Mawqif al-Adabi* 1/2 (May/June 1973): 137–41.

23. For example, when Shahbandar and his colleagues faced a French military tribunal in 1922, he complained of the conditions of his incarceration. See Hashim ʿUthman, *al-Muhakamat al-Siyasiyya fi Suriya* (Beirut: Riad el-Reyyes, 2004), 40. For a description of prison experiences, see also Munir al-Rayyis's *al-Kitab al-Dhahabi li-l-Thawrat al-Wataniyya fi al-Mashriq al-ʿArabi* (Beirut: Dar al-Taliʿa wa-l-Nashr, 1969).

24. Samir Ruhi al-Faysal, for example, traces the connections between texts dealing with the colonial versus the postcolonial period and argues that literary texts describing imprisonment under colonial occupation but produced and published after independence are allegories of political oppression under the authority of postindependence regimes. See *al-Sijn al-Siyasi fi al-Riwayya al-ʿArabiyya* (Tripoli: Jurus Burus, 1994).

25. The story was also written as a play and published in 1963, but I have been unable to locate a copy of either the original short story collection or the dramatic version of the text.

26. While the Baʿth party constitution declares freedom of speech and assembly as one of its main principles, under the provisions of the State of Emergency Law officially implemented in 1963 and ended nominally in 2011, the state has the right to control publication, broadcasting, and the visual arts. See again Middle East Watch, *Syria Unmasked*.

27. Lisa Wedeen, *Ambiguities of Domination: Politics, Rhetoric, and Symbols in Contemporary Syria* (Chicago: Univ. of Chicago Press, 1999), 6, 88. Wedeen is well aware of "other forms of coercive control," which include incarceration and corporal punishment, and she also makes the point that despite "authoritarian circumstances," oppositional movements and uprisings occur, and intellectual life can flourish in spite of the dictates of the regime (27, 148). Given her focus on "as if" political practices by the Syrian state and its citizenry, Wedeen necessarily downplays the impact that the direct oppression of overt political opposition in Syria has on the perceived mass acceptance of the cult of Asad.

28. Wedeen, *Ambiguities*, 88. I have retained Wedeen's transliteration of the term. Its derivatives, *tanfiseh* and *tanfisiyeh* are also used in Syrian colloquial Arabic.

29. Ibid., 89.

30. Ibid., 90–92. miriam cooke also discusses *tanfis* as "commissioned criticism" in *Dissident Syria: Making Oppositional Arts Official* (Durham, NC: Duke Univ. Press, 2007). cooke critiques the possibilities of publication under the auspices of *tanfisiyeh* culture. I find Wedeen's emphasis on *tanfis* as "a locus of struggle" more productive, with the recognition that former political prisoners as authors are consciously aware of and engage with the system of censorship in Syria in order to publish or disseminate their works locally. See also Rebecca Joubin's critique of cooke's views on *tanfis* in *The Politics of Love: Sexuality, Gender, and Marriage in Syrian Television Drama* (Lanham, MD: Lexington, 2013).

31. For analyses of several plays depicting interrogation and torture, including those prior to 1970 thru 2013, especially works by Muhammad al-Maghut, see Edward Ziter, *Political Performance in Syria: From the Six Day War to the Syrian Uprising* (Hampshire, UK: Palgrave Macmillan, 2015), 204–39, Kindle.

32. Andrei Plesu, "Intellectual Life under Dictatorship," *Representations* 49 (Winter 1995): 61–71.

33. See cooke, *Dissident Syria* and "Ghassan al-Jaba'i: Prison Literature in Syria after 1980," *World Literature Today* 75, no. 2 (2001): 237–45, for a discussion of the history of the publication of al-Jaba'i's works. Many of al-Jaba'i's texts were written in and smuggled out of prison. Perhaps one of the reasons permission was granted for the publication of his work was that he agreed to delete the dates and place of writing from the text. Accordingly, the lack of specific reference to time and place in his works on prison made the possibility of publication greater.

34. Human Rights Watch, "Torture Archipelago: Arbitrary Arrests, Torture, and Enforced Disappearances in Syria's Underground Prisons since March 2011," Human Rights Watch, July 3, 2012, accessed March 27, 2019, www.hrw.org/report/2012/07/03/torture-archipelago/arbitrary-arrests-torture-and-enforced-disappearances-syrias. The report cited identifies at least twenty-seven known interrogation branches across the country, and several other smaller intelligence services beyond the four main ones exist to police political dissent. My intention here is not to provide a full accounting of conditions in or a history of Syria's entire prison system. This is not only due to space limitations but also the lack of access to available archival sources. Rather, throughout the book I explore individual detainees' experiences of conditions in Syrian prisons as represented in literary texts.

35. For an overview of prison conditions in Syria in the 1980s and early 1990s, see especially chapter 5 of Middle East Watch, *Syria Unmasked*. For a more recent report on conditions in interrogation branches, see Human Rights Watch, "Torture Archipelago."

36. See Amnesty International, "Human Slaughterhouse."

37. My thanks to Mehran Kamrava for pointing out the need to clarify this in the introduction.

38. Other examples include an early collection of prison writings from the time of Socrates to that of Mohandas K. Gandhi: Isidore Abramowitz's *The Great Prisoners: The First Anthology of Literature Written in Prison* (New York: E. P. Dutton, 1946); H. Bruce Franklin's anthology *Prison Writing in 20th-Century America* (New York: Penguin, 1998); and the anthology edited by Bell Gale Chevigny and published by the PEN American Center, *Doing Time: 25 Years of Prison Writing* (New York: Arcade, 1999). For an international anthology of women's prison writings, see *Wall Tappings: An International Anthology of Women's Prison Writings, 200 to the Present*, ed. Judith A. Scheffler (New York: Feminist Press, 2002). See also Quentin Miller's edited collection *Prose and Cons: Essays on Prison Literature in the United States* (Jefferson, NC: McFarland, 2005). For a study of the relationship between political prison, subversive resistance, and women's writings from Northern Ireland, South Africa, Egypt, Palestine/Israel, El Salvador, and the United States, see Barbara Harlow's *Barred: Women, Writing, and Political Detention* (Hanover, CT: Wesleyan Univ. Press, 1992). For a literary analysis of Russian prison literature, see Elizabeth Ann Cole's dissertation, "Towards a Poetics of Russian Prison Literature: Writings on Prison by Dostoevsky, Chekhov, and Solzhenitsyn" (PhD diss.,

Yale Univ., 1991). For a comparative study of prison literature in the United States and South Africa, see Richard Edward Lee's dissertation "Guards, Prisoners, and Textuality: A Study of South African and American Twentieth-Century Prison Narratives" (PhD diss., Rutgers Univ., 2000). For a study of the emergence of prison narratives in early modern England, see Ruth Ahnert's *The Rise of Prison Literature in the Sixteenth Century* (Cambridge, UK: Cambridge Univ. Press, 2017). For a survey of modern French writings on the experience of imprisonment, see Andrew Sobanet's *Jail Sentences: Representing Prison in Twentieth-Century French Fiction* (Lincoln: Univ. of Nebraska Press, 2008). Allen Feldman's seminal *Formations of Violence: The Narrative of the Body and Political Terror in Northern Ireland* (1991) deals extensively with the prison experiences of Republican paramilitary fighters.

39. cooke's *Dissident Syria* includes a chapter on Syrian prison literature that summarizes a few key texts as forms of "prison consciousness," particularly the short stories of Ibrahim Samu'il and Ghassan al-Jaba'i. Part of her study is an ethnographic account of her interactions with Syrian writers and intellectuals in the 1990s. Her 2011 article "The Cell Story" offers a survey of texts produced after 2000, including Mustafa Khalifa's *Al-Qawqa'a* (*The Shell*). In *"Anticipating" the 2011 Arab Uprisings*, Rita Sakr examines literary works in Egypt, Libya, and Syria and argues that in Syria specifically, prison literature was an important part of shaping the political and cultural geography that led to the uprising. However, she focuses only on three novels published after 2005, effectively discounting prison literature produced prior to that date, as well as poetry, plays, and short stories—works that, I would argue, were more widely circulated and read. Though focused on drama rather than the genre of prison literature, Edward Ziter's *Political Performance in Syria* includes a chapter with analysis of the representation of torture, particularly in the plays of Muhammad al-Maghut.

40. See, for example, Cole, "Towards a Poetics of Russian Prison Literature."

41. For an examination of the shift toward literary experimentalism in Arabic literature since the 1960s, see Sabry Hafez, "The Transformation of Reality and the Arabic Novel's Aesthetic Response," *Bulletin of the School of Oriental and African Studies* 57 (1994): 93–112; Walid Hamarneh, "Some Narrators and Narrative Modes in the Contemporary Arabic Novel," in *The Arabic Novel since 1950: Critical Essays, Interviews, and Bibliography*, ed. Issa J. Boullata (Cambridge, UK: Dar Mahjar, 1994), 205–36; Roger Allen, *The Arabic Novel: An Historical and Critical Introduction* (Syracuse, NY: Syracuse Univ. Press, 1995); and Stefan G. Meyer, *The Experimental Arabic Novel: Postcolonial Literary Modernism in the Levant* (Albany: State Univ. of New York Press, 2001).

42. Roger Allen, *An Introduction to Arabic Literature* (Cambridge, UK: Cambridge Univ. Press, 2000), 90. For more detailed analyses of the concept of commitment in Arabic literature and art, see the introduction and essays in Friederike Pannewick and Georges Khalil, eds., *Commitment and Beyond: Reflections on/of the Political in Arabic Literature since the 1940s* (Wiesbaden: Dr. Ludwig Reichert Verlag, 2015).

43. Meyer, *Experimental Arabic Novel*, 97–98.

44. Ibid., 98.

45. To what extent classical social realism remained the dominant mode of literary style in Syria under the time period in question is contestable given that several of the authors Meyer cites as representing the vanguard of social realism, such as Hanna Mina and Hani al-Rahib, take a sharp turn away from social realism in their later works.

46. It is in this sense that parts of Theodor Adorno's critique of commitment literature is relevant to the Syrian case. For Adorno, "commitment . . . even if politically intended remains politically ambiguous as long as it does not reduce itself to propaganda," and such a reduction to the "obliging shape" of propaganda merely "mocks any commitment on the part of the subject." See Theodor W. Adorno, *Notes to Literature*, vol. 2, trans. Shierry Weber Nicholsen (New York: Columbia Univ. Press, 1992), 77.

47. For an examination of the shift away from commitment literature and social realism in Syria literary production after 1967, see Alexa Firat, "Post-67 Discourse and the Syrian Novel: The Construction of an Autonomous Literary Field" (PhD diss., Univ. of Pennsylvania, 2010).

48. Throughout my study, I draw inspiration from works such as Barbara Harlow's *Barred*, Schaffer and Smith's *Human Rights and Narrated Lives*, Joseph Slaughter's *Human Rights, Inc.: The World Novel, Narrative Form, and International Law* (New York: Fordham Univ. Press, 2007); Lynn Hunt's *The Invention of Human Rights: A History* (New York: W. W. Norton, 2007); Elizabeth Swanson Goldberg and Alexandra Schultheis Moore's *Theoretical Perspectives on Literature and Human Rights*, (New York: Routledge, 2012), Kindle; Elizabeth S. Anker's *Fictions of Dignity: Embodying Human Rights and World Literature* (Ithaca, NY: Cornell Univ. Press, 2012); Sophia A. McClennan's and Alexandra Schultheis Moore's *The Routledge Companion to Literature and Human Rights* (Abingdon, UK: Routledge, 2016); and James Dawes's *The Novel of Human Rights* (Cambridge, MA: Harvard Univ. Press, 2018), Kindle.

49. An important exception, and one that was published prior to September 11, 2001, is Harlow's *Barred*. Additionally, Anker analyzes Nawal al-Sa'dawi's *A Woman At Point Zero* (Imra'a 'ind Nuqtat al-Sifr) in *Fictions of Dignity*. Another notable recent text is McClennan and Moore's *Routledge Companion to Literature and Human Rights*, which includes essays on Palestinian and Israeli literature, as well as on the poetry of Guantanamo Bay detainees, including some in Arabic. For an examination of Ghassan Kanafani's classic *Men in the Sun* (Rijal fi al-Shams, 1963) as a human rights narrative, see Eleni Coundouriotis, "In Flight: The Refugee Experience and Human Rights Narrative," in *The Routledge Companion to Literature and Human Rights*, ed. Sophia A. McClennan and Alexandra Schultheis Moore, (Abingdon, UK: Routledge, 2016), 78–85, Kindle. For a brief discussion of cynical views of human rights and Palestinian and Israeli literature, see Anna Bernard, "States of Cynicism: Literature and Human Rights in Israel/Palestine," in *The Routledge Companion to Literature and Human Rights*, ed.

Sophia A. McClennan and Alexandra Schultheis Moore (Abingdon, UK: Routledge, 2016), 373–79, Kindle. For a discussion of poems written by Guantanamo detainees, see Marc D. Falkoff, "'Where Is the World to Save Us from Torture': The Poets of Guantanamo Bay," in *The Routledge Companion to Literature and Human Rights*, ed. Sophia A. McClennan and Alexandra Schultheis Moore (Abingdon, UK: Routledge, 2016), 351–60, Kindle.

50. The focus in this book is not on the debates about the universal nature of human rights as inaugurated by the Universal Declaration of Human Rights in 1948. Regardless of the numerous, valid, and accurate critiques of the Eurocentrism of the international human rights regime and the use of human rights as a form of moral imperialism, the language of human rights is consistently deployed as a form of political opposition in various contexts around the world, including in the Middle East, the Arab World, and Syria. As Mark Philip Bradley and Patrice Petro point out in their discussion of issues of representation in human rights claims, a "new human rights politics," along with "a circulation of norms, networks, and representations that give it shape and form," are a central part of the phenomenon of globalization. See their introduction in Bradley and Petro, eds., *Truth Claims: Representation and Human Rights* (New Brunswick, NJ: Rutgers Univ. Press, 2002), 1. Rights activists and defenders in the non-West or global South are well aware of the links between the international human rights regime and forms of imperialism, as well as the issue of Eurocentrism in a particularly privileged origin story of human rights. They know all too well the cynical and selective use and manipulation of human rights to serve the interests of the US and other "Western" states. Nevertheless, activists and defenders still often work within and through human rights institutions, local and international, and deploy the lexicon of international human rights as one tool among many in the arsenal in their struggles against forms of oppression and their confrontations with injustice. Many of the authors whose literary works are analyzed in this study have been or are actively involved in civil society, women's rights, and human rights movements in Syria, and they explicitly evoke the concept and language of human rights in their writings beyond those about prison. For a collection of essays critiquing the modern deployment of human rights as cultural, moral, and political imperialism, see Berta Esperanza Hernández-Truyol, ed. *Moral Imperialism: A Critical Anthology* (New York: New York Univ. Press, 2002). For an overview of the history of the debates about human rights, see Michael Freeman, *Human Rights*; Jack Donnelly, *Universal Human Rights*; and Micheline R. Ishay, *The History of Human Rights: From Ancient Times to the Globalization Era* (Berkeley: Univ. of California Press, 2004). For compelling and thorough critiques of the history, development, and concept of human rights see Costas Douzinas, *The End of Human Rights* (Oxford, UK: Hart, 2000); Baxi, *Future of Human Rights*; Makau Mutua, *Human Rights: A Political and Cultural Critique* (Philadelphia: Univ. of Pennsylvania Press, 2002), Kindle; Costas Douzinas, *Human Rights and Empire: The Political Philosophy of Cosmopolitanism* (Abingdon, UK: Routledge, 2007); and Stephen Hopgood, *The*

End-Times of Human Rights, (Ithaca, NY: Cornell Univ. Press, 2015), Kindle. For a compelling analysis of cynical views of human rights institutions and movements in Palestine, see Lori Allen, *The Rise and Fall of Human Rights: Cynicism and Politics in Occupied Palestine* (Stanford, CA: Stanford Univ. Press, 2013).

51. Elizabeth Swanson Goldberg and Alexandra Schultheis Moore, "Introduction: Human Rights and Literature: The Development of an Interdiscipline," in *Theoretical Perspectives on Human Rights and Literature*, ed. Elizabeth Swanson Goldberg and Alexandra Schultheis Moore (New York: Routledge, 2012), Kindle.

52. McClennan and Moore, "Introduction," 1. For more on the link between storytelling and human rights activism, see James Dawes, *That the World May Know: Bearing Witness to Atrocity* (Cambridge, MA: Harvard Univ. Press, 2007), Kindle.

53. Schaffer and Smith, *Human Rights*, 3.

54. Slaughter, "Question of Narration," 407.

55. McClennan and Moore, "Introduction," 2.

56. Goldberg and Moore, "Introduction," 2.

57. Ibid., 3.

58. McClennan and Moore, "Introduction," 3, 8.

59. Hopgood, *End-Times of Human Rights*, viii.

60. Ibid, 60.

61. Goldberg and Moore, "Introduction," 1.

1. Prison Literature, Genre, and Truth Effects

1. Rosa Yaseen Hasan, *Nighatif: Min Dhakira al-Mu'taqalat al-Surriyat* (*Negative: From the Memory of Female Syrian Detainees*), (Cairo: Markaz al-Qahira li Dirasat Huquq al-Insan, 2008), 7.

2. Ibid., 8.

3. Ibid.

4. James Dawes, *The Novel of Human Rights* (Cambridge, MA: Harvard Univ. Press, 2018), Kindle.

5. Hasan, *Nighatif* (*Negative*), 14.

6. See Rosa Yaseen Hasan, "Adab al-Sujun fi Suriya: Masirat Alf Mil," al-Hiwar al-Mutamaddin, April 7, 2006, www.m.ahewar.org/s.asp?aid=69138&r=0, accessed November 1, 2018.

For articles that mention *Negative* as a work of prison literature, see, for example, Muhammad Sharif, "Adab al-Sujun fi Suriya: al-Kitaba Did al-Nisiyan," *Swissinfo*, May 4, 2014, www.swissinfo.ch/ara/-الكتابة-ضد--أو--سوريا-في--السجون--أدب--_-العربية-الثقافات-رواق-في--ندوة 38498508/-سيان-الن, accessed November 1, 2018.

7. Yassin al-Haj Saleh, *Bi-l-Khalas Ya Shabab! Sittin 'Aman fi al-Sujun al-Suriyya* (*At Last, Boys! Sixteen Years in Syrian Prisons*) (Beirut: Dar al-Saqi, 2012), 9. The first part

of the title can also be translated as "Salvation, Boys!" Excerpts reprinted with permission of Yassin al-Haj Saleh.

8. Al-Haj Saleh, *Bi-l-Khalas Ya Shabab!* (*At Last, Boys!*), 9.

9. Ibid.

10. Ibid., 10. In an interview included in the collection, al-Haj Saleh draws a distinction between his writings and literature; on the term *literature* itself he remarks: "I suppose prison literature is literature, the short story or novel, especially, that is written about prison, whether the writers themselves experience prison or not" (208).

11. Throughout this study, I use the term *prison literature* as opposed to *prison writing* because the term *adab al-sijn* or *adab al-sujūn* (literally the literature of prison or the literature of prisons) is much more frequently used than *prison writing* (*kitābat al-sijn*).

12. Dylan Rodríquez, "Against the Discipline of 'Prison Writing': Toward a Theoretical Conception of Contemporary Radical Prison Praxis," *Genre* 35 (Fall/Winter 2002): 409. Rodríguez uses the term *prison writing* as a label for the written cultural production, regardless of content or form, of the detainee, as opposed to the term *prison literature*.

13. I am not arguing that writings produced by US-based prisoners are not produced in an environment of dissent or that members of organized oppositional, dissident movements in the US have not produced prison writings. Rather, my point is that the concept of prison literature in the cultural field in the Arab context is generated specifically out of the experience of political detention—the imprisonment of opponents of authoritarian states for their perceived oppositional activities. Although I acknowledge that the terms *political detention* and *political prisoner* are problematic ones because all prisoners are political, I use the term here because the distinction is made in the writings of Syrian detainees. For a discussion of the terms *political prisoner* and *prison*, see the introduction of Dylan Rodríguez, *Forced Passages: Imprisoned Radical Intellectuals and the U.S. Prison Regime* (Minneapolis: Univ. of Minnesota Press, 2006).

14. Literary critics and scholars have used various designations—prison literature, prison writings, prison narratives—to describe texts related to the experience of detention. In his study of American prison literature, for example, H. Bruce Franklin notes: "My subject is literature created by those members of the oppressed classes who have become artists with words through their experience of being defined by the state as criminals. All the works studied in this book were produced by 'criminals' who spent time physically incarcerated for their actions or beliefs or social status." H. Bruce Franklin, *Prison Literature in America: The Victim as Criminal and Artist* (New York: Oxford Univ. Press, 1989), xxxi. In their study of writings from or about Chinese prisons, Philip F. Williams and Yenna Wu include four different categories of texts: nonfictional writings (including memoirs, diaries, collections of letters, autobiographies, and testimonials written by former People's Republic of China prison inmates), nonfictional reportage (including journalistic writings and interviews), fictional works by former prison inmates,

and fiction or drama set in prison camps but written by writers who have not been imprisoned. Philip F. Williams and Yenna Wu, *The Great Well of Confinement: The Chinese Prison Camp through Contemporary Fiction and Reportage* (Berkeley: Univ. of California Press, 2004), 155–57.

15. John Frow, *Genre* (London: Routledge, 2005), 52.

16. Ibid., 125.

17. Ibid., 53.

18. For an example of the comparison of al-Haj Saleh to Václav Havel, see Kaelen Wilson-Goldie, "Price of Freedom," *Artforum*, January 15, 2015, www.artforum.com/film/-49756, accessed December 10, 2018.

19. In a few articles as well her book *Dissident Syria*, miriam cooke attempts to trace the emergence of what she calls "prison consciousness" in Arabic literature in general and in the works of two Syrian writers, Ghassan al-Jaba'i and Ibrahim Samu'il, in particular. cooke, like other critics, does not elaborate on an exact definition of *prison literature*; for her, prison literature consists of those texts that demonstrate what she terms "prison consciousness." See miriam cooke, "Ghassan al-Jaba'i: Prison Literature in Syria after 1980," *World Literature Today* 75, no. 2 (2001): 237–45. Whether she is addressing Arabic literature in general or the works of Samu'il and al-Jaba'i in particular, her discussion is restricted to texts, both fictional and nonfictional, that have been written by authors who have been imprisoned. cooke observes: "Prison-consciousness is the best way to describe the awareness of the significance but also the danger inherent in the literary project which may be the cause or outcome of the prison experience. In authoritarian systems, writers and readers share in the realization of the power and danger of the written word. Prison is almost a condition for becoming a public intellectual" (cooke, "Ghassan al-Jaba'i," 238).

20. Jacques Derrida, "The Law of Genre," trans. Avital Ronnell, *Critical Inquiry* 7, no. 1 (1980): 56.

21. Ibid., 57.

22. Tzvetan Todorov, *Genres in Discourse* (Cambridge, UK: Cambridge Univ. Press, 1990), 19–20.

23. M. M. Bakhtin and P. N. Medvedev, *The Formal Method in Literary Scholarship*, trans. Albert Wehrle (Baltimore: John Hopkins Univ. Press, 1991), 137. See also M. M. Bakhtin, *Speech Genres and Other Late Essays* (Austin: Univ. of Texas Press, 1986).

24. M. M. Bakhtin, *Speech Genres*, 60.

25. Frow, *Genre*, 14.

26. Ibid., 25.

27. Ibid., 26.

28. Ibid.

29. Ibid., 19.

30. Ibid., 2.

31. I am borrowing the term *truth claims* from Mark Philip Bradley and Patrice Petro. Although the term is used in the title of their edited collection, they do not actually define the term in their introduction; nor is it defined by the contributors to the volume. See Mark Philip Bradley and Patrice Petro, eds., *Truth Claims: Representation and Human Rights* (New Brunswick, NJ: Rutgers Univ. Press), 2002. I use the term here with the acknowledgment that its meaning can be interpreted in a variety of ways. These meanings include, within human rights regimes, the idea of a legal claim made by both victims of human rights abuses and the organizations that represent victims and survivors.

32. Frow, *Genre*, 25.

33. Sophia A. McClennan and Alexandra Schultheis Moore, "Introduction: Aporia and Affirmative Critique: Mapping the Landscape of Literary Approaches to Human Rights," in *The Routledge Companion to Literature and Human Rights*, ed. Sophia A. McClennan and Alexandra Schultheis Moore (New York: Routledge, 2016), 14.

34. As Goldberg and Moore note, "Prioritization of factual veracity occurs within the epistemological tenets of individualist western notions, contexts, and applications of truth value. Indeed, some of the most important recent rights work has occurred in legal, psychoanalytic, and literary testimonial forums in which such limits to the forms and contexts of legitimated 'truth-telling,' including truth and reconciliation commissions, have been challenged." See Elizabeth Swanson Goldberg and Alexandra Shultheis Moore, "Introduction: Human Rights and Literature: The Development of an Interdiscipline," in *Theoretical Perspectives on Human Rights and Literature*, ed. Elizabeth Swanson Goldberg and Alexandra Shultheis Moore (New York: Routledge, 2012), 8.

35. See Barbara Harlow, *Barred: Women, Writing, and Political Detention* (Hanover, CT: Wesleyan Univ. Press, 1992), and Joseph Slaughter *Human Rights, Inc.: The World Novel, Narrative Form, and International Law* (New York: Fordham Univ. Press, 2007), for discussion of the ways in which human rights discourse and international human rights law have been shaped by particular generic conventions and genres. As Kay Schaffer and Sidonie Smith remind us, the human rights regime can only "offer an imperfect response to the problem of human suffering in the world. It reifies the identities of 'victim' and 'perpetrator.' It stages the plurality of voices but controls the terms of their witnessing. It attempts to manage the chaotic forces of affect, thereby directing political awareness into privatized emotional response. It depends on the politics of shame. It reproduces a circuit of demand in which the powerful and relatively privileged retain the right to confer or refuse recognition" (Kay Schaffer and Sidonie Smith, *Human Rights and Narrative Lives: The Ethics of Recognition* [New York: Palgrave Macmillan, 2004], 232).

36. Frow, *Genre*, 19.

37. Rosalie Colie, *The Resources of Kind: Genre Theory in the Renaissance* (Berkeley: Univ. of California Press, 1973), as quoted in Frow, *Genre*, 19.

38. Frow, *Genre*, 19, emphasis in original.

39. My contention here is not, of course, that realist genres do provide transparent truth telling. Rather, they have the appearance of being so or are regarded as such by their multiple audiences.

40. Schaffer and Smith, *Human Rights*, 3.

41. Frow, *Genre*, 41.

42. Schaffer and Smith, *Human Rights*, 37.

43. See chapter 4 for a discussion of Bayraqdar's case.

44. Nabil Sulayman, "Nahwa Adab al-Sujun" ("Toward Prison Literature"), *al-Mawqif al-Adabi* 1/2 (May/June 1973): 137–41. Sulayman's essay contains the earliest mention of the term I have located in my research after surveying several major literary journals of the 1950s, 1960s, and 1970s. The essay is primarily a summary and critique of Iraqi writer Fadil al-'Azzawi's *al-Qal'a al-Khamisa*, but Sulayman also notes that several months earlier, in January 1973, the Egyptian literary magazine *al-Hilal* had published an edition titled "Littérateurs behind Bars" (Udaba' wara' al-Qudban), which mostly focused on writers from the classical and medieval periods who were imprisoned.

45. Nazih Abu Nidal, *Adab al-Sujūn* (*Prison Literature*), (Beirut: Dar al-Hadatha, 1981), 20. A number of studies and anthologies of prison literature were published in the 1980s and 1990s after Abu Nidal's book; analyses that focus on the themes of imprisonment and captivity in classical and early modern Arabic literature, particularly poetry, far outnumber the quantity of criticism produced on more contemporary writings. These include: Hasan Na'isa, *Shu'ara' wara'a al-Qudban* (*Poets behind Bars*) (Beirut: Dar al-Haqa'iq, 1986), an anthology of poetry on the themes of imprisonment and exile, as well as brief biographical sketches of poets that range from Abu Firas al-Hamadani to Ibn Zaydun to al-Bayyati; Wadih al-Samad, *al-Sujun wa 'Athruha fi al-Adab al-'Arabi* (*Prisons and Their Influence on Arabic Literature*) (Beirut: al-Mu'assasa al-Jami'iyya li-l-Dirasat wa-l-Nashr wa al-Tawzi', 1995), a survey of the theme and descriptions of prison in Arabic literature, primarily poetry, from the Jahiliyya period to the Umayyad period; Ahmad Mukhtar al-Bizra, *al-'Asr wa-l-Sijn fi al-Shi'r al-'Arabi* (*Captivity and Prison in Arabic Poetry*) (Damascus: Mu'assasat 'Ulum al-Quran, 1985), a survey of prison poetry from the Jahiliyya through the Abbasid period. Both al-Samad and al-Bizra begin their examinations of classical Arabic prison poetry with a discussion of the development of prisons and incarceration in both the pre-Islamic and early Islamic historical periods, but even more importantly, both argue that one of the most important elements of classical prison poetry is its truthfulness or believability (*ṣidq*), a much discussed theme in classical Arabic rhetoric. The notion that well-written prison poetry is truthful marks the way in which both the poetry and the poets' prison experiences are discussed and allows the critic to interpret and catalogue such poetic texts as social, psychological, and political documentation. Additionally, Sabry Hafez makes the debatable point that Arabic literature is unique in having a "distinct literary genre known as the 'prison novel,'"

which came into existence due to the fact that many writers have themselves faced arrest, imprisonment, and torture by authorities. See Sabry Hafez, "Torture, Imprisonment, and Political Assassination in the Arab Novel," *al-Jadid* 8, no. 38 (2002), www.aljadid.com /features/0838hafez.html, accessed September 8, 2008.

46. For another example, see Samir Ruhi al-Faysal, *al-Sijn al-Siyasi fi al-Riwayya al-'Arabiyya* (*Political Prison in the Arabic Novel*) Tripoli: Jurus Burus, 1994. Similarly, in al-Faysal's book, one finds a detailed discussion of phases of arrest and imprisonment and forms of torture represented in the novels under discussion rather than an examination of the aesthetic implications of divergent narrative strategies used by authors. This is also replicated in Abdel-Qader Abou Shariefeh, "The Prison in the Contemporary Arabic Novel" (PhD diss., Univ. of Michigan, 1983).

47. McClennan and Moore, "Introduction," 14.

48. Abu Nidal, *Adab al-Sujun*, 117.

49. Ibid., 117–18.

50. Frederic Jameson, *The Political Unconscious: Narrative as a Socially Symbolic Act* (Ithaca, NY: Cornell Univ. Press, 1981), 141.

51. *That Smell* is also discussed in chapter 6 with respect to its metafictional tendencies.

52. Sabry Hafez, "The Transformation of Reality and the Arabic Novel's Aesthetic Response," *Bulletin of the School of Oriental and African Studies* 57 (1994): 93–112.

53. Samia Mehrez, *Egyptian Writers between Fiction and History* (Cairo: American Univ. in Cairo Press, 1994).

54. Jameson, *Political Unconscious*, 230.

55. Ibid., 231.

56. Harlow, *Barred*, xii.

57. Gerard Genette, *Paratexts: Thresholds of Interpretation* (New York: Cambridge Univ. Press, 1997), 5.

58. Hasan, *Nighatif* (*Negative*), 15.

59. Ibid., 20.

60. Genette, *Paratexts*, 332.

61. See, for example, Middle East Watch, *Syria Unmasked: The Suppression of Human Rights by the Asad Regime* (New Haven, CT: Yale Univ. Press, 1991). More recent reports on human rights abuses in Syria have a special focus on women. See, for example, Human Rights Watch, "Syria: Detention and Abuse of Female Activists," Human Rights Watch, June 24, 2013, www.hrw.org/news/2013/06/24/syria-detention-and-abuse-female-activists, accessed December 1, 2017.

62. Julie Kristeva, "World, Dialogue, and Novel," in *The Kristeva Reader*, ed. Toril Moi (New York: Columbia Univ. Press, 1986), 34–62.

63. Hasan, *Nighatif* (*Negative*), 13.

64. Ibid.

2. Vulnerability, Sentimentality, and the Politics of Recognition

1. For a journalist's description of the events in Dar'a in March 2011, including the detention of the children, see Ghassan Sa'ud, "Dar'a Madinat al-Ashbah: Rihla fi Thawra Lam Tulid Ba'd," *al-Akhbar*, March 25, 2011, www.al-akhbar.com/node/7549/, accessed April 30, 2016. See also Paul Gabriel Hilu Pinto, "Syria," in *Dispatches from the Arab Spring: Understanding the New Middle East*, ed. Paul Amar and Vijay Prashad (Minneapolis: Univ. of Minnesota Press, 2013), Kindle. For more on the protests leading up to the March 2011 events in Dar'a, see Robin Yassin-Kassab and Leila al-Shami, *Burning Country: Syrians in Revolution and War* (London: Pluto, 2016), Kindle.

2. Faraj Bayraqdar, "'Awal Thawra fi al-Tarikh Yaqdahu Shararataha al-Atfal," al-Hiwar al-Mutamaddin, June 10, 2011, www.ahewar.org/debat/show.art.asp?aid=262727, accessed April 30, 2016. For examples of poems dedicated to Hamza al-Khatib, see selections on the website of the Rabitat Kuttab al-Thawra al-Suriyya, syrianrevolution writers.blogspot.com/2012/05/blog-post_7359.html/, accessed April 30, 2016; and You-Tube videos such as "Qasidat Hamza al-Khatib," June 2, 2011, www.youtube.com/watch ?v=_Grq1rIGw3Y/. Multiple testimonials about and from the children of Dar'a can also be viewed on YouTube. See, for example: "Ahad al-Atfal Alladhina Katabu Awla Shi'arat al-Hurriyya 'ala Jidran al-Madrasa fi Dar'a," March 18, 2014, www.youtube.com/watch ?v=hlN2mAXHLYM/, and "15 Tilmidh Shabab Indila' al-Thawra al-Suriyya Haqiqa La Tusdiq," January 30, 2012, www.youtube.com/watch?v=STikjAh0XXs.

3. Mudawwana Muwatina Suriyya, May 29, 2011, syrians4change.wordpress.com /حتى-السوري-النظام-عذبه-طفل-الخطيب-حمزة/, accessed April 30, 2016. /2011/05/29/

4. Rita Sakr, *"Anticipating" the 2011 Arab Uprisings: Revolutionary Literatures and Political Geographies* (New York: Palgrave Macmillan, 2013), Kindle.

5. I am mindful of the issues involved in using the term *sentimental education*. It is not my intention to evoke the term as formulated by Richard Rorty in "Human Rights, Rationality, and Sentimentality," in *The Politics of Human Rights*, ed. Obrad Savic (London: Verso, 2002), 67–83. Rather, I'm drawing on the work of Margaret Cohen, including *The Sentimental Education of the Novel* (Princeton, NJ: Princeton Univ. Press, 2002); Joseph Slaughter, *Human Rights, Inc.: The World Novel, Narrative Form, and International Law* (New York: Fordham Univ. Press, 2007); and Lynn Hunt, *The Invention of Human Rights: A History* (New York: W. W. Norton, 2007). Slaughter has critiqued Rorty's vision of sentimental identification and sentimental education; he highlights the fact that in Rorty's vision the "sentimental model of reading has a tendency to become a patronizing humanitarianism that is enabled by and subsists on socioeconomic and political disparities." Slaughter, *Human Rights*, 325; see also 324–28; Joseph Slaughter, "Humanitarian Reading," in *Humanitarianism and Suffering: The Mobilization of Empathy*, ed. Richard Ashby Wilson and Richard D. Brown (Cambridge, UK: Cambridge Univ. Press, 2009), 88–107. For more critiques of Rorty's positions on human rights and sentimentality, see

Upendra Baxi, *The Future of Human Rights* (New Delhi: Oxford Univ. Press, 2002); Bruce Robbins, "Sad Stories in the International Public Sphere: Richard Rorty on Culture and Human Rights," *Public Culture* 9 (1997): 209–32; and Costas Douzinas, *Human Rights and Empire: The Political Philosophy of Cosmopolitanism* (Abingdon, UK: Routledge, 2007), 72–73, 79, 84.

6. For an examination of Samuil's and other authors' short stories as prison portraiture and through the lens of theorizations of the genre of short fiction, see chapter 2 of Shareah Taleghani, "The Cocoons of Language, The Betrayals of Silence" (PhD diss., New York Univ., 2009).

7. Ibrahim Samu'il, *Ra'ihat al-Khatw al-Thaqil* (*The Stench of the Heavy Step*) (Damascus: Dar al-Jundi, 1990), 34.

8. Ibid., 17.

9. Ibid., 18.

10. Margaret Cohen, "Sentimental Communities," in *The Literary Channel: The Inter-National Invention of the Novel*, ed. Margaret Cohen and Carolyn Dever (Princeton, NJ: Princeton Univ. Press, 2001), 108. Cohen uses the term *spectacle* rather than *scene*. I have deliberately elided the term *spectacle* here because Samu'il's and al-Jaba'i's narratives do not necessarily emit excessive or overwrought sentiment or depict the spectacular; rather, both authors focus on what I would describe as scenes of everyday, sometimes muted, suffering.

11. Lauren Berlant, "The Subject of True Feeling: Pain, Privacy, and Politics," in *Cultural Pluralism, Identity Politics, and the Law*, ed. Austin Serat and Thomas R. Kearns (Ann Arbor: Univ. of Michigan Press, 1999), 53.

12. Ibid.

13. Ibid., 54.

14. Lauren Berlant, "Poor Eliza," *American Literature* 70, no. 3 (1998): 641. As Kathleen Woodward notes, one of Berlant's key concerns is that "the experience of being moved by these sentimental scenes of suffering, whose ostensible purpose is to awaken us to redress injustice" can work, instead, "to return us to a private world far removed from the public sphere," which leads to passivity rather than action. Kathleen Woodward, "Calculating Compassion," in *Compassion: The Cultural Politics of an Emotion*, ed. Lauren Berlant (New York: Routledge, 2004), 59–86.

15. Berlant, "Poor Eliza," 655.

16. Ibid., 655–56.

17. Terence Cave, *Recognitions: A Study in Poetics* (Oxford: Clarendon, 2002).

18. Ibid., 2.

19. Ibid., 2, 33.

20. As Joseph Slaughter has noted, in drafting the UDHR's preamble, the United Nations "deduces the need for a speech act of recognition that identifies human rights as inherent and inalienable, and it declares *this* declaration to be *that* speech act of common

recognition and understanding." Slaughter, *Human Rights, Inc.*, 64, emphasis in the original.

21. In her critique of human rights, Hannah Arendt observes that despite the "best intentions" of international human rights declarations, a "sphere that is above the nation does not exist." Hannah Arendt, *The Origins of Totalitarianism* (New York: Houghton Mifflin Harcourt, 1994), 298, Kindle. Thus the implementation and enforcement of international human rights law becomes problematic, if not impossible, in the face of the self-interests of sovereign nation-states. For additional discussion of the nation-state as both principle violator and essential protector of human rights, see Jack Donnelly, *Universal Human Rights in Theory and Practice* (Ithaca, NY: Cornell Univ. Press, 2003), 34–37. See also Costas Douzinas, *Human Rights*.

22. Bryan S. Turner, *Vulnerability and Human Rights* (University Park, PA: Penn State Univ. Press, 2006), Kindle.

23. Ibid., 46.

24. Ibid., 58.

25. Judith Butler, *Precarious Life: The Powers of Mourning and Violence* (London: Verso, 2004), 43.

26. Ibid.

27. Likewise, in describing the ways in which an "ethics of recognition" functions in human rights discourse, Kay Schaffer and Sidonie Smith observe: "Whether or not storytelling in the field of human rights results in the extension of human justice, dignity, and freedom depends on the willingness of those addressed to hear the stories and take responsibility for the recognition of others and claims. In the transits of multi-vectored space there are many flows, but also many detours, undercurrents, dams and blockages." Kay Schaffer and Sidonie Smith, *Human Rights and Narrated Lives: The Ethics of Recognition* (New York: Palgrave Macmillan, 2004), 5.

28. In her critiques of the relationship between conceptions of humanity and human rights, Samera Esmeir has cogently argued that human rights law "transforms humanity into a juridical status, which precedes, rather than follows or describes, all humans" (1544). This form of what she calls "juridical humanity" conflates the human with a requisite legal status and transforms "humanity into a status conferred by the proactive work of the law" that leads to the "renaming of human rights violations as practices of dehumanization." But for Esmeir, juridical humanity is based on the falty assumption that "humanity can be taken away or given back." It erases alternative conceptions of humanity not tied to the law, and "shares affinities with colonial rationalities" (1545). Samera Esmeir, "On Making Dehumanization Possible," *PMLA* 121, no. 5 (2006): 1544–51.

29. As Barbara Harlow has noted, "recognition scenes" in prison writings usually counter any form of narrative or ideological restoration or closure. Barbara Harlow, *Barred: Women, Writing, and Political Detention* (Hanover, CT: Wesleyan Univ. Press, 1992), 72–73.

30. Hans Robert Jauss, "The Identity of the Poetic Text in the Changing Horizon of Understanding," in *Reception Study: From Literary Theory to Cultural Studies*, ed. James L. Machor and Philip Goldstein (New York: Routledge, 2001), 7–28.

31. Ibid., 7.

32. Lynn Hunt, *Inventing Human Rights: A History* (New York: W. W. Norton, 2007), 61.

33. James Dawes, *The Novel of Human Rights* (Cambridge, MA: Harvard Univ. Press, 2018), Kindle.

34. Jauss, "Identity," 9.

35. Ghassan Jaba'i, *Asabi' al-Mawz (Banana Fingers)* (Damascus: Wizarat al-Thaqafa, 1994); Angus Fletcher, *Allegory: The Theory of a Symbolic Mode* (Ithaca, NY: Cornell Univ. Press, 1970), 2. Fletcher also notes that literary analysis of allegory must always be aware of the "political overtones" rooted in the Greek understanding of the term because "censorship may produce devious ways of speaking," a point that is highly relevant to interpreting texts about political detention, such as al-Jaba'i's short stories and other works of Syrian prison literature. Fletcher also considers irony a form of "condensed allegory." Fletcher, *Allegory*, 230.

36. Shawqi Baghdadi, "Introduction," in *Asabi' al-Mawz (Banana Fingers)*, by Ghassan al-Jaba'i (Damascus: Wizarat al-Thaqafa, 1994), 13.

37. Jeremy Tambling, *Allegory* (New York: Routledge, 2009), 92.

38. Al-Jaba'i, *Asabi' al-Mawz (Banana Fingers)*, 59.

39. Butler, *Precarious Life*, 33.

40. Al-Jaba'i, *Asabi' al-Mawz (Banana Fingers)*, 77, ellipses in the original.

41. Linda Hutcheon, *Irony's Edge: The Theory and Politics of Irony* (London: Routledge, 2005), 4, 10, Kindle.

42. Al-Jaba'i, *Asabi' al-Mawz (Banana Fingers)*, 115. Quotation marks and ellipses in the original.

43. Ibid., 123. Quotation marks and ellipses in the original.

44. Ibid., 128.

45. Turner, *Vulnerability*, 27.

46. As Hutcheon notes, irony is "an interpretative and intentional move" in that the reader as interpreter must make or infer "meaning in addition to and different from what is stated, together with an attitude toward both the said and unsaid." The presence of irony in the narrative thus adds to the forms of recognition a reader undergoes. Hutcheon, *Irony's Edge*, 11.

47. Butler, *Precarious Life*, 34.

48. 'Abd al-Salam al-'Ujayli, *Majhula 'ala al-Tariq* (London: Riyad El-Rayyes, 1997).

49. Turner, *Vulnerability*.

50. Wadi' Ismandar, *al-Rajul al-'Ari (The Naked Man)* (Beirut: Dar al-Quds, 1979).

51. See, for example, Faraj Bayraqdar's *Khiyanat al-Lugha wa-l-Samt* (*The Betrayals of Language and Silence*) (Beirut: Dar al-Jadid, 2006); and Malik Daghastani's novel *Duwar al-Hurriyya* (*The Vertigo of Freedom*) (Damascus: Dar al-Balad, 2002).

52. Samu'il, *Ra'ihat al-Khatw al-Thaqil* (*The Stench of the Heavy Step*), 34.

53. Mikhail Bakhtin, *Problems of Dostoevsky's Poetics* (Minneapolis: Univ. of Minnesota Press, 2003), 6.

54. Samu'il, *Ra'ihat al-Khatw al-Thaqil* (*The Stench of the Heavy Step*), 34.

55. Ibid., 34–35.

56. Ibid., 37.

57. Ibid., 37–38.

58. Ibid., 38–39.

59. Ibid., 39.

60. Turner, *Vulnerability*, 27.

61. Michael Camille, "Simulacrum," in *Critical Terms for Art History*, ed. Robert S. Nelson and Richard Shiff (Chicago: Univ. of Chicago Press, 2003), 35.

62. Cave, *Recognitions*, 1.

63. Turner, *Vulnerability*.

64. Samu'il, *Ra'ihat al-Khatw al-Thaqil* (*The Stench of the Heavy Step*), 38.

65. Douzinas, *Human Rights*, 39.

66. Kelly Oliver, *Witnessing: Beyond Recognition* (Minneapolis: Univ. of Minnesota Press, 2001).

3. Rescripting Torture

1. Maher Arar v. John Ashcroft et al. United States District Court, Eastern District of New York, *Center for Constitutional Rights*, January 22, 2004, ccrjustice.org/ourcases /current-cases/arar-v.-ashcroft#files, accessed November 24, 2008.

2. Ibid., 16.

3. Michel Foucault, *Discipline and Punish: The Birth of the Prison*, trans. Alan Sheridan (New York: Vintage, 1992), 297. For a discussion of the US government's outsourcing of torture, see Jane Mayer, "Outsourcing Torture: The Secret History of America's 'Extraordinary Rendition' Program," *New Yorker*, February 14, 2005, www.newyorker.com /archive/2005/02/14/050214fa_fact6, accessed May 10, 2007, and Laleh Khalili, *Confinement in Counterinsurgencies* (Stanford, CA: Stanford Univ. Press, 2013). See also Wendy Patten, "Human Rights Watch Report to the Canadian Commission of Inquiry into the Actions of Canadian Officials in Relation to Maher Arar," Human Rights Watch, June 7, 2005, hrw.org/backgrounder/eca/canada/arar/, May 10, 2007. For a thorough historical overview of the use of torture in Western democracies, see Darius Rejali's monumental study *Torture and Democracy* (Princeton, NJ: Princeton Univ. Press, 2007), Kindle.

4. Although it is no longer active, Arar had his own personal website to publicize his case, which included a section titled "Maher's Story." The original URL was www.maher arar.ca/, accessed May 10, 2007.

5. See the introduction and chapter 1 for the debates about the definition of prison literature.

6. Elaine Scarry, *The Body in Pain: The Making and Unmaking of the World* (New York: Oxford Univ. Press, 1985), 54.

7. Ibid., 20, 54.

8. Ibid., 20.

9. Ibid., 56.

10. Ibid.

11. In his scorching review of the book, Peter Singer critiques Scarry for ahistoricism, logical fallacies, and inaccurate descriptions of torture. See Peter Singer, "Unspeakable Acts," *New York Review of Books*, February 27, 1986, www.nybooks.com/articles /1986/02/27/unspeakable-acts/. For an overview of critiques of Scarry, see Clifford van Ommen, John Cromby, and Jeffrey Yen, "The Contemporary Making and Unmaking of Elaine Scarry's *The Body in Pain*," *Subjectivity* 9, no. 4 (2016): 333–42.

12. Ñacuñán Sáez, "Torture: A Discourse on Practice," in *Tattoo, Torture, Mutilation, and Adornment: The Denaturalization of the Body in Culture and Text*, ed. Frances E. Mascia-Lees and Patricia Sharpe (Albany: State Univ. of New York Press, 1992), 138; Patrice Douglass and Frank Wilderson, "The Violence of Presence: Metaphysics in a Blackened World," *Black Scholar* 43, no. 4 (2013): 117–23. Sáez also calls into question Scarry's notion that torture destroys language and the victim's capacity to speak by examining the problem of false confession and deliberate misinformation provided by victims of torture. In confirmation of Sáez's argument, Arar attests that he signed a false confession. Additionally, Scarry has been criticized for assuming an "already constituted subject" in her analysis due in part to the archival materials (human rights reports) she uses to draw her conclusions (Crystal Parikh, personal communication). See also Bibi Bakare-Yusuf, "The Economy of Violence: Black Bodies and the Unspeakable Terror," in *Feminist Theory and the Body: A Reader*, ed. Janet Price and Margrit Shildrick (Edinburgh: Edinburgh Univ. Press, 1999), 311–23.

13. Elizabeth S. Anker, *Fictions of Dignity: Embodying Human Rights and World Literature* (Ithaca, NY: Cornell Univ. Press, 2012), 31.

14. Ibid., 30–31.

15. Ibid., 30.

16. Kay Schaffer and Sidonie Smith, *Human Rights and Narrated Lives: The Ethics of Recognition* (New York: Palgrave Macmillan, 2004), 3.

17. Costas Douzinas, *Human Rights and Empire: The Political Philosophy of Cosmopolitanism* (Abingdon, UK: Routledge, 2007), 40; Robert M. Cover, "Violence and the Word," *Yale Law Journal* 95, no. 8 (1986), 1601.

18. Schaffer and Smith, *Human Rights*, 3. See also Gillian Whitlock, *Postcolonial Narratives: Testimonial Translations* (Oxford: Oxford Univ. Press, 2015), 182.

19. Another, more detailed account of the events of Arar's case was offered on his website; this account provides "Maher's Story" in narrative segments separated under dated headings. See www.maherarar.ca/, accessed November 24, 2008. The television program *60 Minutes* conducted a lengthy interview with Arar: "His Year in Hell," *60 Minutes*, January 21, 2004, www.cbsnews.com/stories/2004/01/21/60II/main594974.shtml, accessed November 24, 2008. Having filed the complaint on behalf of Arar, the Center for Constitutional Rights also created a number of videos about Arar's case, including a video in which Arar tells his story in the first person. See "Maher Arar Speaks about His Rendition and Torture," October 3, 2017, www.youtube.com/watch?v=RFdFvihF_NM&t =67s, accessed June 24, 2020.

20. The portions of Arar's 2003 statement quoted here, originally posted on the website of the CBC, are available through the Rendition Project. See www.therendition project.org.uk/prisoners/arar.html, accessed June 24, 2020.

21. Bryan S. Turner, *Vulnerability and Human Rights* (University Park, PA: Penn State Univ. Press, 2006), Kindle.

22. Middle East Watch, *Syria Unmasked: The Suppression of Human Rights by the Asad Regime*, (New Haven, CT: Yale Univ. Press, 1991); Amnesty International, "Syria: Torture by the Security Forces," Amnesty International, September 1984, 18–21.

23. See, for example, Amnesty International, "Syria," *Amnesty International Annual Report 2005*, www.amnesty.org/en/documents/pol10/0001/2005/en/. See also a public statement issued by Amnesty International on September 23, 2004, regarding Syria's accession to the convention: www.amnesty.org/en/documents/MDE24/069/2004/en/.

24. Middle East Watch, *Syria Unmasked*, 149–51. Under the direction of Lokman Slim and Monika Borgmann, the Lebanese organization UMAM has also published a dictionary and reference guide for terminology related to Syrian prisons. See Mahmud al-Hamadi, *Mafatih al-Sijn al-Suri: Mustalahat min wara' al-Qudban* (Beirut: Umam li-l-Tawthiq wa-l-Abhath, 2012).

25. Richard A. Posner, "Torture, Terrorism, and Interrogation," in *Torture: A Collection*, ed. Sanford Levison (Oxford: Oxford Univ. Press, 2004), 291. A consistent internationally or universally accepted definition of *torture* has been a source of debate since promulgation of the 1948 Universal Declaration of Human Rights (UDHR), as well as the UN Convention against Torture and Other Cruel, Inhuman, or Degrading Treatment or Punishment, adopted by the UN General Assembly in 1984. For discussions of the debates over the definition of *torture* in the context of the US government's "war on terrorism," see Sanford Levison, "Contemplating Torture: An Introduction," in *Torture: A Collection* (Oxford: Oxford Univ. Press, 2004), 23–43, and John Parry, "Escalation and Necessity: Defining Torture at Home and Abroad," in *Torture: A Collection*, ed. Sanford Levison (Oxford: Oxford Univ. Press, 2004), 145–64.

26. Slaughter, "A Question of Narration: The Voice in International Human Rights Law." *Human Rights Quarterly* 19, no. 2 (1997), 407.

27. The absence or marginalization of depictions of torture in Samu'il's numerous prison stories has been noted by numerous critics, including Mamduh 'Adwan, Isabella D'Afflitto, and miriam cooke. When depicted, physical assault is usually shown only indirectly or via the soundscape of prison, as in the conclusion of the short story "al-Nahnahat." Ibrahim Samu'il, *al-Nahnahat* (*Ahem, Ahem*) (Damascus: Dar al-Jundi), 1990.

28. Other writers, such as Ghassan al-Jaba'i, choose to render their depictions of torture through an allegorical lens in which the pain caused by torture is narrated in the voice of a humanized but inanimate object, as in the story "The Barrel," discussed in chapter 2.

29. Although it was published in 1972, the novel has been read as depicting the imprisonment of secular political opponents under Adib al-Shishakli's rule (1951–54). However, the only major reference to specific historical events in the text is a discussion that takes place among prisoners about their solidarity with imprisoned Algerian *mujāhidīn* who are fighting the French.

30. For an analysis of Sulayman's and Bu 'Ali Yasin's *Literature and Ideology in Syria 1967–1973*, see Alexa Firat, "Cultural Battles on the Literary Playing Field," paper presented at the Middle East History and Theory Conference, University of Chicago, May 11–12, 2007.

31. For elaboration on the notion and negative connotations of "the ideology of prison," see Yassin al-Haj Saleh, *Bi-l-Khalas Ya Shabab! Sittin 'Aman fi al-Sujun al-Surriya* (*At Last, Boys! Sixteen Years in Syrian Prisons*) (Beirut: Dar al-Saqi, 2012), especially 108–17. Excerpts reprinted with permission of Yassin al-Haj Saleh.

32. Ibid., 112.

33. Nabil Sulayman, *Al-Sijn* (*The Prison*), 19–20.

34. Ibid., 21.

35. Ibid., 21–22.

36. Faraj Bayraqdar was born in 1951 in Tir al-Ma'alla, near Homs in central Syria. He began publishing poetry while still in high school. At the University of Damascus, he and a group of friends started a literary journal, and certain texts published in it led to his arrest and imprisonment for three months. His first poetry collection, *You Are Not Alone*, came out in 1979 (Beirut: Dar al-Haqa'iq). He stopped writing in the early 1980s due to activities in Communist Action Party. In 1987 Bayraqdar was arrested again. His imprisonment lasted fourteen years, in three different prisons (Palestine Division, Tadmur, and Saydnaya). See also chapter 4 for a discussion of the publication process and an analysis of Bayraqdar's poetry collection, *Hamama Mutlaqat al-Jinahayn* (*Dove in Free Flight*) (Beirut: n.p., 1997).

37. The memoir was published in the cultural supplement of the Lebanese newspaper *al-Nahar* and disseminated widely on the internet long before he could find a publisher

who would agree to print and distribute it. The most famous passage details a gruesome scene at the infamous Tadmur Military Prison, in which a guard arbitrarily takes a prisoner out to the courtyard and forces him to swallow a dead mouse whole.

38. Faraj Bayraqdar, *Khiyanat al-Lugha wa-l-Samt* (*The Betrayals of Language and Silence*) (Beirut: Dar al-Jadid, 2006), 28. Excerpts reprinted with permission of Faraj Bayraqdar.

39. Ibid.

40. Elizabeth Swanson Goldberg and Alexandra Shultheis Moore, "Introduction: Human Rights and Literature: The Development of an Interdiscipline," in *Theoretical Perspectives on Human Rights and Literature*, ed. Elizabeth Swanson Goldberg and Alexandra Shultheis Moore (New York: Routledge, 2012), Kindle.

41. Terence Cave, *Recognitions: A Study in Poetics* (Oxford: Clarendon, 2002), 33.

42. Ibid., 2.

43. Bayraqdar, *Khiyanat al-Lugha wa-l-Samt* (*The Betrayals of Language and Silence*), 29, emphasis mine.

44. Carolyn Forché, "Reading the Living Archives: the Witness of Literary Art," Poetry Foundation, May 2, 1011, www.poetryfoundation.org/poetrymagazine/articles/69680 /reading-the-living-archives-the-witness-of-literary-art, accessed December 12, 2019.

45. Bayraqdar, *Khiyanat al-Lugha wa-l-Samt* (*The Betrayals of Language and Silence*), 30.

46. See, for example, Middle East Watch, *Syria Unmasked*.

47. Bayraqdar, *Khiyanat al-Lugha wa-l-Samt* (*The Betrayals of Language and Silence*), 30–32.

48. Ibid., 30.

49. Born in 1958 into an 'Alawi family, 'Abd al-Rahman moved from a small impoverished village north of Latakia to Damascus while she was still a child. Having developed an interest in oppositional politics in secondary school, she became active in underground political activities in her late teens. She was detained by Syrian state security for prolonged periods four times, including from 1986 to 1991, also due to her membership in the Communist Action Party.

50. Noted in author interview with 'Adnan Husayn Ahmad, *Al-Zaman*, March 4, 2002.

51. Joanna Bourke, *The Story of Pain: From Prayer to Painkillers* (Oxford: Oxford Univ. Press, 2014), 5, Kindle. Bourke notes that an event is "one of those recurring occurrences that we regularly experience and witness that participates in the constitution of our sense of self and other. An event is designated 'pain' if it is identified as such by the person claiming that kind of consciousness."

52. The siege of and massacres in the city of Hama in February 1982 are generally viewed as the nadir of a series of Syrian government crackdowns on and reprisals against oppositional forces—both secular and religious, militant and pacifist—between 1976

and 1982. The city was considered a major stronghold of Islamist opposition to the Ba'th Party beginning in 1963, and it had been the site of major government repressive measures in both 1964 and 1981, which included the massacre of protestors. On February 2, 1982, government forces entered the city to disarm militias of the Muslim Brotherhood and other groups based there. A call for general insurrection was issued by the Muslim Brotherhood, and for ten days a series of clashes between government troops and the armed opposition ensued until upward of thirty thousand Syrian troops occupied the city. In response to the armed resistance, the government's forces destroyed large sections of the city indiscriminately, with little regard for civilian life. The Syrian Muslim Brotherhood has estimated that the number of people killed by government forces was as high as twenty-five thousand. Most English-language historical accounts give the range of those killed as between five thousand and ten thousand, but suggest that the numbers could be higher. Some local human rights organizations, such as the Syrian Human Rights Committee, have estimated the number of people murdered at much higher numbers, such as thirty thousand to forty thousand victims. See their declaration: "Majzarat Hama (1982): Mas'uliyyat al-Qanun Tastawjib al-Muhasaba," February 22, 1999 (reissued February 4, 2004), web.archive.org/web/20130528222037/http://www.shrc.org/data/aspx/d3/53.aspx. See Middle East Watch, *Syria Unmasked*, 17–21, for a detailed account of the siege and the events leading up to it. See also Lisa Wedeen's discussion of the Syrian regime's rhetoric and "official narrative" of the events at Hama in February 1982: Lisa Wedeen, *Ambiguities of Domination: Politics, Rhetoric, and Symbols in Contemporary Syria* (Chicago: Univ. of Chicago Press, 1999), 46–49. Since the publication of 'Abd al-Rahman's novel, more authors have depicted the siege in their literary works, including Manhal al-Sarraj in her novel *Kama Yanbaghi li-Nahr: Riwayya* (*As a River Should*) (Beirut: al-Dar al-'Arabiyya li-l-'Ulum, 2007) and Khalid Khalifa in his novel *Madih al-Karahiyya* (*In Praise of Hatred*) (Beirut: Dar al-Adab, 2008). Alfoz Tanjour's (Alfuz Tanjur) poignant documentary film *al-Dhakira bi-l-Lawn al-Khaki* (*A Memory in Khaki*), 2016, features the artist Khaled al-Khani (Khalid al-Khani) describing his family's and others' experiences of the massacre. For a more elaborate English-language analysis of testimonies about the massacre in Hama as well as al-Sarraj's novel, see also chapter 4 in Salwa Ismail, *The Rule of Violence: Subjectivity, Memory, and Government in Syria* (Cambridge, UK: Cambridge Univ. Press, 2018).

53. Mohja Kahf, "The Silences of Contemporary Syrian Literature," *World Literature Today* 75, no. 2 (2001): 229.

54. Steve Larocco, "Pain as Semiosomatic Force: The Disarticulation and Rearticulation of Subjectivity," *Subjectivity* 9, no. 4 (2016): 343.

55. Ibid., 344.

56. Jacques Derrida, *Writing and Difference* (Chicago: Univ. of Chicago Press, 1980), 11.

57. 'Abd al-Rahman, *al-Sharnaqa* (*The Cocoon*), 107.

58. Ibid., 263.

59. There is also a very brief description of the character Lama's torture by a guard who knew her from childhood, in the chapter titled "The Decisive Battle."

60. Scarry, *Body*, 35, 32.

61. Larocco, "Pain," 343.

62. Ibid., 355

63. Scarry, *Body*, 50.

64. Larocco, "Pain," 359.

65. Scarry, *Body*, 33.

66. As Larocco notes, "Pain is not, in the manifold forms of its experience, nearly as isolating as Scarry claims" ("Pain," 346).

67. 'Abd al-Rahman, *al-Sharnaqa* (*The Cocoon*), 24.

68. Ibid., 27, ellipses in the original.

69. Ibid., 29.

70. Ibid., 34, ellipses in the original.

71. Ibid., 34, ellipses in the original.

72. Ana Douglass and Thomas A. Vogler, "Introduction," in *Witness and Memory: The Discourse of Trauma*, ed. Ana Douglass and Thomas A. Vogler (New York: Routledge, 2003), 22.

73. Pierre Nora, "The Return of the Event," trans. Arthur Goldhammer, in *Histories: French Constructions of the Past*, ed. Jacques Revel and Lynn Hunt (New York: New Press, 1998), 432.

74. Ibid., 432, 433.

75. Michel Foucault, *Power/Knowledge: Selected Interviews and Other Writings, 1972–1977* (New York: Pantheon, 1980), 114.

76. 'Abd al-Rahman, *al-Sharnaqa* (*The Cocoon*), 41, 42. Adding to the ambiguities of the text, throughout the novel very few proper names of places and very few dates are given; for example, Aleppo is referred to as the "Northern City" and Damascus as the "Capital." 'Abd al-Rahman's references to particular historical events must be interpreted through her descriptions, as is the case with the 1982 siege of Hama.

77. Ibid., 42.

78. Ibid., 131.

79. Jacques Ranciere, *The Names of History*, trans. Hassan Melehy (Minneapolis: Univ. of Minnesota Press, 1994), 30.

4. On Forms of Life

1. Yassin al-Haj Saleh, *Bi-l-Khalas Ya Shabab! Sittin 'Aman fi al-Sujun al-Suriyya* (*At Last, Boys! Sixteen Years in Syrian Prisons*) (Beirut: Dar al-Saqi, 2012), 29. Excerpts reprinted with permission of Yassin al-Haj Saleh. The chapter cited here, "On Life and

Time in Prison," was originally published as an independent essay on June 30, 2004, on the website al-Hiwar al-Mutamaddin, which at that time was a major forum for writers opposing the current Syrian political regime.

2. Al-Haj Saleh, *Bi-l-Khalas Ya Shabab!* (*At Last Boys!*), 29–30.

3. Although the representation of biopolitics in prison literature is not the focus my analysis, a link can be drawn between al-Haj Saleh's discussion of prison as a form of life (*namaṭ li-l-ḥayāa*) and Giorgio Agamben's conception of forms-of-life in *Means without End: Notes on Politics*, trans. Vincenzo Binetti and Cesare Casarino (Minneapolis: Univ. of Minnesota Press, 2000), and *Homo Sacer: Sovereign Power and Bare Life*, trans. Daniel Heller-Roazen (Stanford, CA: Stanford Univ. Press, 1998). The phrase "prison as a form of life" (*namaṭ li-l-ḥayāa*) carries multiple connotations: the word *namaṭ* in Arabic can mean "form" but it also means "way, mode, or manner." For more details on the connection between al-Haj Saleh's writings and Agamben's notion of bare life, see the appendix of R. Shareah Taleghani, "The Cocoons of Language, The Betrayals of Silence" (PhD diss., New York Univ., 2009).

4. See the introduction and chapter 3 for discussions of human rights reports on torture and deaths in custody both prior to and during the Syrian Revolution.

5. Al-Haj Saleh, *Bi-l-Khalas Ya Shabab!* (*At Last Boys!*), 16. In the first essay he notes, "Every year, when the anniversaries of my arrest and release approach, once more, the feeling plagues me—of the necessity of writing my story. . . . But every year, the avoidance reoccurs and the confrontation is postponed again. The years pass, and I feel more and more that I am betraying myself, that I am betraying my friends who died in prison or after their release, and that I am betraying the mothers and fathers who died waiting, or perhaps I am abandoning their corpses out in the open. . . . Rather, it's as if they [the official powers] . . . want us [to take] from memory just enough to keep us afraid and [to take] from forgetting just enough to prevent [us from] demanding anything more" (15–16).

6. For reference to and discussion of al-Haj Saleh's conception of the "ideology of prison," see chapter 3, as well as R. Shareah Taleghani, "The Cocoons of Language: Torture, Voice, Event," in *Human Rights, Suffering, and Aesthetics in Political Prison Literature*, ed. Yenna Wu and Simona Livescu (Lanham, MD: Lexington, 2011).

7. Al-Haj Saleh, *Bi-l-Khalas Ya Shabab!* (*At Last Boys!*), 30. In the 2004 version of this essay, al-Haj Saleh uses the expression *taming time* (*tarwīḍ al-waqt*) in lieu of the phrase *buying time*.

8. Al-Haj Saleh, *Bi-l-Khalas Ya Shabab!* (*At Last Boys!*), 30.

9. Ibid.

10. Al-Haj Saleh is not suggesting that time cannot be coercive, and neither am I. The period of detention is always dictated by the state, and more often than not the length of the sentence is arbitrary. Al-Haj Saleh was detained for eleven years without charge and then sentenced to fifteen years in prison for his membership in the Syrian Communist Party Political Bureau. Having served nearly all of his original fifteen-year sentence, he

was not released. Instead, he was sent to Tadmur at the beginning of 1996 for another year as an additional punishment for refusing to renounce his political activities and cooperate with the authorities.

11. See chapter 5 for a more detailed examination of the history of and literature on Tadmur Military Prison.

12. Michael Fiddler, "Four Walls and What Lies Within: The Meaning of Space and Place in Prisons," *Prison Service Journal* 187 (2010): 3.

13. The term *istiḥbās* is a tenth-form derivative of the root of the letters *ḥa-ba-sīn*, meaning "to obstruct, cut off, confine, or imprison." Al-Haj Saleh defines his understanding of the term *istiḥbās* in a footnote as a "basic, repeated idea in this book. It means that the prisoner settles into or takes up residence in prison. For he comes to the point as if it is his home and he relaxes in it, and time stops being exclusively an enemy to him." Al-Haj Saleh, *Bi-l-Khalas Ya Shabab!* (*At Last Boys!*), 95. While al-Haj Saleh presents his own experience with entering a state of *istiḥbās* as positive, other political detainees, such as Lu'ay Husayn, view this same state in a far more negative light. In his writings on prison, Husayn also discusses *istiḥbās*: it is "a term that is a product of the length of years of prison. The prisoners apply it to one who identifies with prison and begins to lose his mind. I began to *astaḥbis*; rather I began to not pay attention to the differences of things and issues: I knew these differences but I didn't pay attention to which of them are there or are not there. For everything and everything else was equal to me. . . . I became a nonentity." For Husayn, a prisoner is eager for his release prior to reaching the state of *istiḥbās*, but once in that state, the prisoner cannot distinguish between himself and the prison, and this renders the detainee "unhuman" or "nonhuman." See Lu'ay Husayn, *al-Faqd: Hikayat min Dhakira Mutakhayyala li-Sajin Haqiqi* (Beirut: al-Furat, 2006), 70.

14. Michel Foucault, *Discipline and Punish: The Birth of the Prison*, trans. Alan Sheridan (New York: Vintage, 1992), 187.

15. Leila M. Harris and Helen D. Hazen, "Power of Maps: (Counter) Mapping for Conservation," *ACME: An International E-Journal for Critical Geographies* 4, no. 1 (2005): 99–130.

16. Ibid., 115.

17. In using the term *visibility*, I mean to evoke and expand on Joseph Slaughter's frequent use of the term *legibility*, which is also relevant to the notion of readability in representations of torture as discussed in chapter 3. Slaughter uses the term *legibility* in multiple ways, but here I'm drawing on his discussion of how international human rights law and the development of the modern human rights establishment was inspired by particular literary and narrative forms, including the bildungsroman, to produce and legitimize a seemingly transparent but unwritten vision of "universal" human rights, as well as a particular construction of the modern human rights subject. I also use the term *visibility* with Michel Foucault's much-disseminated and much-critiqued discussion of Jeremy Bentham's theorized, but never fully realized, panopticon model in mind. See

Joseph Slaughter, *Human Rights, Inc.: The World Novel, Narrative Form, and International Law* (New York: Fordham Univ. Press, 2007).

18. Ben Crewe, Jason Warr, Peter Bennett, and Alan Smith, "The Emotional Geography of Prison Life," *Theoretical Criminology* 18, no. 1 (2013): 60.

19. Liz Bondi, Joyce Davidson, and Mick Smith, "Introduction: Geography's 'Emotional' Turn," in *Emotional Geographies*, ed. Liz Bondi, Joyce Davidson, and Mick Smith (Hampshire, UK: Ashgate, 2012), 3, Kindle.

20. Joyce Davidson and Christine Milligan, "Embodying Emotion Sensing Space: Introducing Emotional Geographies," *Social and Cultural Geography* 5, no. 4 (2004): 523.

21. "Amnesty International: Facts," NobelPrize.org, 2014, www.nobelprize.org/nobel_prizes/peace/laureates/1977/amnesty-facts.html, accessed September 1, 2017.

22. Middle East Watch, *Syria Unmasked: The Suppression of Human Rights by the Asad Regime* (New Haven, CT: Yale Univ. Press, 1991), 54–77.

23. Ibid., 69.

24. Ibid., 75–76.

25. The word *mahja'* (pl. *mahāji'*) can be translated as "military barracks" or "dorms," and is the term for communal or dormitory cells or cellblocks. The term also indicates a link between political detention and military rule, given that many of the detention and interrogation facilities, including Tadmur, were originally built as prisons for military personnel who had committed ordinary crimes or for use by the military security branches of the Syrian intelligence services.

26. For a discussion of the use of Google Earth in tracking human rights violations, see Jeremy W. Crampton, "Cartography: Maps 2.0," *Progress in Human Geography* 33, no. 1 (2009): 91–100.

27. A second map on the same webpage showing interrogation centers around Syria does include brief quotations from six detainees detailing the forms of torture they endured, but it does not include their personal descriptions of the prisons' physical spaces. The report concludes with a lengthy chart of every known interrogation center in Syria, the branches of the Syrian intelligence agency in charge of each center, the cities where they are located, and the names of the military officers in charge, when known. In a separate article I hope to analyze the ways in which recent online (as opposed to conventional hard copy) reports have allowed for the increased presence of the voices and stories of individual survivors of human rights abuses while at the same time problematically rendering human rights reportage into a video game–like interactive spectacle.

28. Amnesty International and Forensic Architecture, "Saydnaya: Inside a Syrian Torture Prison," Amnesty International, undated (c. August 2016), saydnaya.amnesty.org/?kind=explore, accessed December 15, 2016.

29. J. B. Harley, "Silence and Secrecy: The Hidden Agenda of Cartography in Early Modern Europe," *Imago Mundi* 40 (1988): 66.

30. Barbara Harlow, *Barred: Women, Writing, and Political Detention* (Hanover, CT: Wesleyan Univ. Press, 1992), 24. Foucault's study was originally published in French as *Surveiller et punir* (Paris: Gallimard, 1975), and translated into English as *Discipline and Punish* by Alan Sheridan (New York: Pantheon, 1977). For an overview of the numerous critiques of Foucault in the field of carceral geography, see Bettina van Hoven and David Sibley, "'Just Duck': The Role of Vision in the Production of Prison Spaces," *Environment and Planning D: Society and Space* 26, no. 6 (2008): 1002–17. See also the detailed discussion of critiques of Foucault in Dominique Moran, *Carceral Geography: Spaces and Practices of Incarceration* (New York: Routledge, 2016), Kindle. For an analysis of prison as a heterotopic space, drawing on Foucault's later writings, see Mason McWatters, "Poetic Testimonies of Incarceration: Towards a Vision of Prison as Manifold Space," in *Carceral Spaces: Mobility and Agency in Imprisonment and Migrant Detention*, ed. Dominique Moran, Nick Gill, and Deidre Conlon (Burlington, VT: Ashgate, 2013), Kindle.

31. Foucault, *Discipline*, 200.

32. See Aaron Schutz, "The Metaphor of 'Space' in Educational Theory: Henry Giroux through the Eyes of Hannah Arendt and Michel Foucault," in *Philosophy of Education*, ed. Susan Laird (Urbana, IL: Philosophy of Education Society, 1998), 352–60. Drawing on the work of Henri Lefebvre, Schutz argues that in failing to account for space as dynamic and humanly constructed, Foucault denies any "spatial approach to liberation," and because he rejects the spatial metaphor as having any potential for liberation, Foucault cannot articulate concrete forms of human agency (352).

33. Lisa Wedeen, *Ambiguities of Domination: Politics, Rhetoric, and Symbols in Contemporary Syria* (Chicago: Univ. of Chicago Press, 1999).

34. Foucault, *Discipline*, 187.

35. Fayezaq, "Alhorrah Heba Aldabbagh Speech in Windsor, Canada during the Syrian Protest with English Translation," posted May 15, 2011, accessed August 1, 2017, www.youtube.com/watch?v=lov4zryISgE.

36. For a report on the detention, torture, rape, and abuse of women by the regime and the *shabīḥa* from 2011 to 2013, see Human Rights Watch, "Syria: Detention and Abuse of Female Activists," Human Rights Watch, June 24, 2013, www.hrw.org/news/2013/06/24/syria-detention-and-abuse-female-activists, accessed December 1, 2017. Several journalists and news networks have covered the human rights abuses suffered by female detainees. In English, see Bethan McKernan, "Inside Assad's Prisons: Horrors Facing Female Inmates in Syrian Jails Revealed," *Independent*, August 28, 2017. See also the episode "al-Muʿtaqalat al-Suriyat: Bayn Ijram al-Nizam wa Nabdh al-Mujtamiʿ," from the Al Jazeera program "Li-l-Qissa Baqiyya," aired in 2017 on Al Jazeera, www.aljazeera.net/programs/rest-of-the-story/2017/2/3/13-الابتزاز-سلاح-الأسد-بسجون-معتقلة-ألف, accessed January 7, 2018. In December 2017, France 2 also aired a documentary, *Syria: The Strangled Cry* (Suriya: al-Sarkha al-Makhnuqa), focusing on Syrian female detainees.

37. A 2007 version of the memoir in both English and Arabic is available on the web-site of the Syrian Human Rights Committee: www.shrc.org/en/?p=20427, accessed June 24, 2020. Revealing another connection between works of prison literature in different parts of the Arab world, the Arabic version of Dabbagh's memoir includes an introduc-tion written by the Egyptian Islamist activist and founder of the Muslim Women's Union, Zaynab al-Ghazzali, who herself was imprisoned from 1965 to 1971 and wrote of her prison experiences and the treatment of Muslim Brotherhood detainees in Egypt in her book *Ayyam min Hayati* (*Days from My Life*), 1978, translated into English by A. R. Kid-wai in 1989. Although Dabbagh's memoir is one of the first works of Syrian prison litera-ture to be translated into English, translations of other such works have recently become available; these include Muhammad Salim Hammad's *Tadmur: Witnessed and Observed, 1930–1991*, published in 1998 and translated by the Syrian Human Rights Committee in 2017, and Mustafa Khalifa's novel, *al-Qawqa'a* (*The Shell*), published in 2008 and trans-lated in 2016 by Paul Starkey.

38. CAGE posted the interview with Dabbagh on May 14, 2014; at the time, Begg was imprisoned in the UK for alleged involvement in terrorist activities in Syria. According to CAGE's website, after his release from Guantanamo, Begg has been known to refer to and promote Dabbagh's memoir. See Heba Dabbagh, "Interview: Heba al-Dabbagh Speaks to CAGE," CAGE, May 14, 2014, cage.ngo/uncategorized/interview-heba-al-dabbagh-speaks-cage/, accessed August 10, 2017.

39. See chapter 3 for a brief discussion of the siege of Hama in 1982.

40. Harlow, *Barred*, 133.

41. Stanley Cohen and Laurie Taylor, "Time and the Long-Term Prisoner," in *The Sociology of Time*, ed. John Hassard (New York: St. Martin's, 1990), 178–87.

42. Heba Dabbagh, *Just Five Minutes: Nine Years in the Prisons of Syria*, trans. Bayan Khatib (Toronto: n.p., 2007), 147.

43. Ibid.

44. Ibid.

45. The English translation of Dabbagh's memoir uses a nonstandardized form of Arabic-to-English transliteration. Except for direct quotations from the text, for consis-tency I've retained the simplified *IJMES* transliteration system for the spelling of Arabic terms, including prison names, that is used throughout this book.

46. See, for example, her descriptions of Qatana (Katana) and Duma (Dooma) pris-ons: Dabbagh, *Just Five Minutes*, 137–38, 219. She compares the layouts and structures of both prisons to "old Arab style homes."

47. R. Murray Schafer, *The Soundscape: Our Sonic Environment and the Tuning of the World* (Rochester, VT: Destiny, 1994), 3.

48. Tiffany Lopez, "Critical Witnessing in Latina/o and African-American Prison Narratives," in *Prose and Cons: Essays on Prison Literature in the United States*, ed. Quen-tin Miller (Jefferson, NC: McFarland, 2005), 68.

49. Cohen and Taylor, "Time," 180.

50. Dabbagh, *Just Five Minutes*, 65.

51. Teresa Dirsuweit, "Carceral Spaces in South Africa: A Case Study of Institutional Power, Sexuality, and Transgression in a Women's Prison," *Geoforum* 30, no. 1 (1999): 75.

52. Dabbagh, *Just Five Minutes*, 66.

53. Katie Hemsworth, "'Feeling the Range': Emotional Geographies of Sound in Prisons," *Emotion, Space, and Society* 20 (August 2016): 90. See also Suzanne G. Cusick, "Towards an Acoustemology of Detention in the 'Global War on Terror,'" in *Music, Sound, and Space: Transformations of Public and Private Experience*, ed. Georgina Born (Cambridge, UK: Cambridge Univ. Press, 2013), 275–91.

54. Yvonne Jewkes, *Captive Audience: Media, Masculinity, and Power in Prisons* (Portland, OR: Willan, 2002), as cited in Hemsworth, "'Feeling the Range,'" 92.

55. Dabbagh, *Just Five Minutes*, 22.

56. Schafer, *Soundscape*, 8.

57. Tom Rice, "Sounds Inside: Prison, Prisoners and Acoustical Agency," *Sound Studies* 2, no. 1 (2016): 6–20.

58. Yi-Fu Tuan, *Space and Place: The Perspective of Experience* (Minneapolis: Univ. of Minnesota Press, 2001), 15.

59. Ibid., 16.

60. Dabbagh, *Just Five Minutes*, 51, 67.

61. Hemsworth, "'Feeling the Range,'" 93.

62. Dabbagh, *Just Five Minutes*, 37–38.

63. Ibid., 38.

64. Ibid., 40.

65. Dabbagh, *Just Five Minutes*, 55.

66. Dabbagh, *Just Five Minutes*. See, for example, pages 75–81, 102–5, and 174–78.

67. For more details of the siege of, and massacres in, the city of Hama in 1982, see chapter 3.

68. Dabbagh, *Just Five Minutes*, 246–47.

69. Amal Hanano, "The Cell of Survival: Bara Sarraj," *Jadaliyya*, December 12, 2011, www.jadaliyya.com/pages/index/3500/the-cell-of-survival_bara-sarraj, accessed February 18, 2016.

70. He continues to maintain a very active presence on Twitter and Facebook; see twitter.com/Tadmor_Harvard. Throughout this chapter I am retaining the transliteration of Tadmur according to the modified *IJMES* guidelines followed throughout this book, except when directly quoting from the text. The name of the prison is also frequently transliterated as Tadmor, which is how Sarraj and some human rights organizations spell it in English.

71. The full title of the memoir is *Min Tadmur ila Harvard: Rihlat Sajin 'Adim al-Ra'i* (*From Tadmur to Harvard: The Journey of a Prisoner Lacking an Opinion*). The subtitle

is Sarraj's play on one of the Arabic terms for "prisoner of conscience" (*sajīn al-ra'i*). He observes that he was not involved in politics when he was arrested, and thus at the time he was "lacking an opinion." In both the memoir and his tweets against the regime, he comments that he has an opinion now and is no longer afraid to express it.

72. Bara Sarraj (Bara' al-Sarraj), *Min Tadmur ila Harvard: Rihlat Sajin 'Adim al-Ra'i* (*From Tadmur to Harvard: The Journey of a Prisoner Lacking an Opinion*) (Middletown, DE: n.p., 2016), 3. The PDF file was initially circulated by Sarraj himself and downloadable from 4Shared. In February 2016 it was published as a printed book available on Amazon. An English translation is forthcoming. Text reproduced with permission of Bara Sarraj.

73. Hanano, "The Cell of Survival."

74. Sarraj, *Min Tadmur* (*From Tadmur*), 194.

75. Crampton, "Cartography," 91.

76. Sarraj, *Min Tadmur* (*From Tadmur*), 194.

77. Harley, "Silence," 57.

78. Images of the interiors of Syrian prisons have circulated more frequently since the 2011 Revolution, after antiregime forces took over prisons and detention centers and photographed them. The most prominent example of this is Tadmur, where ISIS members photographed and videotaped the prison; these images are discussed in chapter 5.

79. Sarraj, *Min Tadmur* (*From Tadmur*), 7, ellipses in the original.

80. Ibid., 29–30.

81. Crewe et al., "Emotional Geography," 66.

82. Bill Hillier and Julienne Hanson, *The Social Logic of Space* (Cambridge, UK: Cambridge Univ. Press, 1984), 2, as quoted in Fiddler, "Four Walls," 3.

83. Sarraj, *Min Tadmur* (*From Tadmur*), 34.

84. See chapter 5 for a more detailed discussion of the history of and writings about Tadmur Military Prison.

85. Sarraj, *Min Tadmur* (*From Tadmur*), 33. Due to the overcrowded conditions, prisoners were forced to sleep on their sides, with heads facing the feet of other prisoners, and also had to take turns standing up while others slept. Other writers refer to this sleeping arrangement as *musayyafa*—a term also derived from the word for *sword* in Arabic.

86. Sarraj, *Min Tadmur* (*From Tadmur*), 35.

87. Ibid., 36.

88. Ibid., 148.

89. Ibid., 53, 93–94, 124.

90. Ibid., 87.

91. Ibid., 149.

92. See, for example, Sarraj's description of those who volunteered to be at the head or end of the line when exiting and entering the communal cells of Tadmur: Sarraj, *Min Tadmur* (*From Tadmur*), 104, 128.

93. Ibid., 13.

94. Ibid., 150.

95. Ibid., 60.

96. Ibid., 58.

97. Although I'm aware of its connotations in Christian religious practices, for simplicity I translate *nashīd/anāshīd* here as "hymn"/"hymns."

98. Sarraj, *Min Tadmur* (*From Tadmur*), 73.

99. Hemsworth, "'Feeling the Range,'" 93.

100. Sarraj, *Min Tadmur* (*From Tadmur*), 72.

101. Ibid., 164.

102. Faraj Bayraqdar, *Hamama Mutlaqat al-Jinahayn* (*Dove in Free Flight*) (Beirut: n.p., 1997). Excerpts reprinted with permission of Faraj Bayraqdar.

103. Abdelke was arrested again in 2013 after signing a declaration calling for the removal of Bashar al-Asad.

104. See chapter 1 for a discussion of how translation can affect the cases of individual political prisoners.

105. Due to the fraught process of its compilation and editing, the original 1997 Arabic edition contained many mistakes, which in some cases completely changed the poet's intended meaning. After Bayraqdar's release, he reedited the manuscript. The translations used in this chapter are based on a copy of the reedited manuscript obtained from the poet and translated by the New York Translation Collective, a group of students and scholars based in New York, of which I am a member. The translation is forthcoming from UpSet Press.

106. Edward W. Soja, *Thirdspace: Journeys to Los Angeles and Other Real-and-Imagined Places* (Malden, MA: Blackwell, 1996), 39, as quoted in Fiddler, "Four Walls," 7.

107. Fiddler, "Four Walls," 7.

108. See chapter 1.

109. Faraj Bayraqdar, personal communication with the author, August 15, 2005.

110. Fiddler, "Four Walls," 7.

111. Ibid., 3.

112. Bondi, Davidson, and Smith, "Introduction," 12.

113. Ibid., 7.

5. On "The Kingdom of Death and Madness"

1. Greg Botelho and Khushbu Shah, "ISIS Is 'Everywhere' in Syria's Ancient City of Palmyra," CNN, May 22, 2015, www.cnn.com/2015/05/21/middleeast/isis-syria-iraq /index.html, accessed September 10, 2017.

2. Omur Harmansah, "ISIS, Heritage, and the Spectacles of Destruction in Global Media," *Near Eastern Archaeology* 78, no. 3 (2015): 170.

3. Kareem Shaheen, "Palmyra: Historic Syrian City Falls under Control of ISIS," *Guardian*, May 21, 2015.

4. Botelho and Shah, "ISIS."

5. One video featured Palmyra's ancient amphitheater; at the time the militants used it to stage the execution of more than twenty captured men who were allegedly Syrian regime soldiers. Months later the amphitheater was destroyed. See Kimberly Hutcherson, "ISIS Video Shows Execution of 25 Men in Ruins of Syrian Amphitheater," CNN, July 5, 2015, edition.cnn.com/2015/07/04/middleeast/isis-execution-palmyra-syria/, accessed October 20, 2017. ISIS members also captured, tortured, and executed renowned eighty-one-year-old Syrian archaeologist Khalid al-As'ad after he refused to reveal the location of valuable artifacts, leaving his body for public display in the ruins. Kareem Shaheen and Ian Black, "Beheaded Syrian Scholar Refused to Lead ISIS to Hidden Palmyra Antiquities," *Guardian*, August 19, 2015.

6. For an analysis of ISIS visual propaganda, as well as Arab comedic parodies of the same discourse, see Nathaniel Greenberg, "Mythical State: The Aesthetics and Counter-Aesthetics of the Islamic State of Iraq and Syria," *Middle East Journal of Culture and Communication* 10, no. 1 (2017): 255–71.

7. Human Rights Watch, "Syria's Tadmor Prison: Dissent Still Hostage to a Legacy of Terror," Human Rights Watch, April 1996. www.hrw.org/reports/1996/Syria2.htm, accessed September 8, 2007.

8. This was noted on the now-defunct website Tadmor8k.com, which did not provide any direct information on who constructed or funded the website when I accessed it in 2009. The site served as a platform for testimonial literature on the experiences of detainees affiliated with the Muslim Brotherhood, and included the testimonies of officers who participated in the Tadmur Massacre of 1980 as well as a few testimonies from female prisoners detained there. In his memoir Muhammad Salim Hammad also notes that political prisoners were detained in Tadmur once the Ba'th party took power in the 1960s. See Muhammad Saleem Hammad, *Tadmur: Witnessed and Observed*, trans. Syrian Human Rights Committee, (N.p: Syrian Human Rights Committee, n.d.), 8, www.shrc.org/en/wp-content/uploads/2017/02/Tadmur-Witnessed-and-Observed-Final-1.pdf, accessed December 20, 2017. I have slightly modified the title's translation. Hiba Dabbagh includes the stories of a number of female prisoners who were transferred out of Tadmur after being held there in the 1980s. See Dabbagh, *Just Five Minutes: Nine Years in the Prisons of Syria*. Syrian Human Rights Committee, trans. Bayan Khatib (Toronto: N.p., 2007), 184–85.

9. Amnesty International, "Syria: Torture, Despair, and Dehumanisation in Tadmur Military Prison," September 18, 2001, 7, www.amnesty.org/download/Documents/132000/mde240142001en.pdf, accessed September 8, 2008.

10. Ibid., 1.

11. Human Rights Watch, "Syria's Tadmor Prison."

12. Later, after the appearance of the video depicting the prison's destruction, all three news outlets featured articles on Tadmur Military prison. See, for example, BBC, "Inside Tadmur: The Worst Prison in the World?" *BBC Magazine*, June 20, 2015, www .bbc.com/news/magazine-33197612, accessed October 15, 2017.

13. Amnesty International, "Syria: Harrowing Torture, Summary Killings in Secret ISIS Detention Centers," Amnesty International, December 19, 2013, www.amnesty.org/en /latest/news/2013/12/syria-harrowing-torture-summary-killings-secret-isis-detention -centres/, accessed October 21, 2017.

14. Bara Sarraj (@Tadmor_Harvard) tweeted, "3D Tadmor prison, #Syria. Thanks Google maps," Twitter, March 5, 2013. See chapter 4 for a more detailed examination of Sarraj's use of Google satellite imagery as a form of countermapping in his memoir, *Min Tadmur ila Harvard: Rihlat Sajin 'Adim al-Ra'i* (*From Tadmur to Harvard: The Journey of a Prisoner Lacking an Opinion*) (Middletown, DE: n.p, 2016).

15. An example of the image of those killed in the massacre could be seen on the website of Palmyra Monitor, palmyra-monitor.net/tag/مجزرة-سجن-تدمر/, accessed October 10, 2017. The site is no longer active. In retaliation for an attempt to assassinate Hafez al-Asad on June 27, 1980, the Syrian Defense Brigades, led by the then-president's younger brother, Rif'at al-Asad, entered the prison and ordered the summary execution of at least one thousand prisoners with hand grenades and guns. Some of the soldiers who perpetrated the massacre later provided testimonials, confessing to their participation. Victims of the massacre were reportedly buried in unmarked collective graves in the desert outside the prison. The assassination attempt and retaliatory prison massacre was followed by the regime's drafting and implementation of Law 49, which made membership in or any affiliation with the Muslim Brotherhood a capital crime in Syria. It culminated in the siege of and massacre at the city of Hama in 1982, which quelled public displays of dissent and armed resistance in the country until the death of Hafez al-Asad in 2000. See chapter 3 for a discussion of the siege of Hama. For a description of the massacre at Tadmur, see also Syrian Human Rights Committee, "Tadmur Prison: A Special Report," Syrian Human Rights Committee, May 27, 2015, www.shrc.org/en/?p=25060, accessed October 10, 2017.

16. Mohammad's documentary features a group conversation that was filmed en route from Damascus to Tadmur. Shot clandestinely to avoid censorship and harassment from state security agents, the film later aired as part of Al Jazeera's series on prison literature in 2006.

17. In 2000–2001, after the death of Hafez al-Asad and in the period of the Damascus Spring, the state granted a general amnesty for several hundred political prisoners and declared that Tadmur was officially closed. See Human Rights Watch, "A Wasted Decade: Human Rights in Syria during Bashar al-Asad's First Ten Years in Power," Human Rights Watch, July 16, 2010, www.hrw.org/report/2010/07/16/wasted-decade/human -rights-syria-during-bashar-al-asads-first-ten-years-power, accessed October 23, 2017.

The prison was reportedly reopened in 2011 to house activists detained for participation in the Revolution.

18. See, for example, Syrian Human Rights Committee, "Tadmur Prison"; Amnesty International, "Syria: Torture, Despair, and Dehumanisation"; and Human Rights Watch, "Syria's Tadmor Prison."

19. My thanks again to Sinan Antoon for pointing out this analogy.

20. Al-Haj Saleh, *Bi-l-Khalas, Ya Shabab! Sittin 'Aman fi al-Sujun al-Suriyya (At Last, Boys! Sixteen Years in Syrian Prisons)* (Beirut: Dar al-Saqi, 2012), 38–39, ellipses in the original. Excerpts reprinted with permission of Yassin al-Haj Saleh.

21. Former prisoners have written a wide range of works on Tadmur, and due to space limitations only a few can be addressed in this chapter. Among the memoirs of those affiliated with the Muslim Brotherhood, or accused of being so affiliated, are Khalid Fadil's 1985 "Fi al-Qa': Sanatayn fi Sijn Tadmur al-Sahrawi" ("In the Abyss: Two Years in Tadmur Desert Prison"), Syrian Human Rights Committee, February 29, 2004, www .shrc.org/?p=7502, accessed September 29, 2018; 'Abdullah al-Naji's 1992 "Hammamat al-Damm fi Sijn Tadmur" ("Bloodbaths in Tadmur Prison"), Syrian Human Rights Committee, July 16, 2008, www.shrc.org/wp-content/uploads/2008/07/tadmurbloodbaths.pdf, accessed September 9, 2018; Muhammad Salim Hammad's "Tadmur: Witness and Witnessed" ("Tadmur: Shahid wa Mashhud") Syrian Human Rights Committee, July 16, 2007, www.shrc.org/?p=15321, accessed September 18, 2018; and Bara Sarraj's *Min Tadmur ila Harvard (From Tadmur to Harvard)*. Additionally, Ali Abou Dehn, who was arrested under accusations of supporting the South Lebanese Army during Syria's occupation of Lebanon, wrote a memoir titled *'A'id min al-Jahannam (Returning from Hell)*, 5th ed. (Beirut: Dar al-Jadid wa Umam li-l-Tawthiq wa-l-Abhath, 2012). Memoirs by leftist or Marxist-oriented detainees that deal with Tadmur include Faraj Bayraqdar's *Khiyanat al-Lugha wa-l-Samt (The Betrayals of Language and Silence)* (Beirut: Dar al Jadid, 2006). Yassin al-Haj Saleh discusses Tadmur in a number of essays in his collection *Bi-l-Khalas, Ya Shabab! Sittin 'Aman fi al-Sujun al-Suriyya (At Last Boys! Sixteen Years in Syrian Prisons)* (Beirut: Dar al-Saqi, 2012). More recently, 'Abbas 'Abbas's *Longing for Life (Tawqan ila al-Haya,* 2015) was published three years after the author's death. Novels that deal entirely or briefly with Tadmur include Mustafa Khalifa's *al-Qawqa'a (The Shell)* (Beirut: Dar al-Adab, 2008); Riyad Mu'as'as's *Hammam Zunubiya (Zenoubia's Bath)* (Tunis: Dar al-Junub li-l-Nashr, 2012); Khalid Khalifa's *Madih al-Karahiyya (In Praise of Hatred)* (Beirut: Dar al-Adab, 2008); and Manhal al-Sarraj's *Kama Yanbaghi li-Nahr (As the River Should)* (Beirut: al-Dar al-'Arabiyya li-l-'Ulum, 2007). Jordanian author Ayman 'Attum, who spent several years in prison, based his novel *Yasma'un Hasisha (They Hear Her Faint Sound)* (Beirut: al-Mu'assasa al-'Arabiyya li-l-Dirasat wa-l-Nashr, 2012) on the story of a former Tadmur detainee. Playwright and short-story writer Ghassan al-Jaba'i composed some of the short stories in his collection *Asabi' al-Mawz (Banana Fingers)* (Damascus: Wizarat al-Thaqafa, 1994) while in Tadmur, and in particular the story "Over the Sand,

Under the Sun" ("Fawq al-Raml, Taht al-Shams") references the desert prison. Filmmaker Muhammad Malas used the title of this story for his 1998 film on political detention. While several of the memoirs mention that a small number of female prisoners were imprisoned at Tadmur in the 1980s and 1990s, at the time of writing I have not encountered any works written by them, although reference to the stories of female political prisoners in Tadmur are made in Heba Dabbagh's *Just Five Minutes*. There was one testimonial from a female detainee available on the Brotherhood affiliated Tadmor8K website, but the site is no longer available.

22. My thanks, again, to Sinan Antoon for drawing this to my attention.

23. Bayraqdar, *Khiyanat al-Lugha wa-l-Samt* (*The Betrayals of Language and Silence*), 63. Excerpts reprinted with permission of Faraj Bayraqdar.

24. Bettina van Hoven and David Sibley, "'Just Duck:' The Role of Vision in the Production of Prison Spaces," *Environment and Planning D: Society and Space* 26, no. 6 (2008): 1002.

25. Ibid., 1012.

26. For the purposes of this chapter, I'm using the Syrian Human Rights Committee's anonymous English translation of Hammad's memoir, which does not use standardized transliteration. Muhammad Salim Hammad, *Tadmur: Witnessed and Observed*, 7. I have slightly modified the title's translation.

27. Ibid., 7.

28. Ibid.

29. Ibid., 145–46. He writes, "We were commanded to open our eyes and look around normally. When I did so, I surveyed my surroundings and found myself face to face with this terrorizing place that had held us hostage."

30. Ibid., 43.

31. Ibid.

32. Ibid., 45.

33. See chapter 4 for a discussion of the emotional geographies of the prison soundscape. Hammad, like other authors of Tadmur memoirs, notes how he and other prisoners served as earwitnesses rather than eyewitnesses in that they witnessed executions aurally rather than visually; those left inside the cells could hear those about to be executed yelling "*Takbir!*" See, for example, Hammad, *Tadmur: Witnessed and Observed*, 66–67.

34. Hammad, *Tadmur*, 50.

35. Ibid.

36. Ibid., 54.

37. Ibid., 111.

38. Ibid., 71.

39. Ibid.

40. Ibid., 72.

41. Ibid., 73.

42. Khalifa never directly names the prison as Tadmur; instead, throughout the novel he uses the phrase "the desert prison." Mustafa Khalifa, *The Shell*, trans. Paul Starkey (Northampton, MA: Interlink, 2017).

43. Khalifa, *Shell*, 3.

44. Ibid.

45. Ibid., The term use for confession (*'itirāf*) also means recognition, and in this case both meanings are suggested.

46. My thanks to Regine Joseph for suggesting the term *autosurveillance*. For a discussion of how the novel depicts the prisoners' internalization of the regime's mechanisms of power and fear, see Anne-Marie McManus, "Plucking Out the Heart of Power: al-Qawqa'a," Jadaliyya, November 16, 2011, www.jadaliyya.com/Details/24622/Plucking -Out-the-Heart-of-Power-Al-Qawqa%60a, accessed April 11, 2018.

47. Mir Adnan Ali and Steve Mann, "The Inevitability of the Transition from a Surveillance-Society to a Veillance-Society: Moral and Economic Grounding for Sousveillance," IEEE International Symposium on Technology and Society (ISTAS), Toronto, June 2013. My thanks to Karly Alderfer for bringing the idea of sousveillance to my attention.

48. Van Hoven and Sibley, "'Just Duck,'" 1001.

49. Khalifa, *Shell*, 15–16.

50. Ibid., 22.

51. Ibid., 23

52. Ibid.

53. Ibid., 48.

54. Hasiba 'Abd al-Rahman, *al-Sharnaqa* (*The Cocoon*) (N.p.: n.p., 1999).

55. Ibid., 252.

56. Initially after his release in 2000 Bayraqdar had great difficulty finding a publisher for the memoir because of fears of retaliation by the Syrian security apparatus due to the book's contents and its indictment of the Asad regime. However, he was able to publish excerpts from the memoir in the cultural supplement of *al-Nahar*.

57. See especially the chapter titled "Interval" and "On the Brink of Insight," which is discussed in chapter 3. Bayraqdar, *Khiyanat al-Lugha wa-l-Samt* (*The Betrayals of Language and Silence*), 19–32.

58. Bayraqdar, *Khiyanat al-Lugha wa-l-Samt* (*The Betrayals of Language and Silence*), 57–58; ellipses in original.

59. Sophia A. McClennan and Alexandra Schultheis Moore, "Introduction: Aporia and Affirmative Critique: Mapping the Landscape of Literary Approaches to Human Rights," in *The Routledge Companion to Literature and Human Rights*, ed. Sophia A. McClennan and Alexandra Schultheis Moore (New York: Routledge, 2016), 14.

60. Bayraqdar, *Khiyanat al-Lugha wa-l-Samt* (*The Betrayals of Language and Silence*), 60.

61. Ibid., 61.

62. Ibid.

63. Ibid., 62.

64. Ibid.

65. John Corbin, "Images of War: Picasso's Guernica," *Visual Anthropology* 13, no. 1 (2010): 1–21.

66. Carolyn Forché, "Reading the Living Archives: The Witness of Literary Art," *Poetry Magazine*, May 2, 1011, www.poetryfoundation.org/poetrymagazine/articles/69680 /reading-the-living-archives-the-witness-of-literary-art, accessed December 12, 2019.

67. According to Monika Borgmann, via Bara Sarraj, the main political prison may not have actually been destroyed and can still be seen via Google satellite photos, and the structure featured in the video was actually the civilian prison in the city of Tadmur. Monika Borgmann, personal communication, November 30, 2017. At the time of writing I was unable to confirm to what extent the prison was still intact or in use.

6. The Stairwell of Solitary Days

1. Hasiba 'Abd al-Rahman, "Shahadat Kitabat al-Riwayya Kharajit min al-Qalb wa-l-Dhakira" ("The Testimony of Writing a Novel that Came Out of the Heart and Memory"). *Dirasat Istirakiyya*, nos. 182/183 (2000): 425–27.

2. 'Abbas Mahmud 'Abbas, *Tawqan ila al-Haya: Awraq Sajin* (*Longing for Life: A Prisoner's Papers*) (Beirut: Dar al-Khayal, 2015), 18.

3. Ibid.

4. Yusif Bazzi, "Tawqan ila al-Haya: Awraq 'Abbas 'Abbas fi Sujun Suriya," al-Mudun, May 26, 2017, www.almodon.com/culture/2017/5/26/توقا-إلى-الحياة-أوراق-عباس- عباس-في-السجون-السورية, accessed September 10, 2018.

5. 'Abbas, *Tawqan ila al-Haya* (*Longing for Life*), 28.

6. Ibid.

7. Ibid.

8. Ibid.

9. Heba Dabbagh, *Just Five Minutes: Nine Years in the Prisons of Syria*, trans. Bayan Khatib (Toronto: n.p., 2007), 7.

10. James Dawes, *The Novel of Human Rights* (Cambridge, MA: Harvard Univ. Press, 2018), Kindle; Barbara Harlow, *Resistance Literature* (New York: Metheun & Co., 1987), 120.

11. Joseph Slaughter, "A Question of Narration: The Voice in International Human Rights Law," *Human Rights Quarterly* 19, no. 2 (May 1997): 413.

12. See, for example, Bayraqdar's poem "Story" (in *Hamama Mutlaqat al-Jinahayn* (*Dove in Free Flight*) (Beirut: n.p., 1997), as well as Sarraj's *Min Tadmur ila Harvard: Rihlat Sajin 'Adim al-Ra'i* (*From Tadmur to Harvard: The Journey of a Prisoner Lacking an Opinion*) (Middletown, DE: n.p, 2016), as discussed in chapter 4; and al-Jaba'i's "Memoirs of

a Barrel" (in *Asabi' al-Mawz* [*Banana Fingers*] [Damascus: Wizarat al-Thaqafa, 1994]), as discussed in chapter 2. See also the representation of writing in Mustafa Khalifa's *al-Qawqa'a* (*The Shell*) (Beirut: Dar al-Adab, 2008), as noted in chapter 5. References to writing can also be seen throughout Hasiba 'Abd al-Rahman's *al-Sharnaqa* (*The Cocoon*) (N.p.: n.p., 1999), particularly the portrayal of the character Tuhama writing in her diaries. Some authors, like 'Abd al-Rahman in her short story "Letters from Strangers," in *Sagata Sahwan* (*It Fell Inadvertently*)(N.p.: n.p., 2002); Rosa Yaseen Hasan in her novel *Huras al-Hawa'* (*Guardians of Air*) (Beirut: Dar al-Kawkab, 2009); and Ibrahim Samu'il in his short story "The Peering Eyes" ("al-'Ayun al-Mushri'"), in his collection *Ra'ihat al-Khatw al-Thaqil* (*The Stench of the Heavy Step*) (Damascus: Dar al-Jundi, 1990), incorporate traces of the act of writing as a framing device or as an integral element of the plot of a story, thus drawing attention to the both the significance, for prisoners, of writing as a means of resistance and communication with the outside world.

13. Jamil Hatmal, *al-Majmu'a al-Qisasiyya al-Khams* (*The Five Story Collections*) (Beirut: al-Mu'assasa al-'Arabiyya li-l-Dirasat wa-l-Nashr, 1998); Malik Daghastani, *Duwar al-Hurriyya* (*The Vertigo of Freedom*) (Damascus: Dar al-Balad, 2002).

14. In coining the term *carceral metafiction*, I'm drawing inspiration from Linda Hutcheon's work on historiographic metafiction and postmodernism. See Linda Hutcheon, "Historiographic Metafiction," in *Metafiction*, ed. Mark Currie (New York: Routledge, 2013), Kindle. Hutcheon argues that historiographical metafiction is unique to the poetics of postmodernism and that such works challenge the transparency and assumptions of the realist novel as well as historical narratives. I would assert that carceral metafiction in Arabic literature is uniquely generated and has become prevalent as a response to the era of the postcolonial, authoritarian state in Syria and elsewhere. I am deliberately avoiding the term *postmodern* in my analysis due to the debates about the validity of applying it to particular works of modern and contemporary Arabic literature.

15. Patricia Waugh, "What Is Metafiction and Why Are They Saying Such Awful Things about It?" in *Metafiction*, ed. Mark Currie (New York: Longman, 1995), 40.

16. For a more detailed analysis of metafiction in these two novels, as well as Sinan Antoon's *I'jam* (Beirut: Dar al-Adab, 2004), Elias Khoury's *Yalu* (Beirut: Dar al-Adab, 2002), and Sami al-Jundi's *Sadiqi Ilyas* (*My Friend Elias*) (Beirut: Dar al-Nahar, 1969), see R. Shareah Taleghani, "Writing against the Regime: Metafiction in the Arabic Prison Novel," in *Prison Writing and the Literary World: Imprisonment, Institutionality, and Questions of Literary Practice*, ed. Michelle Kelly and Claire Westall (New York: Routledge, 2020).

17. See Sabry Hafez, "The Transformation of Reality and the Arabic Novel's Aesthetic Response," *Bulletin of the School of Oriental and African Studies*, 57 (1994): 93–112. For an examination of Ibrahim's early works, including their reception and publication, see also Samia Mehrez, *Egyptian Writers between History and Fiction* (Cairo: American Univ. in Cairo Press, 1994).

18. My thanks to Nader Uthman for pointing this out.

19. One can add to this list Jamal al-Ghittani's 1974 novel *al-Zayni Barakat* (Beirut: Dar al-Shuruq, 1994), which also references torture and detention and can be considered a work of historiographic metafiction in Hutcheon's terms.

20. Waugh, "What Is Metafiction," 40.

21. Mark Currie, ed., *Metafiction* (New York: Longman, 1995), 2.

22. Ibid., 15.

23. See chapter 3 for a discussion of the concept of truth claims with reference to representations of torture and the narrative imperative.

24. Hatmal, *al-Majmu'a al-Qisasiyya al-Khams* (*The Five Story Collections*), 78.

25. 'Abd al-Rahman Munif, "Introduction," in *al-Majmu'a al-Qisasiyya al-Khams*, by Jamil Hatmal (Beirut: al-Mu'assasa al-'Arabiyya li-l-Dirasat wa-l-Nashr, 1998), 6.

26. Kofi Anyidoho, "Prison as Exile/Exile as Prison: Circumstance, Metaphor, and a Paradox of Modern African Literatures," in *The Word Behind Bars and the Paradox of Exile*, ed. Kofi Anyidoho (Evanston, IL: Northwestern Univ. Press, 1997), 3.

27. Ibid., 11, 2.

28. Ella Shohat, *Taboo Memories, Diasporic Voices* (Durham, NC: Duke Univ. Press, 2006), 308.

29. 'Abd al-Rahman Munif, *al-Katib wa-l-Manfa* (*The Writer and Exile*) (Beirut: Dar al-Fikr al-Jadid, 1992), 85.

30. In making this point, Munif draws a direct connection between Hatmal and exiled Iraqi poet Badr Shakir al-Sayyab. See Munif, "Introduction," 8–9.

31. Ibid., 12.

32. Edward Said, *Reflections on Exile and Other Essays* (Cambridge, MA: Harvard Univ. Press, 2000), 186.

33. Ibid.

34. Michael Hanne, "Creativity and Exile: An Introduction," in *Creativity in Exile*, ed. Michael Hanne (Amsterdam: Rodopi, 1994), 4, 5.

35. Abani cites Homi Bhabha, Arjun Appadurai, and Salman Rushdie in this respect. Chris Abani, "Resisting Anomie: Exile and the Romantic Self," *Creativity in Exile*, ed. Michael Hanne (Amsterdam: Rodopi, 1994), 22. See also the chapter "The Banality of Exile" in Zeina G. Halabi, *The Unmaking of the Arabic Intellectual: Prophecy, Exile, and the Nation* (Edinburgh: Edinburgh Univ. Press, 2017), Kindle.

36. Ibid., 22.

37. Said, as quoted in Abani, "Resisting Anomie," 23. Said writes, "Exile is neither aesthetically nor humanistically comprehensible: at most the literature about exile objectifies an anguish and a predicament most people rarely experience first hand; but to think of the exile informing this literature as beneficially humanistic is to banalize its mutilations, the losses it inflicts on those who suffer them, the muteness with which it responds to any attempt to understand it 'as good for us.'" Said, *Reflections*, 174.

38. Al-Jundi, *Sadiqi Ilyas* (*My Friend Ilyas*), 67.

39. Abani, "Resisting Anomie," 23.

40. Ibid., 24.

41. Also thanks to Nader Uthman for drawing this point out in his comments on an earlier draft of this chapter.

42. I am taking my citations of Hatmal's stories from his collected works that were published in a single volume in 1998 (*al-Majmu'a al-Qisasiyya al-Khams*). There are, of course, several exceptions to this assertion, including stories such as "The Policeman." The longest story directly depicting prison is in his last collection and is titled "It Happened Twelve Years Ago." My point here is not to say that prison is not a central focus of Hatmal's writings but rather that in his stories the experience of prison is often inscribed and depicted indirectly, and in some cases secondarily, via the psychological states and memories of his characters and narrators, or through the depictions of characters outside prison. Very few of the stories that take place within prison provide, for example, a physical description of prison space.

43. See chapter 2 for a discussion of the absence of politics in Ibrahim Samu'il's short stories.

44. Hatmal published four collections of short stories before his death: *al-Tifla Dhat al-Quba'a al-Bayda'* (*The Girl with the White Hat*, 1981), *Infi'alat* (*Reactions*, 1985), *Hayna La Balad* (*When There's No Country*, 1993), and *Qisas al-Mard, Qisas al-Junun* (*Stories of Illness, Stories of Madness*, 1994). His fifth collection, *Sa'aqul Lahum* (*I Will Tell Them*) is published only in the complete collection of his works that appeared in 1998, four years after his death.

45. Defamiliarization ("to make strange") is a key term used by Russian formalist Viktor Shklovsky. According to Shklovsky, the purpose of literature is to "make objects unfamiliar, to make forms difficult, to increase the difficulty and length of the perception process." Joseph W. Childers and Gary Hentzi, *The Columbia Dictionary of Modern Literary and Cultural Criticism* (New York: Columbia Univ. Press, 1995), 76. This is a key component of Hatmal's use of metafiction.

46. Said, *Reflections*, 180, 177.

47. Ibid., 177.

48. The metafictional references in Hatmal's texts are too numerous to mention here. However, another example of the theme of writing is the imaginary pledge written by a tenant conceding his rights to an unethical cement company and an official deposition written by a man who claims he didn't know his tenant was involved in politics ("A Mud House in the 'Amara District"). Also at the conclusion of the story "The Room under the Stairs," security officers force a battered student to write and sign an informer's report. Hatmal presents a familiar scene of a prisoner being forced to write a confession—to register his own guilt in official form and to inform on those around him. Yet in one of the few depictions of staunchly enacted resistance in the author's stories, the student does not

write about his cousin, he only writes about himself. In this case and in that of another story ("White Beds") that depicts an informer writing reports on his fellow prisoners, Hatmal juxtaposes the destructive capacities of official or authoritative writing with the tropes of inscription that his narratives both depict and embody. In "The Room Under the Stairs" the student who is forced to sign the confession resists this destructive capacity by remaining silent about his cousin.

In "The Policeman" the officer takes refuge in writing poetry and mourns the loss of his notebooks, which are taken from him while he is in prison. The loss of his ability to write in his notebooks causes Sami, the police officer, to suffer a breakdown, and at the end of the story, once he is released from prison, he begins to write on the walls of his house, "insulting the sergeant, the police, the government, and automobiles" (Hatmal, *al-Majmuʿa al-Qisasiyya al-Khams* [*The Five Story Collections*], 64). Writing, in this story, might be seen as a form of directly confronting the corruption of the state, but the loss of writing also signifies the advent of madness for the main character.

49. The collection is divided into three sections, titled "Reactions," "People," and "States." There are four stories in the first section, the three discussed here and a fourth one titled "Stay This Night, and for This Night Only" which can be linked to the three previous stories by the use of the same anonymous, first-person narrator. I have not included a discussion here of "Stay This Night" because it does not reference writing; nor does it speak as clearly as the other stories to the connection between writing, exile, and prison.

50. Hatmal, *al-Majmuʿa al-Qisasiyya al-Khams* (*The Five Story Collections*), 73.

51. Ibid.

52. Ibid., 74.

53. Ibid., 76.

54. Hatmal also uses the technique of revealing the narrator to be in prison at the conclusion of the narrative in several other stories. One example is "The Door," in which the narrator's revelry is broken at the end by the voice of an interrogator.

55. Hatmal, *al-Majmuʿa al-Qisasiyya al-Khams* (*The Five Story Collections*), 77.

56. Ibid., 78.

57. Ibid.

58. Ibid.

59. Ibid., 79.

60. Ibid.; ellipses in the original.

61. Ibid.

62. Said, *Reflections*, 179

63. Philip F. Williams and Yenna Wu, *The Great Wall of Confinement: The Chinese Prison Camp through Contemporary Ficton and Reportage* (Berkeley: Univ. of California Press, 2004), 173. See in particular Williams's and Wu's discussion of Cong Weixi's works.

64. This story can also be considered emblematic of the depiction of space in contemporary Syrian prison literature—particularly with the juxtaposition of the inside of

prison versus the outside as constructed through memory. See chapter 4 for discussions of the representations of prison space in other works.

65. Hatmal, *al-Majmuʻa al-Qisasiyya al-Khams* (*The Five Story Collections*), 97, ellipses in the original.

66. For example, a nostalgic, scenic description of the entrance to the protagonist's home village and allusions to his impending arrest are coupled with the mention of a cousin who will later be revealed as the informer who turned Abu Salih in to the authorities.

67. See chapter 3 for a discussion of ʻAbd al-Rahman's novel.

68. Hatmal, *al-Majmuʻa al-Qisasiyya al-Khams* (*The Five Story Collections*), 99, ellipses in the original.

69. Ibid., 100.

70. Ibid., 101.

71. Ibid., 102. In the original text, in several places where they would normally appear, question marks are not used; thus several of the sentences are stated as questions but punctuated as statements of fact. I have retained the original punctuation in my translation.

72. Said, *Reflections*, 179.

73. Munif, "Introduction," 13, 6.

74. Ibid., 6.

75. Anyidoho, "Prison," 16.

76. Said, *Reflections*, 173.

77. See chapter 3 for a discussion of Nabil Sulayman's novel and Yassin al-Haj Saleh's definition of the "ideology of prison."

78. Jacques Derrida, *Writing and Difference*, trans. Alan Bass (Chicago: Univ. of Chicago Press, 1980), 11.

79. Daghastani, *Duwar al-Hurriyya* (*The Vertigo of Freedom*), 20.

80. Ibid., 26.

81. Ibid., 26–27, ellipses in the original.

82. Ibid., 28, 29.

83. Ibid., 29.

84. Ibid.

85. Ibid., 55.

86. Ibid., 59, 61.

87. An example of this can be seen when he comments: "And suddenly the palm of my hand relaxed on her hip, and the truth is that my saying the word 'suddenly' is something unjustly crude to the spirit of what was happening" (Daghastani, *Duwar al-Hurriyya* [*The Vertigo of Freedom*], 81).

88. Daghastani, *Duwar al-Hurriyya* (*The Vertigo of Freedom*), 84–85; ellipses in the original.

89. Ibid., 92.

Coda

1. Zainab Saleh, "A Dream's End: Temporalities in Abounaddara's Emergency Cinema," In Media Res, February 8, 2016, mediacommons.org/imr/2016/02/06/dreams-end -temporalities-abounaddaras-emergency-cinema, accessed February 9, 2017.

2. Ibid.

3. Popan, Elena R., "Building New Platforms for Civil Society: The Right to Image in Syrian Abounaddara Collective's Cinema of Emergency," *Spectra: The Aspect Journal*, 5, no. 2 (2016), spectrajournal.org/articles/10.21061/spectra.v5i2.379/, accessed February 8, 2017.

4. As Cherif Kizwan has stated, "We try not to obey the media agenda. You are surprised because usually you see Syrian—always, always they are defined as Muslim against Christians, Sunni against Alawites. And in our films, people are represented as human beings." Kizwan as quoted in Popan, "Building."

5. Popan, "Building."

6. Ibid.

7. Ibid.

8. Abounaddara, "A Right to the Image for All: Concept Paper for the Coming Revolution," *Post: Notes on Modern and Contemporary Art Around the Globe*, October 19, 2015, post.at.moma.org/content_items/719-a-right-to-the-image-for-all-concept-paper-for -a-coming-revolution, accessed February 2, 2017.

9. Ibid.

10. Ibid.

11. Ibid.

12. James Dawes, *The Novel of Human Rights* (Cambridge, MA: Harvard Univ. Press, 2018), Kindle; Abounaddara, "Right to the Image."

13. Abounaddara, "Regarding the Spectacle: What Happens When a Society No Longer Has the Ability to Defend Itself Post-Truth?," *Nation*, December 2, 2016, www .thenation.com/article/regarding-the-spectacle/, accessed February 2, 2019.

14. My thanks to Glenn Urieta for explaining this and Alexa Firat for pointing me to the concept of stop-motion illustration.

15. For a description of the background and process of making the film, see Muhammad Malas, *Mufakkirat Film: al-Kullu fi Makanihi wa Kullu Shay' 'ala Ma Ya Ram Sidi al-Dabit (Damascus: Dar al-Mada, 2003).*

16. Abounaddara, "Right to the Image."

17. See Costas Douzinas, *The End of Human Rights* (Oxford, UK: Hart, 2000), and *Human Rights and Empire: The Political Philosophy of Cosmopolitanism* (Abingdon, UK: Routledge, 2007); Stephen Hopgood, *The End-Times of Human Rights* (Ithaca, NY: Cornell Univ. Press, 2015), Kindle; and Colin Dayan, *The Law Is a White Dog*, Princeton, NJ: Princeton Univ. Press, 2011.

18. Douzinas, *Human Rights and Empire*, 66.

Arabic Bibliography

Note: Some texts included in this bibliography lack complete information due to the circumstances of their publication.

'Abbas, 'Abbas Mahmud. *Tawqan ila al-Haya: Awraq Sajin* (*Longing for Life*). Beirut: Dar al-Khayal, 2015.

'Abd al-'Aziz, Ahmad. *Qadiyyat al-Sijn wa-l-Hurriyya fi Shi'r al-Andalus* (*The Issue of Prison and Freedom in the Poetry of al-Andalus*). Cairo: Maktabat al-Anjlu al-Misriyya, 1990.

'Abd al-Qadir, Salim. "Nuqta . . . Intaha al-Tahqiq" ("Point . . . the Interrogation Has Ended"). N.p.: Nashirun bila Hudud, 2006.

———. *Al-Qadimun al-Khidr* (*The Green Arrivals*). N.p.: Maktabat Bayt al-Muqaddas, n.d.

'Abd al-Rahman, Hasiba. *Saqata Sahwan* (*It Fell Inadvertently*). N.p: n.p., 2002.

———. "Shahadat Kitabat al-Riwayya Kharajit min al-Qalb wa-l-Dhakira" ("The Testimony of Writing a Novel that Came Out of the Heart and Memory"). *Dirasat Ishtirakiyya*, nos. 182/183 (2000): 425–27.

———. *Al-Sharnaqa* (*The Cocoon*). N.p.: n.p., 1999.

Abou Dehn, Ali (Abu Dahn, 'Ali). *'A'id min al-Jahannam* (*Returning from Hell*), 5th edition. Beirut: Dar al-Jadid wa Umam li-l-Tawthiq wa-l-Abhath, 2012.

Abounaddara (Abu Naddara), dir. *Al-Mu'taqal Ghayr Mawjud* (*The Detainee is Not Present*). 2012. Vimeo, vimeo.com/45297139.

———. *Sijn Saydnaya . . . Yarwihi al-Suri Alladhi Arada al-Thawra* (*Saydnaya Prison . . . as Narrated by the Syrian Who Wanted the Revolution*). 2016. Vimeo, vimeo.com/159464122.

———. *Al-Marid al-Suri* (*The Syrian Patient*). 2016. Vimeo, vimeo.com/1829 82740.

Abu Nidal, Nazih. *Adab al-Sujun* (*Prison Literature*). Beirut: Dar al-Hadatha, 1981.

'Adwan, Mamduh. "Introduction." In *Ra'ihat al-Khatw al-Thaqil* (*The Stench of the Heavy Step*), by Ibrahim Samu'il. Damascus: Dar al-Jundi, 1990.

Antoon, Sinan (Antun, Sinan). *I'jam*. Beirut: Dar al-Adab, 2004.

'Arsan, 'Ali 'Uqla. *Al-Sajin 95* (Prisoner 95). Damascus: Munshurat Ittihad al-Kuttab al-'Arab, 1974.

al-Atassi, Muhammad 'Ali. "Hiwar: al-Sha'ir Faraj Bayraqdar Yarwi Tajribatahu al- I'tiqal wa-l-Hurriyya" ("Interview: The Poet Faraj Bayraqdar Tells of His Experience of Detention and Freedom"). Al-Hiwar al-Mutamaddin, January 2, 2002. www.ahewar.org/debat/show.art.asp?aid=651. Accessed September 8, 2018.

———, dir. *Ibn al-'Amm* (*Cousin*). 2001; Syria.

'Attum, Ayman. *Yasma'un Hasisha* (*They Hear Her Faint Sound*). Beirut: al-Mu'assasa al-'Arabiyya li-l-Dirasat wa-l-Nashr, 2012.

'Azzam, Mamduh. *Ma'raj al-Mawt* (*The Ascension of Death*). Damascus: Dar al-Balad, 2003.

al-'Azzawi, Fadil. *Al-Qal'a al-Khamisa* (*Cellblock Five*). Cologne: al-Jamal, 2000.

Baghdadi, Shawqi. "Introduction." In *Asabi' al-Mawz* (Banana Fingers), by Ghassan al-Jaba'i. Damascus: Wizarat al-Thaqafa, 1994.

Bayraqdar, Faraj. "Awal Thawra fi al-Tarikh Yaqdahu Shararataha al-Atfal" ("The First Revolution in History That's Spark Was Ignited Children"). Al-Hiwar al-Mutamaddin, June 10, 2011. www.ahewar.org/debat/show.art.asp?aid=262727. Accessed April 30, 2016.

———. *Hamama Mutlaqat al-Jinahayn* (*Dove in Free Flight*). Beirut: n.p., 1997.

———. *Khiyanat al-Lugha wa-l-Samt* (*The Betrayals of Language and Silence*). Beirut: Dar al-Jadid, 2006.

———. *Al-Khuruj min al-Kahf: Yawmiyat al-Sijn wa-l-Hurriyya* (*Exiting the Cave: Chronicles of Prison and Freedom*). Beirut: al-Mu'assasa al-'Arabiyya li-l-Dirasat wa-l-Nashr, 2013.

———. "Tahiyya ila Adunis: Raddan li-l-Jamil" ("Greetings to Adonis: A Response to the Kindness"). Al-Hiwar al-Mutamaddin, April 1, 2006. www.ahewar.org/debat/show.art.asp?aid=61100&r=0. Accessed July 1, 2020.

———. *Taqasim Asawiyya* (*Asian Improvisations*). Damascus: Dar al-Hawran, 2001.

———. *Wa Ma Inta Wahdak* (*You Are Not Alone*). Beirut: Dar al-Haqa'iq, 1979.

Bazzi, Yusif. "Tawqan ila al-Haya: Awraq 'Abbas 'Abbas fi Sujun Suriya" ("Longing for Life: The Papers of 'Abbas 'Abbas on the Prisons of Syria"). Al-Mudun, May

توقا-إلى-الحياة-أوراق-عباس-عباس/www.almodon.com/culture/2017/5/26 ,2017 ,26
في-السجون-السورية. Accessed September 10, 2018.

al-Bizra, Ahmad Mukhtar. *Al-'Asr wa-l-Sijn fi al-Shi'r al-'Arabi* (*Captivity and Prison in Arabic Poetry*). Damascus: Mu'assasat 'Ulum al-Quran, 1985.

al-Dabbagh, Hiba. *Khams Daqa'iq wa Hasb: Tis' Sanawat fi Sujun Suriya* (*Just Five Minutes: Nine Years in the Prisons of Syria*). Cairo: al-Zahra li-l-'Ilam al-'Arabi, 1998.

Daghastani, Malik. *Duwar al-Hurriyya* (*The Vertigo of Freedom*). Damascus: Dar al-Balad, 2002.

Dughaym, Muhammad Ghanim. *Diwan Tadmur: Wathiqa li-l-Tarikh min Sijn Tadmur al-'Askari* (*The Tadmur Collection: A Document for History from Tadmur Military Prison*). Beirut: Dar al-Nawa'ir, 2013.

Fadil, Khalid. "Fi al-Qa': Sanatayn fi Sijn Tadmur al-Sahrawi" ("In the Abyss: Two Years in Tadmur Desert Prison"). Syrian Human Rights Committee, February 29, 2004. www.shrc.org/?p=7502. Accessed September 29, 2018.

al-Faysal, Samir Ruhi. *Al-Sijn al-Siyasi fi al-Riwayya al-'Arabiyya* (*Political Prison in the Arabic Novel*). Tripoli: Jurus Burus, 1994.

Faris, Muhammad 'Adil. *La'nahum Qalu La* (*Because They Said No*). N.p.: Nashi-run Bila Hudud, 2006.

al-Ghazzali, Zaynab. *Ayyam min Hayati* (*Days from My Life*). 1978. Reprint, Cairo: Dar al-Tawzi' wa-l-Nashr al-Islamiyya, 1999.

al-Ghittani, Jamal. *Al-Zayni Barakat.* 1974. Reprint, Beirut: Dar al-Shuruq, 1994.

Haddad, Lutfi. *Riyad Turk: Mandila Suriya* (*Riyad Turk: The Mandela of Syria*). Newburg: Mu'assasat Judhur al-Thaqafa, 2005.

Haddad, Rida. "Muqtitafat min Shahadat al-Sahafi Rida Haddad" ("Excerpts from the Testimony of the Journalist Rida Haddad"). Syrian Human Rights Committee, January 11, 2004. www.shrc.org/?p=6891. Accessed September 10, 2018.

al-Haj Saleh, Yassin (al-Hajj Salih, Yasin). *Bi-l-Khalas, Ya Shabab! Sittin 'Aman fi al-Sujun al-Suriyya* (*At Last, Boys! Sixteen Years in Syrian Prisons*). Beirut: Dar al-Saqi, 2012.

———. "Hal Yamkan li-l-Sijn an Yakun Namat li-l-Haya?" ("Is It Possible for Prison to Be a Form of Life?" Al-Hiwar al-Mutamaddin, June 20, 2004. www.rezgar.com. Accessed August 30, 2005.

———. "Su'bat al-Tadhakkur wa Istihalat al-Nisiyan" ("The Difficulty of Remembering and the Impossibility of Forgetting"). Al-Hiwar al-Mutamaddin, December 24, 2003. www.rezgar.com. Accessed August 30, 2005.

Halasa, Ghalib. *Al-Khamasin*. Cairo: Dar al Thaqafa al-Jadida, 1975.

al-Hamadi, Mahmud. *Mafatih al-Sijn al-Suri: Mustalahat min wara' al-Qudban* (*Keys to Syrian Prison: Terms from behind Bars*) Beirut: Umam li-l-Tawthiq wa-l-Abhath, 2012.

Hammad, Muhammad Salim. "Tadmur: Shahid wa Mashhud, 1980–1991" ("Tadmur: Witness and Witnessed, 1980–1991"). Syrian Human Rights Committee, July 16, 2007. www.shrc.org/?p=15321. Accessed September 18, 2018.

Hasan, Rosa Yaseen (Hasan, Ruza Yasin). "Adab al-Sujun fi Suriya: Masirat Alf Mil" ("Prison Literature in Syria: The Journey of a Thousand Miles"). Al-Huwar al-Mutamaddin, April 7, 2006. www.m.ahewar.org/s.asp?aid=69138&r=0. Accessed November 1, 2018.

———. *Huras al-Hawa* (*Guardians of Air*). Beirut: Dar al-Kawkab, 2009.

———. *Nighatif: Min Dhakirat al-Mu'taqalat al-Surriyat* (*Negative: From the Memory of Female Syrian Detainees*). Cairo: Markaz al-Qahira li-Dirasat Huquq al-Insan, 2008.

Hatmal, Jamil. *al-Majmu'a al-Qisasiyya al-Khams* (*The Five Story Collections*). Beirut: al-Mu'assasa al-'Arabiyya li-l-Dirasat wa-l-Nashr, 1998.

Hawrani, Faysal. *Al-Muhasarun* (*The Besieged*). Damascus: N.p., 1973.

Hawraniyya, Sa'id. "Al-Mahja' al-Rabi'" ("The Fourth Barracks"). In *Sanatayn wa Tahtariq al-Ghaba* (*Two Years and the Forest Burns*). Damascus: Dar al-Mada, 2000.

Haydar, Haydar. *Walima li-l-A'shab al-Bahr* (*A Feast for Seaweed*). Damascus: Dar al-Ward, 2000.

Himmich, Bensalem (Himmish, Binsalim). *Majnun al-Hukm* (*The Theocrat*). London: Riad el-Rayyes, 1990.

Husayn, Lu'ay. *Al-Faqd: Hikayat min Dhakira Mutakhayyala li-Sajin Haqiqi* (*Loss: Stories from an Imaginary Memory of a True Prisoner*). Beirut: Dar al-Furat, 2006.

Ibrahim, Sun'allah. *Sharaf*. Cairo: Dar al-Hilal, 1997.

———. *Tilka Ra'iha wa Qisas 'Ukhra* (*That Smell and Other Stories*). 1966. Reprint, Cairo: Dar al-Mustaqbal, 1993.

———. *Yawmiyat al-Wahat* (*The Diaries of the Oases*). Cairo: Dar al-Mustaqbal al-'Arabi, n.d.

Ibrahim, Talib Kamil. *As'ila* (*Questions*). Damascus: Dar Hawran, 2004.

———. *Shu'a' al-Shams* (*Sun Rays*). N.p.: n.p, 2002.

Ikhlasi, Walid. *Al-Dahisha fi al-'Uyun al-Qasiyya* (*The Surprise in Cruel Eyes*). Damascus: Wizarat al-Thaqafa, 1972.

Isma'il, Sidqi. *Al-'Usa'* (*The Rebels*). Beirut: Manshurat Dar al-Tali'a, 1964.

Ismandar, Wadi'. *Al-Rajul al-'Ari* (*The Naked Man*). Beirut: Dar al-Quds, 1979.

———. *Sirat Rajul Ma* (*The Biography of Some Man*). Damascus: Wizarat al-Thaqafa, 1979.

al-Jaba'i, Ghassan. *Asabi' al-Mawz* (*Banana Fingers*). Damascus: Wizarat al-Thaqafa, 1994.

———. *Thalath Masrahiyat* (*Three Plays*). Damascus: Wizarat al-Thaqafa, 1995.

———. *Al-Wahl* (*The Mud*). Damascus: Wizarat al-Thaqafa, 1999.

Jaridat al-Zaytun wa Markaz li-l-Tufula wa-l-Ta'hil. *Hayna Tatahaddath al-Zanazin: 'An Mu'taqalin min Idlib Qadu taht al-Ta'dhib* (*When the Prison Cells Speak: Detainees from Idlib Who Died under Torture*). Gaziantep: Nun 'Arb'a li-l-Nashr wa-l-Taba'a wa-l-Tawzi', 2018.

al-Jundi, 'Asim. *Al-Ightiyal* (*The Assassination*). Beirut: Dar al-Farabi, 1999.

al-Jundi, Sami. *Sadiqi Ilyas* (*My Friend Elias*). Beirut: Dar al-Nahar, 1969.

Kanafani, Ghassan. *Rijal fi al-Shams* (*Men in the Sun*). 1963. Reprint, Beirut: Mu'assasat al-Abhath al-'Arabiyya, 1998.

Karabit, Aram. *Al-Rahil ila al-Majhul: Yawmiyati fi Sujun Suriya* (*Journey to the Unknown: My Diaries in Syrian Prisons*). Alexandria: Jidar li-l-Thaqafa wa-l-Nashr, 2010.

Kassab, Jurj. *Al-Jallad: 'Ashrat Ayyam fi Sijn al-Mezzeh* (*The Executioner: Ten Days in al-Mezzeh Prison*). Beirut: Dar Saydun, 1983.

al-Kawni, Ibrahim. *Al-Qafs* (*The Cage*). Limassol: Dar al-Tanwir, 1992.

Khadir, Khalifa. *Al-Kana'is: Shahadat min Sujun Tanzim al-Dawla fi Suriya* (*The Kana'is: Testimonies from the Prison of ISIS in Syria*). Damascus: Dar Mamduh 'Adwan li-l-Nashr wa-l-Tawzi', 2018.

Khalifa, Khalid. *Madih al-Karahiyya* (*In Praise of Hatred*). Beirut: Dar al-Adab, 2008.

Khalifa, Mustafa. *Al-Qawqa'a* (*The Shell*). Beirut: Dar al-Adab, 2008.

al-Khatib, Muhammad Kamil. *Al-Mudun al-Sahiliyya* (*The Coastal Cities*). Beirut: Dar Ibn Rushd, 1979.

Khoury, Elias (Khuri, Ilyas). *Yalu*. Beirut: Dar al-Adab, 2002.

Khust, Nadya. *Fi Sijn 'Akka* (*In the Prison of Acre*). Damascus: Manshurat Wizarat al-Thaqafa, 1984.

al-Kurdi, 'Ali. *Mawkib al-Batt al-Bari'* (*The Procession of Innocent Ducks*). Damascus: Dar al-Kan'an, 1998.

al-Lajna al-Suriyya li-Huquq al-Insan (Syrian Human Rights Committee). "Majzarat Hama (1982): Mas'uliyyat al-Qanun Tastawjib al-Muhasaba"

("The Massacre of Hama [1982]: The Responsibilities of the Law Require Accountability"), February 22, 1999 (reissued February 14, 2004), web. archive.org/web/20130528222037/http://www.shrc.org/data/aspx/d3/53 .aspx.

Maghout, Jalal (Maghut, Jalal), dir. *Suleima*. 2014; France.

al-Maghut, Muhammad. *A'mal Muhammad al-Maghut* (*The Works of Muhammad al-Maghut*). Damascus: Dar al-Mada, 1998.

———. *Al-Muharrij* (*The Jester*). Damascus: Dar al-Mada, 1998.

———. *Sa'akhun Watani* (*I Will Betray My Nation*). Damascus: Dar al-Mada, 2001.

———. *Al-'Usfur al-Ihdab* (*The Hunchback Sparrow*). Beirut: al-Dar al-Sharqiyya, 1967.

Mahfouz, Najib. *Al-Karnak*. Cairo: Dar Misr, 1986.

Majed, Ziad (Majid, Ziyad). *Suriya: al-Thawra al-Yatima* (*Syria: The Orphaned Revolution*). Beirut: Sharq al-Kitab, 2014.

Malas, Muhammad. *Mufakkirat Film: al-Kullu fi Makanihi wa Kullu Shay' 'ala Ma Ya Ram Sidi al-Dabit* (*A Film Notebook: Everything Is in Its Place and Is as It Should Be, Officer, Sir*). Damascus: Dar al-Mada, 2003.

———, dir. *Ahlam al-Madina* (*Dreams of the City*). 1984; Syria.

———, dir. *Bab al-Maqam* (*Passion*). 2005; Tunisia, France, Syria.

———, dir. *Fawq al-Raml, That al-Shams* (*Over the Sand, Under the Sun*). 1998; France.

———, dir. *Al-Kullu fi Makanihi wa Kullu Shay' 'ala Ma Ya Ram Sidi al-Dabit* (*Everything Is in Its Place and Is as It Should Be, Officer, Sir*). 1974; Moscow.

———, dir. *Sullam ila Dimashq* (*Ladder to Damascus*). 2013; Qatar, Lebanon, Syria.

Mina, Hanna. *Al-Masabih al-Zurq* (*The Blue Lanterns*). Beirut: Dar al-Adab, 1982.

———. *Al-Thalj Ya'ti min al-Nafidha* (*The Snow Comes from the Window*). Beirut: Dar al-Adab, 1999.

Minassa, May. *Awraq Dafatir Sajin* (*Papers of a Prisoner's Notebooks*). Beirut: Dar al-Nahar, 2001.

Mohammad, Hala (Muhammad, Hala), dir. *Rihla ila al-Dhakira* (*A Journey into Memory*). 2006; Syria.

Mu'as'as, Riyad. *Hammam Zunubiya* (*Zenoubia's Bath*). Tunis: Dar al-Junub li-l-Nashr, 2012.

Munif, ʿAbd al-Rahman. *Alan . . . Huna aw Sharq al-Mutawassit Marratan 'Ukhra* (*Here . . . Now or East of the Mediterranean Once Again*). Beirut: al-Muʾassasa al-ʿArabiyya li-l-Dirasat wa-l-Nashr, 1997.

———. "Introduction." In *Al-Majmuʿa al-Qisasiya al-Khams*, by Jamil Hatmal. Beirut: al-Muʾassasa al-ʿArabiyya li-l-Dirasat wa-l-Nashr, 1998.

———. *Al-Katib wa-l-Manfa* (*The Writer and Exile*). Beirut: Dar al-Fikr al-Jadid, 1992.

———. *Sharq al-Mutawassit* (*East of the Mediterranean*). 1977. Reprint, Beirut: al-Muʾassasa al-ʿArabiyya li-l-Dirasat wa-l-Nashr, 1999.

Naʿisa, Hasan. *Shuʿaraʾ waraʾ al-Qudban* (*Poets Behind Bars*). Beirut: Dar al-Haqaʾiq, 1986.

al-Naji, ʿAbdullah. "Hammamat al-Damm fi Sijn Tadmur" ("Bloodbaths in Tadmur Prison"). Syrian Human Rights Committee, July 16, 2008. www.shrc .org/wpcontent/uploads/2008/07/tadmurbloodbaths.pdf. Accessed September 9, 2018.

Naqqash, Farida. *Al-Sijn . . . al-Watn* (*The Prison . . . The Nation*). Beirut: Dar al-Kalima li-l-Nashr, 1980.

Qasir, Samir. *Dimuqratiyyat Suriya wa Istiqlal Lubnan: al-Bahth ʿan Rabiʿ Dimashq* (*The Democracy of Syria and the Independence of Lebanon: The Search for the Damascus Spring*). Beirut: Dar al-Nahar li-l-Nashr, 2004.

al-Rabiʿi, ʿAbd al-Rahman Majid. *Al-Washm* (*The Tattoo*). Beirut: Dar al-ʿAwda, 1972.

al-Rayyis, Munir. *Al-Kitab al-Dhahabi li-l-Thawrat al-Wataniyya fi al-Mashriq al-ʿArabi* (*The Golden Book of the National Revolutions in the Arab Mashriq*). Beirut: Dar al-Taliʿa li-l-Tibaʿa wa-l-Nashr, 1969.

Razzaz, Munif. *Al-Tajriba al-Murra* (*The Bitter Experience*). Beirut: Dar Ghandur, 1967.

Rifaʿiyya, Yasin. *Al-Rijal al-Khatirun* (*Dangerous Men*). Beirut: Dar al-Taliʿa, 1979.

al-Sabaʿi, Fadil. *Huzn Hata al-Mawt* (*Sorrow Until Death*). Damascus: Dar Ishbiliya, 2002.

———. *Al-Ibtisamat fi al-Ayyam al-Sʿaba* (*Smiles on Difficult Days*). Damascus: Dar Ishbiliya, 2002.

al-Safadi, Mutaʿ. "Al-Shams Khalf al-Qudban" ("The Sun Behind Bars"). *Al-Adab* 7, no. 2–4 (1964): 66–68.

Saʿid, Rifʿat. *Al-Basaqa* (*Spit*). Beirut: Dar Ibn Khaldun, 1980.

Salama, ʿAbdallah ʿIsa. *Baʾis fi Firdus al-Shaytan* (*Wretched in the Paradise of the Devil*). Amman: Dar al-Ammar, 2010.

al-Samad, Wadih. *Al-Sujun wa ʾAthruha fi al-Adab al-ʿArabi* (*Prisons and Their Influence on Arabic Literature*). Beirut: al-Muʾassasa al-Jamiʿiyya li-l-Dirasat wa-l-Nashr wa-l-Tawziʿ, 1995.

Samuʾil, Ibrahim. *Al-Nahnahat* (*Ahem, Ahem*). Damascus: Dar al-Jundi, 1990.

———. *Raʾihat al-Khatw al-Thaqil* (*The Stench of the Heavy Step*). Damascus: Dar al-Jundi, 1990.

Sarraj, Bara (al-Sarraj, Baraʾ). *Min Tadmur ila Harvard: Rihlat Sajin ʿAdim al-Raʾi* (*From Tadmur to Harvard: The Journey of a Prisoner Lacking an Opinion*). Middletown, DE: n.p, 2016.

al-Sarraj, Manhal. *Kama Yanbaghi li-Nahr: Riwayya* (*As a River Should: A Novel*). Beirut: al-Dar al-ʿArabiyya li-l-ʿUlum, 2007.

Saʿud, Ghassan. "Darʿa Madinat al-Ashbah: Rihla fi Thawra Lam Tulid Baʿd" ("Darʿa, the City of Ghosts: A Journey in a Revolution Not Yet Born"). *Al-Akhbar*, March 25, 2011. www.al-akhbar.com/node/7549/. Accessed April 30, 2016.

Sawwah, Waʾil. *Limadha Mat Yusif al-Najjar* (*Why Did Joseph the Carpenter Die*). N.p.: Dar al-Haqaʾiq, 1979.

———. *Qalit Iman* (*Iman Said*). N.p: n.p, n.d.

Sharif, Muhammad. "ʿAdab al-Sujun fi Suriya: al-Kitaba did al-Nisiyan" ("Prison Literature in Syria: Writing Against Forgetfulness"). Swissinfo, May 4, 2014. www.swissinfo.ch/ara/ندوة--في-رواق-الثقافات-العربية-_-أدب--السجون--في--سوريا-- أو--الكتابة-ضد-الن-سيان/38498508. Accessed November 1, 2018.

Shiha, ʿImad. *Baqaya min Zaman Babil* (*Remnants from the Time of Babel*). Damascus: Dar al-Sawsan, 2007.

———. *Ghubar al-Talʿ* (*Pollen*). Beirut: al-Markaz al-Thaqafi al-ʿArabi, 2006.

———. *Mawt Mushtahin* (*A Desired Death*). Damascus: Dar al-Sawsan, 2005.

Sulayman, Nabil. "Nahwa Adab al-Sujūn" ("Toward Prison Literature"). *Al-Mawqif al-Adabi* 1/2 (May/June 1973): 137–41.

———. *Samar al-Layali* (*Nightly Conversations*). Latakia: Dar al-Hiwar, 2000.

———. *Al-Sijn* (*The Prison*). 1972. Reprint, Latakia: Dar al-Hiwar, 1999.

Sulayman, Nabil, and Bu ʿAli Yasin. *Al-Idiulujiyya wa-l-Adab fi Suriya 1967–1973* (*Ideology and Literature in Syria, 1967–1973*). Latakia: Dar al-Hiwar, 1985.

Tamir, Zakariya. *Al-Numur fi al-Yawm al-ʿAshir* (*Tigers on the Tenth Day*). 1978. Reprint, Beirut: Riad el-Rayyes, 2000.

———. *Rabiʿ fi al-Ramad* (*Spring in the Ashes*). Beirut: Riad el-Rayyes, 2001.

———. *Taksir Rakb* (*Breaking Knees*). Beirut: Riad el-Rayyes, 2002.

Tanjour, Alfoz (Tanjur, Alfuz), dir. *Dhakira bi-l-Lawn al-Khaki* (*A Memory in Khaki*). 2016; Qatar.

'Ubayd, Salama. *Abu Sabir: al-Tha'ir al-Mansi Marratayn* (*Abu Sabir: the Twice Forgotten Revolutionary*). Damascus: Manshurat Wizarat al-Thaqafa, 1971.

al-'Ujayli, 'Abd al-Salam. *Majhula 'ala al-Tariq* (*Unknown on the Road*). London: Riad El-Rayyes, 1997.

'Uthman, Hashim. *Al-Muhakamat al-Siyasiyya fi Suriya* (*Political Trials in Syria*). Beirut: Riad el-Reyyes, 2004.

Uthman, Layla. *Al-Muhakama* (*The Trial*). Damascus: Dar al-Mada, 2000.

Wannus, Sa'd Allah. Al-*Malik Huwwa al-Malik* (*The King Is the King*). 1977.

Zakariya, Ghassan. *Fi Sujun al-Ba'th* (*In the Prisons of the Ba'th*). London: Ibla, 1999.

Zarzur, Faris. *Al-La'ijtima'iun* (*The Antisocial Ones*). Damascus: Dar al-Jalil, 1981.

English Bibliography

Abani, Chris. "Resisting Anomie: Exile and the Romantic Self." In *Creativity in Exile*, edited by Michael Hanne, 21–30. Amsterdam: Rodopi, 1994.

'Abd-allah, Umar F. *The Islamic Struggle in Syria*. Berkeley, CA: Mizan, 1983.

Abou Shariefeh, Abdel-Qader. "The Prison in the Contemporary Arabic Novel." PhD diss., University of Michigan, 1983.

Abounaddara. "Regarding the Spectacle: What Happens When a Society No Longer Has the Ability to Defend Itself Post-Truth?" *Nation*, December 2, 2016. www.thenation.com/article/regarding-the-spectacle/. Accessed February 2, 2019.

———. "A Right to the Image for All: Concept Paper for the Coming Revolution." Post: Notes on Modern and Contemporary Art around the Globe, October 19, 2015. post.at.moma.org/content_items/719-a-right-to-the-image-for-all-concept-paper-for-a-coming-revolution. Accessed February 2, 2017.

Abramowitz, Isidore. *The Great Prisoners: The First Anthology of Literature Written in Prison*. New York: E. P. Dutton, 1946.

Adorno, Theodor W. *Notes to Literature*, vol. 2. Translated by Shierry Weber Nicholsen. New York: Columbia Univ. Press, 1992.

Afshar, Sara. "Assad's Syria Recorded Its Own Atrocities: The World Can't Ignore Them." *Guardian*, August 27, 2018. www.theguardian.com/commentisfree/2018/aug/27/assad-syria-atrocities-regime-photographed-murdered. Accessed December 10, 2018.

Agamben, Giorgio. *Homo Sacer: Sovereign Power and Bare Life*. Translated by Daniel Heller-Roazen. Stanford, CA: Stanford Univ. Press, 1998.

———. *Means without End: Notes on Politics*. Translated by Vincenzo Binetti and Cesare Casarino. Minneapolis: Univ. of Minnesota Press, 2000.

———. *Remnants of Auschwitz: The Witness and the Archive*. Translated by Daniel Heller-Roazen. Brooklyn: Zone, 2005.

Ahnert, Ruth. *The Rise of Prison Literature in the Sixteenth Century*. Cambridge, UK: Cambridge Univ. Press, 2017.

Ali, Mir Adnan, and Steve Mann. "The Inevitability of the Transition from a Surveillance-Society to a Veillance-Society: Moral and Economic Grounding for Sousveillance." IEEE International Symposium on Technology and Society (ISTAS). Toronto, June 2013.

Allen, Lori. *The Rise and Fall of Human Rights: Cynicism and Politics in Occupied Palestine*. Stanford, CA: Stanford Univ. Press, 2013.

Allen, Roger. *The Arabic Novel: An Historical and Critical Introduction*. Syracuse, NY: Syracuse Univ. Press, 1995.

———. *An Introduction to Arabic Literature*. Cambridge, UK: Cambridge Univ. Press, 2000.

Amnesty International. "Challenging Repression: Human Rights Defenders in the Middle East and North Africa." Amnesty International, March 11, 2009. www.amnesty.org/en/library/info/MDE01/001/2009/en. Accessed April 10, 2009.

———. "Human Slaughterhouse: Mass Hangings and Extermination at Saydnaya Prison Syria." Amnesty International, February 7, 2017. www.amnesty .org/en/documents/mde24/5415/2017/en/,/. Accessed August 9, 2018.

———. "Syria." *Amnesty International Annual Report 2005*. May 24, 2005. www .amnesty.org/en/documents/pol10/0001/2005/en/.

———. "Syria: Amnesty International Welcomes Syria's Accession to the UN Convention Against Torture." Amnesty International, September 23, 2004, http://web.amnesty.org/library/index/engMDE240692004?open&of=eng -2d2. Accessed September 8, 2008.

———. "Syria: Harrowing Torture, Summary Killings in Secret ISIS Detention Centers." Amnesty International, December 19, 2013. www.amnesty.org/en /latest/news/2013/12/syria-harrowing-torture-summary-killings-secret-isis -detention-centres/. Accessed October 21, 2017.

———. "Syria: Torture by the Security Forces." Amnesty International, September 1984, 18–21.

———. "Syria: Torture, Despair, and Dehumanisation in Tadmor Military Prison." Amnesty International, September 18, 2001. www.amnesty.org/down load/Documents/132000/mde240142001en.pdf. Accessed September 8, 2008.

Amnesty International and Forensic Architecture. "Saydnaya: Inside a Syrian Torture Prison." Amnesty International, undated (c. August 2016). saydnaya .amnesty.org/?kind=explore. Accessed December 15, 2016.

Anker, Elizabeth S. *Fictions of Dignity: Embodying Human Rights and World Literature.* Ithaca, NY: Cornell Univ. Press, 2012.

Anyidoho, Kofi. "Prison as Exile/Exile as Prison: Circumstance, Metaphor, and a Paradox of Modern African Literatures." In *The Word behind Bars and the Paradox of Exile,* edited by Kofi Anyidoho, 1–17. Evanston, IL: Northwestern Univ. Press, 1997.

———, ed. *The Word behind Bars and the Paradox of Exile.* Evanston, IL: Northwestern Univ. Press, 1997.

Arar v. Ashcroft (Maher Arar v. John Ashcroft et al. United States District Court, Eastern District of New York). Center for Constitutional Rights. January 22, 2004. ccrjustice.org/ourcases/current-cases/arar-v.-ashcroft#files. Accessed November 24, 2008.

Arendt, Hannah. *The Origins of Totalitarianism.* 1948. Reprint, New York: Houghton Mifflin Harcourt, 1994. Kindle.

Bahari, Maziar. *Then They Came for Me: A Story of Injustice and Survival in Iran's Most Notorious Prison.* London: Oneworld, 2013.

———, dir. *82 Names: Syria, Please Don't Forget Us.* 2018, USA.

Bakare-Yusuf, Bibi. "The Economy of Violence: Black Bodies and the Unspeakable Terror." In *Feminist Theory and the Body: A Reader,* edited by Janet Price and Margrit Shildrick, 311–23. Edinburgh: Edinburgh Univ. Press, 1999.

Bakhtin, Mikhael. *The Dialogical Imagination.* Austin: Univ. of Texas Press, 1981.

———. *Problems of Dostoevsky's Poetics.* Minneapolis: Univ. of Minnesota Press, 2003.

———. *Speech Genres and Other Late Essays.* Austin: Univ. of Texas Press, 1986.

Bakhtin, M. M., and P. N. Medvedev. *The Formal Method in Literary Scholarship.* Translated by Albert Wehrle. Baltimore: John Hopkins Univ. Press, 1991.

Batatu, Hanna. *Syria's Peasantry, the Descendants of Its Lesser Rural Notables, and Their Politics.* Princeton, NJ: Princeton Univ. Press, 1999.

Baxi, Upendra. *The Future of Human Rights.* New Delhi: Oxford Univ. Press, 2002.

Bayraqdar, Faraj. *Dove in Free Flight.* Translated by New York Translation Collective. Fayetteville, AR: UpSet Press, forthcoming.

———. *Mirrors of Absence.* Translated by John Asfour. Toronto: Guernica, 2015.

BBC. "Inside Tadmur: The Worst Prison in the World?" *BBC Magazine,* June 20, 2015. www.bbc.com/news/magazine-33197612. Accessed October 15, 2017.

Berlant, Lauren. "Poor Eliza." *American Literature* 70, no. 3 (1998): 635–68.

————. "The Subject of True Feeling: Pain, Privacy, and Politics." In *Cultural Pluralism, Identity Politics, and the Law,* edited by Austin Serat and Thomas R. Kearns, 49–82. Ann Arbor: Univ. of Michigan Press, 1999.

Bernard, Anna. "States of Cynicism: Literature and Human Rights in Israel/Palestine." In *The Routledge Companion to Literature and Human Rights,* edited by Sophia A. McClennan and Alexandra Schultheis Moore, 373–79. Abingdon, UK: Routledge, 2016. Kindle.

Bondi, Liz, Joyce Davidson, and Mick Smith. "Introduction: Geography's 'Emotional' Turn." In *Emotional Geographies,* edited by Liz Bondi, Joyce Davidson, and Mick Smith, 1–16. Hampshire, UK: Ashgate, 2012. Kindle.

Boochani, Behrouz. *No Friend but the Mountains.* Translated by Omid Tofighian. London: Picador, 2019.

Booth, Marilyn. "Women's Prison Memoirs in Egypt and Elsewhere: Prison, Gender, Praxis." *MERIP Middle East Report* 149 (November–December 1987): 35–41.

Botelho, Greg, and Khushbu Shah. "ISIS Is 'Everywhere' in Syria's Ancient City of Palmyra." CNN, May 22, 2015. www.cnn.com/2015/05/21/middleeast/isis -syria-iraq/index.html. Accessed September 10, 2017.

Bourke, Joanna. *The Story of Pain: From Prayer to Painkillers.* Oxford: Oxford Univ. Press, 2014. Kindle.

Bradley, Mark Philip and Patrice Petro, eds. *Truth Claims: Representation and Human Rights.* New Brunswick, NJ: Rutgers Univ. Press, 2002.

Butler, Judith. *Precarious Life: The Powers of Mourning and Violence.* London: Verso, 2004.

Camille, Michael. "Simulacrum." In *Critical Terms for Art History,* edited by Robert S. Nelson and Richard Shiff. Chicago: Univ. of Chicago Press, 2003, Kindle.

Cave, Terence. *Recognitions: A Study in Poetics.* Oxford, UK: Clarendon, 2002.

Chase, Anthony. "Introduction: Human Rights and Agency in the Arab World." In *Human Rights in the Arab World: Independent Voices,* edited by Anthony Chase and Amr Hamzawy, 1–17. Philadelphia: Univ. of Pennsylvania Press, 2006.

Chase, Anthony, and Amr Hamzawy, eds. *Human Rights in the Arab World: Independent Voices.* Philadelphia: Univ. of Pennsylvania Press, 2006.

Cheliotis, Leonidas K. *The Arts of Imprisonment: Culture, Resistance, and Empowerment.* Oxon, UK: Routledge, 2016.

Chevigny, Bell Gale. *Doing Time: 25 Years of Prison Writing*. New York: Arcade, 1999.

Childers, Joseph W., and Gary Hentzi. *The Columbia Dictionary of Modern Literary and Cultural Criticism*. New York: Columbia Univ. Press, 1995.

Cohen, Margaret. "Sentimental Communities." In *The Literary Channel: The Inter-National Invention of the Novel*, edited by Margaret Cohen and Carolyn Dever, 106–32. Princeton, NJ: Princeton Univ. Press, 2001.

——. *The Sentimental Education of the Novel*. Princeton, NJ: Princeton Univ. Press, 2002.

Cohen, Stanley, and Laurie Taylor. "Time and the Long-Term Prisoner." In *The Sociology of Time*, edited by John Hassard, 178–87. New York: St. Martin's, 1990.

Cole, Elizabeth Ann. "Towards a Poetics of Russian Prison Literature: Writings on Prison by Dostoevsky, Chekhov, and Solzhenitsyn." PhD diss., Yale University, 1991.

Colie, Rosalie. *The Resources of Kind: Genre-Theory in the Renaissance*. Berkeley: Univ. of California Press, 1973.

cooke, miriam. "The Cell Story: Syrian Prison Stories after Hafez Asad." *Middle East Critique* 20, no. 2 (2011): 169–87.

——. *Dissident Syria: Making Oppositional Arts Official*. Durham, NC: Duke Univ. Press, 2007.

——. "Ghassan al-Jaba'i: Prison Literature in Syria after 1980." *World Literature Today* 75, no. 2 (2001): 237–45.

——. "Living in Truth." *Tradition, Modernity, and Postmodernism in Arabic Literature*, edited by Kamal Abdel-Malek and Wael Hallaq, 203–22. Leiden: Brill, 2000.

Corbin, John. "Images of War: Picasso's Guernica." *Visual Anthropology* 13, no. 1 (2010): 1-21.

Cortazar, Julio. "Some Aspects of the Short Story." In *The New Short Story Theories*, edited by Charles E. May, 245–55. Athens: Ohio Univ. Press, 1994.

Coundouriotis, Eleni. "In Flight: The Refugee Experience and Human Rights Narrative." In *The Routledge Companion to Literature and Human Rights*, edited by Sophia A. McClennan and Alexandra Schultheis Moore, 78–85. Abingdon, UK: Routledge, 2016, Kindle.

Cover, Robert M. "Violence and the Word." *Yale Law Journal* 95, no. 8 (1986): 1601–29.

Cowan, J. M. *The Hans Wehr Dictionary of Modern Written Arabic*. Ithaca, NY: Spoken Language Services, 1994.

Crampton, Jeremy W. "Cartography: Maps 2.0." *Progress in Human Geography* 33, no. 1 (2009): 91–100.

Crewe, Ben, Jason Warr, Peter Bennett, and Alan Smith, "The Emotional Geography of Prison Life." *Theoretical Criminology* 18, no. 1 (2013): 56–74.

Culler, Jonathan. *Literary Theory: A Very Short Introduction*. Oxford, UK: Oxford Univ. Press, 2011. Kindle.

Currie, Mark, ed. *Metafiction*. New York: Longman, 1995.

Cusick, Suzanne G. "Towards an Acoustemology of Detention in the 'Global War on Terror.'" In *Music, Sound, and Space: Transformations of Public and Private Experience*, edited by Georgina Born, 275–91. Cambridge, UK: Cambridge Univ. Press, 2013.

Dabbagh, Heba. "Interview: Heba al-Dabbagh Speaks to CAGE," CAGE, May 14, 2014. cage.ngo/uncategorized/interview-heba-al-dabbagh-speaks-cage/. Accessed August 10, 2017.

———. *Just Five Minutes: Nine Years in the Prisons of Syria*. Translated by Bayan Khatib. Toronto: N.p., 2007.

d'Afflitto, Isabella Camera. "Prison Narratives: Autobiography and Fiction." In *Writing the Self: Autobiographical Writing in Modern Arabic Literature*, edited by Robin Ostle, Ed de Moor, and Stefan Wild, 148–56. London: Saqi, 1998.

Davidson, Joyce, and Christine Milligan. "Embodying Emotion Sensing Space: Introducing Emotional Geographies." *Social and Cultural Geography* 5, no. 4 (2004): 523–32.

Davis, Angela Y. *Are Prisons Obsolete?* New York: Seven Stories Press, 2011. Kindle.

Davison, John, and Stefanie Nebehay. "Amnesty Says Syria Executes, Tortures Thousands at Prison; Government Denies." Reuters, February 6, 2017. www.reuters.com/article/us-mideast-crisis-syria-amnesty-idUSKBN15M00F. Accessed November 10, 2018.

Dawes, James. *The Novel of Human Rights*. Cambridge, MA: Harvard Univ. Press, 2018. Kindle.

———. *That the World May Know: Bearing Witness to Atrocity*. Cambridge, MA: Harvard Univ. Press, 2007. Kindle.

Deleuze, Gilles, and Felix Guattari. *Kafka: Towards a Minor Literature*. Minneapolis: Univ. of Minnesota Press, 1986.

Della Ratta, Donatella. "The Unbearable Lightness of the Image: Unfinished Thoughts on Filming in Contemporary Syria." *Middle East Journal of Culture and Communication* 10, nos. 2–3 (2017): 109–32.

Derrida, Jacques. "The Law of Genre." Translated by Avital Ronnell. *Critical Inquiry* 7, no. 1 (1980): 55–81.

———. *Writing and Difference*. Translated by Alan Bass. Chicago: Univ. of Chicago Press, 1980.

Dikötter, Frank, and Ian Brown. *Cultures of Confinement: A History of the Prison in Africa, Asia, and Latin America*. Ithaca, NY: Cornell Univ. Press, 2007.

Dirsuweit, Teresa. "Carceral Spaces in South Africa: A Case Study of Institutional Power, Sexuality, and Transgression in a Women's Prison." *Geoforum* 30, no. 1 (1999): 71–83.

Donnelly, Jack. *Universal Human Rights in Theory and Practice*. Ithaca, NY: Cornell Univ. Press, 2003.

Dorfman, Ariel. "The Tyranny of Terror: Is Torture Inevitable in Our Century and Beyond?" In *Torture: A Collection*, edited by Sanford Levison, 3–18. Oxford: Oxford Univ. Press, 2004.

Douglass, Ana, and Thomas A. Vogler. "Introduction." In *Witness and Memory: The Discourse of Trauma*, edited by Ana Douglass and Thomas A. Vogler, 1–53. New York: Routledge, 2003.

Douglass, Patrice, and Frank Wilderson. "The Violence of Presence: Metaphysics in a Blackened World." *Black Scholar* 43, no. 4 (2013): 117–23

Douzinas, Costas. *The End of Human Rights*. Oxford, UK: Hart, 2000.

———. *Human Rights and Empire: The Political Philosophy of Cosmopolitanism*. Abingdon, UK: Routledge, 2007.

Edgar, Andrew, and Peter Sedgwick. *Key Concepts in Cultural Theory*. London: Routledge, 1999.

Elias, Chad. "Emergency Cinema and the Dignified Image: Cell Phone Activism and Filmmaking in Syria," *Film Quarterly* 71, no. 1 (2017): filmquarterly .org/2017/09/14/emergency-cinema-and-the-dignified-image-cell-phone -activism-and-filmmaking-in-syria/. Accessed January 10, 2019.

Esmeir, Samera. "On Making Dehumanization Possible." *PMLA* 121, no. 5 (2006): 1544–51.

Falkoff, Marc D. "'Where Is the World to Save Us from Torture': The Poets of Guantanamo Bay." In *The Routledge Companion to Literature and Human Rights*, edited by Sophia A. McClennan and Alexandra Schultheis Moore, 351–60. Abingdon, UK: Routledge, 2016. Kindle.

Farquharson, Danine, ed. *Prison Writings*. Oxford: Interdisciplinary Press, 2003.

Feldman, Allen. *Formations of Violence: The Narrative of the Body and Political Terror in Northern Ireland*. Chicago: Univ. of Chicago Press, 1991.

Fiddler, Michael. "Four Walls and What Lies Within: The Meaning of Space and Place in Prison." *Prison Service Journal* 187 (2010): 3.

Firat, Alexa. "Cultural Battles on the Literary Playing Field." Paper presented at the Middle East History and Theory Conference, University of Chicago, May 11–12, 2007.

———. "Post-67 Discourse and the Syrian Novel: The Construction of an Autonomous Literary Field." PhD diss., University of Pennsylvania, 2010.

Fletcher, Angus. *Allegory: The Theory of a Symbolic Mode*. Ithaca, NY: Cornell Univ. Press, 1970.

Forché, Carolyn. "Reading the Living Archives: The Witness of Literary Art." *Poetry Magazine*, May 2, 1011. www.poetryfoundation.org/poetrymagazine /articles/69680/reading-the-living-archives-the-witness-of-literary-art. Accessed December 12, 2019.

Foucault, Michel. *The Archaeology of Knowledge and the Discourse of Language*. New York: Pantheon, 1972.

———. *Discipline and Punish: The Birth of the Prison*. Translated by Alan Sheridan. New York: Vintage, 1992.

———. "Of Other Spaces." Translated by Jay Miskowiec. *Diacritics* 16, no. 1 (1986): 22–27.

———. *Power/Knowledge: Selected Interviews and Other Writings, 1972–1977*. New York: Pantheon, 1980.

———. "Questions of Method." In *The Foucault Effect: Studies in Governmentality*, edited by Graham Burchell, Colin Gordon, and Peter Miller, 73–86. Chicago: Univ. of Chicago Press, 1991.

Franklin, H. Bruce. *Prison Literature in America: The Victim as Criminal and Artist*. New York: Oxford Univ. Press, 1989.

———. *Prison Writing in 20th-Century America*. New York: Penguin, 1998.

Freeman, Michael. *Human Rights: An Interdisciplinary Approach*. Malden, MA: Polity, 2013.

Frow, John. *Genre*. London: Routledge, 2005.

Furst, Lilian, ed. *Realism*. New York: Longman, 1992.

Genette, Gerard. *Paratexts: Thresholds of Interpretation*. New York: Cambridge Univ. Press, 1997.

George, Alan. *Syria: Neither Bread nor Freedom*. London: Zed, 2003.

Goldberg, Elizabeth Swanson, and Alexandra Schultheis Moore. "Introduction: Human Rights and Literature: The Development of an Interdiscipline." In *Theoretical Perspectives on Human Rights and Literature*, edited by Elizabeth Swanson Goldberg and Alexandra Schultheis Moore. New York: Routledge, 2012. Kindle.

————, eds. *Theoretical Perspectives on Literature and Human Rights*. New York: Routledge, 2012. Kindle.

Green, Tara. *From the Plantation to the Prison: African-American Confinement Literature*. Macon, GA: Mercer Univ. Press, 2008.

Greenberg, Nathaniel. "Mythical State: The Aesthetics and Counter-Aesthetics of the Islamic State of Iraq and Syria." *Middle East Journal of Culture and Communication* 10, no. 1 (2017): 255–71.

Hafez, Sabry. "Torture, Imprisonment, and Political Assassination in the Arab Novel." *al-Jadid* 8, no. 38 (2002). www.aljadid.com/features/0838hafez.html. Accessed September 8, 2008.

————. "The Transformation of Reality and the Arabic Novel's Aesthetic Response." *Bulletin of the School of Oriental and African Studies* 57 (1994): 93–112.

al-Haj Saleh, Yassin. *The Impossible Revolution: Making Sense of the Syrian Tragedy*. Translated by Ibtihal Mahmood. London: C. Hurst and Co., 2017.

Halabi, Zeina G. *The Unmaking of the Arabic Intellectual: Prophecy, Exile, and the Nation*. Edinburgh: Edinburgh Univ. Press, 2017. Kindle.

Halasa, Malu, Zaher Omareen, and Nawara Mahfoud. *Syria Speaks: Art and Culture from the Frontline*. London: Saqi, 2014.

Hamarneh, Walid. "Some Narrators and Narrative Modes in the Contemporary Arabic Novel." In *The Arabic Novel Since 1950: Critical Essays, Interviews, and Bibliography*, edited by Issa J. Boullata, 205–36. Cambridge, UK: Dar Mahjar, 1994.

Hammad, Muhammad Saleem. *Tadmur: Witnessed and Observed*. Translated by Syrian Human Rights Committee. N.p.: Syrian Human Rights Committee, n.d. www.shrc.org/en/wp-content/uploads/2017/02/Tadmur-Witnessed-and-Observed-Final-1.pdf. Accessed December 20, 2017.

Hamzawy, Amr. "Globalization and Human Rights: On a Current Debate among Arab Intellectuals." In *Human Rights in the Arab World: Independent Voices*, edited by Anthony Chase and Amr Hamzawy, 51–63. Philadelphia: Univ. of Pennsylvania Press, 2006.

Hanano, Amal. "The Cell of Survival: Bara Sarraj." *Jadaliyya*, December 12, 2011. www.jadaliyya.com/pages/index/3500/the-cell-of-survival_bara-sarraj. Accessed February 18, 2016.

Hanne, Michael. "Creativity and Exile: An Introduction." In *Creativity in Exile*, edited by Michael Hanne, 1–12. Amsterdam: Rodopi, 1994.

———, ed. *Creativity in Exile*. Amsterdam: Rodopi, 1994.

Harley, J. B. "Silence and Secrecy: The Hidden Agenda of Cartography in Early Modern Europe." *Imago Mundi* 40 (1988): 57–66.

Harlow, Barbara. *Barred: Women, Writing, and Political Detention*. Hanover, CT: Wesleyan Univ. Press, 1992.

———. *Resistance Literature*. New York: Metheun & Co., 1987.

Harmansah, Omar. "ISIS, Heritage, and the Spectacles of Destruction in Global Media." *Near Eastern Archaeology* 78, no. 3 (2015): 170–77.

Harris, Leila M., and Helen D. Hazen, "Power of Maps: (Counter) Mapping for Conservation." *ACME: An International E-Journal for Critical Geographies* 4, no. 1 (2005): 99–130.

Hassan, Abdalla. "Black Humor in Dark Times." *World Press*, June 19, 2003. www.worldpress.org/Mideast/1205.cfm. Accessed October 10, 2018.

Hemsworth, Katie. "'Feeling the Range': Emotional Geographies of Sound in Prisons." *Emotion, Space, and Society* 20 (2016): 90–97.

Hernández-Truyol, Berta Esperanza, ed. *Moral Imperialism: A Critical Anthology*. New York: New York Univ. Press, 2002.

Hillier, Bill, and Julienne Hanson. *The Social Logic of Space*. Cambridge, UK: Cambridge Univ. Press, 1984.

Hinnebusch, Raymond. *Syria: Revolution from Above*. London: Routledge, 2001.

Hopgood, Stephen. *The End-Times of Human Rights*. Ithaca, NY: Cornell Univ. Press, 2015. Kindle.

Hopwood, Derek. *Syria 1945–1986: Politics and Society*. London: Unwin Hyman, 1988.

Human Rights Watch. "If the Dead Could Speak: Mass Death and Torture in Syria's Detention Facilities." Human Rights Watch, December 16, 2015. www.hrw.org/report/2015/12/16/if-dead-could-speak/mass-deaths-and-torture-syrias-detention-facilities#. Accessed December 10, 2018, 26.

———. "No Room to Breathe: State Repression of Human Rights Activists in Syria." Human Rights Watch, October 16, 1997. www.hrw.org/en/reports/2007/10/16/no-room-breathe-0. Accessed September 10, 2007.

————. "Syria: Detention and Abuse of Female Activists." Human Rights Watch, June 24, 2013. www.hrw.org/news/2013/06/24/syria-detention-and-abuse -female-activists. Accessed December 1, 2017.

————. "Syria: Stop Torture of Children." Human Rights Watch, February 3, 2012. www.hrw.org/news/2012/02/03/syria-stop-torture-children. Accessed April 30, 2016.

————. "Syria's Tadmor Prison: Dissent Still Hostage to a Legacy of Terror." Human Rights Watch, April 1996. www.hrw.org/reports/1996/Syria2.htm. Accessed September 8, 2007.

————. "Torture Archipelago: Arbitrary Arrests, Torture, and Enforced Disap-pearances in Syria's Underground Prisons since March 2011." Human Rights Watch, July 3, 2012. www.hrw.org/report/2012/07/03/torture-archipelago /arbitrary-arrests-torture-and-enforced-disappearances-syrias. Accessed March 27, 2019.

————. "A Wasted Decade: Human Rights in Syria during Bashar al-Asad's First Ten Years in Power." Human Rights Watch, July 16, 2010. www.hrw .org/report/2010/07/16/wasted-decade/human-rights-syria-during-bashar -al-asads-first-ten-years-power. Accessed October 23, 2017.

Hunt, Lynn. The Invention of Human Rights: A History. New York: W. W. Norton, 2007.

Hutcheon, Linda. "Historiographic Metafiction." In Metafiction, edited by Mark Currie, 71–91. New York: Routledge, 2013. Kindle.

————. Irony's Edge: The Theory and Politics of Irony. London: Routledge, 2005. Kindle.

Hutcherson, Kimberly. "ISIS Video Shows Execution of 25 Men in Ruins of Syr-ian Amphitheater." CNN, July 5, 2015. edition.cnn.com/2015/07/04/middle east/isis-execution-palmyra-syria/. Accessed October 20, 2017.

Ishay, Micheline R. The History of Human Rights: From Ancient Times to the Glo-balization Era. Berkeley: Univ. of California Press, 2004.

Ismail, Salwa. The Rule of Violence: Subjectivity, Memory, and Government in Syria. Cambridge, UK: Cambridge Univ. Press, 2018.

Ismael, Tareq Y., and Jacqueline S. Ismael. The Communist Movement in Syria and Lebanon. Gainesville: Univ. Press of Florida, 1998.

Jameson, Fredric. The Political Unconscious: Narrative as a Socially Symbolic Act. Ithaca, NY: Cornell Univ. Press, 1981.

Jarvis, Simon. Adorno: A Critical Introduction. New York: Routledge, 1998.

Jauss, Hans Robert. "The Identity of the Poetic Text in the Changing Horizon of Understanding." In *Reception Study: From Literary Theory to Cultural Studies*, edited by James L. Machor and Philip Goldstein, 7–28. New York: Routledge, 2001.

Al Jazeera. "Almost 18,000 Died in Syria's Prisons: Amnesty." Al Jazeera, August 18, 2016. www.aljazeera.com/news/2016/08/18000-died-syria-prisons-amnesty-160818051435301.html. Accessed October 5, 2018.

Jewkes, Yvonne. *Captive Audience: Media, Masculinity, and Power in Prisons*. Portland, OR: Willan, 2002.

Joubin, Rebecca. *The Politics of Love: Sexuality, Gender, and Marriage in Syrian Television Drama*. Lanham, MD: Lexington, 2013.

Kahf, Mohja. "The Silences of Contemporary Syrian Literature." *World Literature Today* 75, no. 2 (2001): 225–36.

Kassab, Elizabeth Suzanne. *Contemporary Arab Thought: Cultural Critique in Comparative Perspective*. New York: Columbia Univ. Press, 2010.

———. *Enlightenment on the Eve of the Revolution: The Egyptian and Syrian Debates*. New York: Columbia Univ. Press, 2019.

Khalifa, Mustafa. *The Shell: Memoirs of a Hidden Observer*. Translated by Paul Starkey. Northampton, MA: Interlink, 2017.

Khalili, Laleh. *Confinement in Counterinsurgencies*. Stanford, CA: Stanford Univ. Press, 2013.

Khoury, Philip S. *Urban Notables and Arab Nationalism: The Politics of Damascus 1860–1920*. Cambridge, UK: Cambridge Univ. Press, 2003.

Kristeva, Julie. "World, Dialogue, and Novel." In *The Kristeva Reader*, edited by Toril Moi, 34–62. New York: Columbia Univ. Press, 1986.

Lane, Edward William. *An Arabic-English Lexicon*. Beirut: Librairie du Liban, 1980.

Larocco, Steve. "Pain as Semiosomatic Force: The Disarticulation and Rearticulation of Subjectivity." *Subjectivity* 9, no. 4 (2016): 343–62.

Larson, Doran. "Towards a Prison Poetics." *College Literature* 37, no. 3 (2010): 143–66.

Lee, Edward Lee. "Guards, Prisoners, and Textuality: A Study of South African and American Twentieth Century Prison Narratives." PhD diss., Rutgers University, 2000.

Lefèvre, Raphaël. *Ashes of Hama: The Muslim Brotherhood in Syria*. New York: Oxford Univ. Press, 2013. Kindle.

Lemke, Thomas. "'A Zone of Indistinction': A Critique of Giorgio Agamben's Concept of Biopolitics." *Outlines: Critical Social Studies* 7, no. 1 (2005): 3–13.

Levison, Sanford. "Contemplating Torture: An Introduction." In *Torture: A Collection*, edited by Sanford Levison, 23–43. Oxford: Oxford Univ. Press, 2004.

————, ed. *Torture: A Collection*. Oxford: Oxford Univ. Press, 2004.

Lopez, Tiffany. "Critical Witnessing in Latina/o and African-American Prison Narratives." In *Prose and Cons: Essays on Prison Literature in the United States*, edited by Quentin Miller, 62–77. Jefferson, NC: McFarland, 2005.

Machor, James L., and Philip Goldstein, eds. *Reception Study: From Literary Theory to Cultural Studies*. New York: Routledge, 2001.

Makdisi, Saree. "Postcolonial Literature in a Neocolonial World: Modern Arabic Culture and the End of Modernity." *boundary 2* 22, no. 1 (1995): 85–115.

Marsden, Peter H., Geoffrey V. Davis, eds. *Towards a Transcultural Future: Literature and Human Rights in a 'Post'-Colonial World*. Amsterdam: Rodopi, 2004.

May, Charles E. "Introduction." *The New Short Story Theories*, edited by Charles E. May, xv–xxvi. Athens: Ohio Univ. Press, 1994.

Mayer, Jane. "Outsourcing Torture: The Secret History of America's 'Extraordinary Rendition' Program." *New Yorker*, February 14, 2005. www.newyorker.com/archive/2005/02/14/050214fa_fact6. Accessed May 10, 2007.

McQuillan, Colin. "The Political Life in Giorgio Agamben." *Kritikos* 2 (July 2005). garnet.acns.fsu.edu/~nr03/mcquillan.htm. Accessed September 8, 2005.

McClennan, Sophia A., and Alexandra Schultheis Moore. "Introduction: Aporia and Affirmative Critique: Mapping the Landscape of Literary Approaches to Human Rights." In *The Routledge Companion to Literature and Human Rights*, edited by Sophia A. McClennan and Alexandra Schultheis Moore. New York: Routledge, 2016. Kindle.

————, eds. *The Routledge Companion to Literature and Human Rights*. Abingdon, UK: Routledge, 2016.

McHugo, John. *Syria: A Recent History*. London: Saqi, 2014.

McKernan, Bethan. "Inside Assad's Prisons: Horrors Facing Female Inmates in Syrian Jails Revealed." *Independent*, August 28, 2017.

McManus, Anne-Marie. "Plucking Out the Heart of Power: *Al-Qawqa'a*." *Jadaliyya*, November 16, 2011. www.jadaliyya.com/Details/24622/Plucking-Out-the-Heart-of-Power-Al-Qawqa%60a. Accessed April 11, 2018.

McWatters, Mason. "Poetic Testimonies of Incarceration: Towards a Vision of Prison as Manifold Space." In *Carceral Spaces: Mobility and Agency in*

Imprisonment and Migrant Detention, edited by Dominique Moran, Nick Gill, and Deidre Conlon. Burlington, VT: Ashgate, 2013. Kindle.

Mehrez, Samia. *Egyptian Writers between Fiction and History*. Cairo: American Univ. in Cairo Press, 1994.

Meyer, Stefan G. *The Experimental Arabic Novel: Postcolonial Literary Modernism in the Levant*. Albany: State Univ. of New York Press, 2001.

Middle East Watch. *Syria Unmasked: The Suppression of Human Rights by the Asad Regime*. New Haven, CT: Yale Univ. Press, 1991.

Miller, Quentin, ed. *Prose and Cons: Essays on Prison Literature in the United States*. Jefferson, NC: McFarland, 2005.

Moore, Alexandra Schultheis. *Vulnerability and Security in Human Rights Literature and Culture*. New York: Routledge, 2016. Kindle.

Moran, Dominique. *Carceral Geography: Spaces and Practices of Incarceration*. New York: Routledge, 2016. Kindle.

Moran, Dominique, Nick Gill, and Deidre Conlon, eds. *Carceral Spaces: Mobility and Agency in Imprisonment and Migrant Detention*. Burlington, VT: Ashgate, 2013. Kindle.

Moyn, Samuel. *The Last Utopia: Human Rights in History*. Cambridge, MA: Belknap, 2010. Kindle.

Mutua, Makau. *Human Rights: A Political and Cultural Critique*. Philadelphia: Univ. of Pennsylvania Press, 2002.

Nora, Pierre. "The Return of the Event." Translated by Arthur Goldhammer. In *Histories: French Constructions of the Past*, edited by Jacques Revel and Lynn Hunt, 421–36. New York: New Press, 1998.

Oliver, Kelly. *Witnessing: Beyond Recognition*. Minneapolis: Univ. of Minnesota Press, 2001.

Pannewick, Friederike, and Georges Khalil, eds. *Commitment and Beyond: Reflections on/of the Political in Arabic Literature since the 1940s*. Wiesbaden: Dr. Ludwig Reichert Verlag, 2015.

Parikh, Crystal. *Writing Human Rights: The Political Imaginaries of Writers of Color*. Minneapolis: Univ. of Minnesota Press, 2017.

Parry, John T. "Escalation and Necessity: Defining Torture at Home and Abroad." In *Torture: A Collection*, edited by Sanford Levison, 145–64. Oxford: Oxford Univ. Press, 2004.

Patten, Wendy. "Human Rights Watch Report to the Canadian Commission of Inquiry into the Actions of Canadian Officials in Relation to Maher Arar."

Human Rights Watch, June 7, 2005. hrw.org/backgrounder/eca/canada/arar/. Accessed May 10, 2007.

PEN America. *The Named and the Nameless: 2018 Prison Writing Awards Anthology*. N.p.: PEN America, 2018.

Pinto, Paul Gabriel Hilu. "Syria." In *Dispatches from the Arab Spring: Understanding the New Middle East*, edited by Paul Amar and Vijay Prashad. Minneapolis: Univ. of Minnesota Press, 2013. Kindle.

Plesu, Andrei. "Intellectual Life under Dictatorship." *Representations* 49 (Winter 1995): 61–71.

Popan, Elena R. "Building New Platforms for Civil Society: The Right to Image in Syrian Abounaddara Collective's Cinema of Emergency." *Spectra: The Aspect Journal* 5, no. 2 (2016). spectrajournal.org/articles/10.21061/spectra .v5i2.379/. Accessed February 8, 2017.

Posner, Richard A. "Torture, Terrorism, and Interrogation." In *Torture: A Collection*, edited by Sanford Levison, 291–98. Oxford: Oxford Univ. Press, 2004.

Ramírez Díaz, Naomí. *The Muslim Brotherhood in Syria: The Democratic Option of Islamism*. New York: Routledge, 2018. Kindle.

Ranciere, Jacques. *The Names of History*. Translated by Hassan Melehy. Minneapolis: Univ. of Minnesota Press, 1994.

Rejali, Darius. *Torture and Democracy*. Princeton, NJ: Princeton Univ. Press, 2007. Kindle.

Rice, Tom. "Sounds Inside: Prison, Prisoners and Acoustical Agency." *Sound Studies* 2, no. 1 (2016): 6–20.

Robbins, Bruce. "Sad Stories in the International Public Sphere: Richard Rorty on Culture and Human Rights." *Public Culture* 9, no. 2 (1997): 209–32.

Rodríquez, Dylan. "Against the Discipline of 'Prison Writing': Toward a Theoretical Conception of Contemporary Radical Prison Praxis." *Genre* 35 (Fall/ Winter 2002): 407–28.

———. *Forced Passages: Imprisoned Radical Intellectuals and the U.S. Prison Regime*. Minneapolis: Univ. of Minnesota Press, 2006.

Rorty, Richard. "Human Rights, Rationality, and Sentimentality." In *The Politics of Human Rights*, edited by Obrad Savic, 67–83. London: Verso, 2002.

Sáez, Ñacuñán. "Torture: A Discourse on Practice." In *Tattoo, Torture, Mutilation, and Adornment: The Denaturalization of the Body in Culture and Text*, edited by Frances E. Mascia-Lees and Patricia Sharpe, 126–44. Albany: State Univ. of New York Press, 1992.

Said, Edward. *Reflections on Exile and Other Essays*. Cambridge, MA: Harvard Univ. Press, 2000.

————. *Representations of the Intellectual*. New York: Vintage, 1996.

Sakr, Rita. *"Anticipating" the 2011 Arab Uprisings: Revolutionary Literatures and Political Geographies*. New York: Palgrave Macmillan, 2013. Kindle.

Saleh, Zainab. "A Dream's End: Temporalities in Abounaddara's Emergency Cinema." *In Media Res*, February 8, 2016. mediacommons.org/imr/2016/02/06 /dreams-end-temporalities-abounaddaras-emergency-cinema. Accessed February 9, 2017.

Samu'il, Ibrahim. "Ahem." Translated by Alexa Firat. *Words without Borders*. www.wordswithoutborders.org/?lab=Ahem. Accessed September 30, 2008.

Savic, Obrad, ed. *The Politics of Human Rights*. London: Verso, 2002.

Scarry, Elaine. *The Body in Pain: The Making and Unmaking of the World*. New York: Oxford Univ. Press, 1985.

Schafer, R. Murray. *The Soundscape: Our Sonic Environment and the Tuning of the World*. Rochester, VT: Destiny, 1994.

Schaffer, Kay, and Sidonie Smith. *Human Rights and Narrated Lives: The Ethics of Recognition*. New York: Palgrave Macmillan, 2004.

Scheffler, Judith A, ed. *Wall Tappings: An International Anthology of Women's Prison Writings, 200 to the Present*. New York: Feminist Press, 2002.

Schutz, Aaron. "The Metaphor of 'Space' in Educational Theory: Henry Giroux through the Eyes of Hannah Arendt and Michel Foucault." In *Philosophy of Education*, edited by Susan Laird, 352–60. Urbana: Philosophy of Education Society, 1998.

Seale, Patrick. *The Struggle for Syria: A Study of Post-War Arab Politics, 1945–1958*. New Haven, CT: Yale Univ. Press, 1986.

Segel, Harold B. *The Walls behind the Curtain: East European Prison Literature, 1945–1990*. Pittsburgh: Univ. of Pittsburgh Press, 2012.

Shaheen, Kareem. "Palmyra: Historic Syrian City Falls under Control of ISIS." *Guardian*, May 21, 2015. www.theguardian.com/world/2015/may/20 /syrian-city-of-palmyra-falls-under-control-of-isis. Accessed September 25, 2017.

Shaheen, Kareem, and Ian Black. "Beheaded Syrian Scholar Refused to Lead ISIS to Hidden Palmyra Antiquities." *Guardian*, August 19, 2015.

Shohat, Ella. *Taboo Memories, Diasporic Voices*. Durham, NC: Duke Univ. Press, 2006.

Singer, Peter. "Unspeakable Acts," *New York Review of Books*, February 27, 1986, www.nybooks.com/articles/1986/02/27/unspeakable-acts/.

60 Minutes. "His Year in Hell." *60 Minutes*, January 21, 2004. www.cbsnews.com /stories/2004/01/21/60II/main594974.shtml. Accessed November 24, 2008.

Slaughter, Joseph. *Human Rights, Inc.: The World Novel, Narrative Form, and International Law*. New York: Fordham Univ. Press, 2007.

———. "Humanitarian Reading." In *Humanitarianism and Suffering: The Mobilization of Empathy*, edited by Richard Ashby Wilson and Richard D. Brown, 88–107. Cambridge, UK: Cambridge Univ. Press, 2009.

———. "Protagonizing Narratives: The Role of the Voice in the Literatures of Trauma and Human Rights." PhD diss., University of Texas at Austin, 1998.

———. "A Question of Narration: The Voice in International Human Rights Law." *Human Rights Quarterly* 19, no. 2 (1997): 406–30.

Slymovics, Susan. *The Performance of Human Rights in Morocco*. Philadelphia: Univ. of Pennsylvania Press, 2005.

Sobanet, Andrew. *Jail Sentences: Representing Prison in Twentieth-Century French Fiction*. Lincoln: Univ. of Nebraska Press, 2008.

Soja, Edward W. *Thirdspace: Journeys to Los Angeles and Other Real-and-Imagined Places*. Malden, MA: Blackwell, 1996.

Sontag, Susan. *Regarding the Pain of Others*. New York: Picador, 2003. Kindle.

Syrian Human Rights Committee, "Tadmur Prison: A Special Report." Syrian Human Rights Committee, May 27, 2015. www.shrc.org/en/?p=25060. Accessed October 10, 2017.

Syrian Network for Human Rights. "Death Toll Due to Torture." Syrian Network for Human Rights, n.d. sn4hr.org/blog/2018/09/24/toll-of-deaths-due-to -torture/. Accessed December 1, 2018.

Taleghani, R. Shareah. "Breaking the Silence of Tadmor Military Prison." *Middle East Report* 275 (Summer 2015). merip.org/2015/06/breaking-the-silence-of -tadmor-military-prison/.

———. "The Cocoons of Language: Torture, Voice, Event." In *Human Rights, Suffering, and Aesthetics in Political Prison Literature*, edited by Yenna Wu and Simona Livescu, 117–38. Lanham, MD: Lexington, 2011.

———. "Writing against the Regime: Metafiction in the Arabic Prison Novel." In *Prison Writing and the Literary World: Imprisonment, Institutionality, and Questions of Literary Practice*, edited by Michelle Kelly and Claire Westall. New York: Routledge, 2020.

Taleghani, Shareah. "The Cocoons of Language, The Betrayals of Silence." PhD diss., New York University, 2009.

Tambling, Jeremy. *Allegory*. New York: Routledge, 2009.

Todorov, Tzvetan. *Genres in Discourse*. Cambridge, UK: Cambridge Univ. Press, 1990.

Tuan, Yi-Fu. *Space and Place: The Perspective of Experience*. Minneapolis: Univ. of Minnesota Press, 2001.

Turner, Bryan S. *Vulnerability and Human Rights*. University Park, PA: Penn State Univ. Press, 2006. Kindle.

van Dam, Nikolaos. *Destroying a Nation: The Civil War in Syria*. London: I. B. Tauris, 2017.

van Hoven, Bettina, and David Sibley. "'Just Duck': The Role of Vision in the Production of Prison Spaces." *Environment and Planning D: Society and Space* 26, no. 6 (2008): 1001–17.

van Ommen, Clifford, John Cromby, and Jeffrey Yen. "The Contemporary Making and Unmaking of Elaine Scarry's *The Body in Pain*." *Subjectivity* 9, no. 4 (2016): 333–42.

Waugh, Patricia. "What Is Metafiction and Why Are They Saying Such Awful Things about It?" In *Metafiction*, edited by Mark Currie, 39–54. New York: Longmann, 1995.

Wedeen, Lisa. *Ambiguities of Domination: Politics, Rhetoric, and Symbols in Contemporary Syria*. Chicago: Univ. of Chicago Press, 1999.

Whitlock, Gillian. *Postcolonial Narratives: Testimonial Translations*. Oxford: Oxford Univ. Press, 2015.

Wieland, Cartson. *Syria—A Decade of Lost Chances: Repression and Revolution from Damascus Spring to Arab Spring*. N.p.: Cune Press, 2012.

Williams, Philip F., and Yenna Wu. *The Great Well of Confinement: The Chinese Prison Camp through Contemporary Fiction and Reportage*. Berkeley: Univ. of California Press, 2004.

Williams, Raymond. *The Long Revolution*. 1961. Reprint, Peterborough, ON, Canada: Broadview, 2001.

Wilson-Goldie, Kaelen. "Price of Freedom." *Artforum*, January 15, 2015. www.artforum.com/film/-49756. Accessed December 10, 2018.

Woodward, Kathleen. "Calculating Compassion." In *Compassion: The Cultural Politics of an Emotion*, edited by Lauren Berlant, 59–86. New York: Routledge, 2004.

Wu, Yenna, and Simona Livescu, eds. *Human Rights, Suffering, and Aesthetics in Political Prison Literature*. Lanham, MD: Lexington, 2011.

Yassin-Kassab, Robin, and Leila al-Shami. *Burning Country: Syrians in Revolution and War*. London: Pluto, 2016. Kindle.

Ziter, Edward. *Political Performance in Syria: From the Six Day War to the Syrian Uprising*. Hampshire, UK: Palgrave Macmillan, 2015. Kindle.

Index

Italic page numbers denote illustrations.

R. Shareah Taleghani is assistant professor and director of Middle East Studies at Queens College, the City University of New York. She is coeditor of *Generations of Dissent: Cultural Production, Intellectuals, and the State in the Middle East and North Africa*.